sweden:
Prototype of Modern Society

STUDIES IN MODERN SOCIETIES

CONSULTING EDITOR:
DENNIS H. WRONG
New York University

A Random House Study in Sociology

SWEDEN:
Prototype of Modern Society

Richard F. Tomasson

THE UNIVERSITY OF NEW MEXICO

RANDOM HOUSE *New York*

Library of Congress Catalog Card Number 71–114565

Composed by Westcott & Thomson, Phila., Pa.

First Edition

2468975

To Nancy, Lars, Leif, Christopher,
and the UNM Sociology Department
without whom this book would have been
finished sooner,
but I have no regrets.

Ten years ago, in *The Future as History*, I wrote that
"With all its glaring and inexcusable failures, the
United States is still probably the most favored and
favorable place for a child to be born and grow up."
Clearly I was wrong then, and even more so today;
the place to ask the stork to drop you is Scandinavia.
—ROBERT L. HEILBRONER

Preface

When this book was first conceived, I intended it to be something like Robin Williams' *American Society*. In some ways it has turned out this way, but in some ways it is quite different.

Like Williams' book this is an attempt to be a general study of the social system of a modern industrial society and we both *do* deal with most of the same institutional areas. On the other hand, Williams writes about his own society, while I am writing about a society not my own and which I see through the eyes of an admiring foreigner. I am sure this perspective has influenced me in ways of which I am not even aware. My book is less than half as long as the third edition of *American Society* (New York: Random House, 1970) and it is less conceptually and theoretically self-conscious and not as systematic, but it is more cross-nationally comparative. Throughout, Swedish institutions are compared, in particular, with those of the other Scandinavian societies, Britain, and the United States. This book is also more developmental and empirical in orientation. These differences are understandable when it is pointed out that Swedish society *achieved* modern values while we were almost born to them; the more empirical orientation is partly a consequence of the magnificent statistical resources of Swedish society and partly my own fundamental empiricism. Another important difference is that I have a point of view, one which is implicit throughout the book, but which really did not emerge clearly to me until it was almost finished. This idea has been put into the

title: Sweden is seen as the "prototype of modern society." I am willing to argue, even though I do not emphasize it here, that Sweden
manifests modern values and a modern social structure to a greater
extent than any other society in the world. Though I would not have
put it quite this way in 1963 when I planned this book, this is what
originally aroused my interest in Sweden.

By modernization I mean the process of institutions adapting to the
changing functions brought about by the continuing increase in man's
knowledge, a result of the scientific revolution which has enabled him to increasingly control his environment. The ramifications
of this simple and abstract definition are, of course, enormous. They
have been neatly spelled out by C. E. Black in his masterful little book
The Dynamics of Modernization (New York: Harper and Row, 1967).
From this vantage point, then, I think my view of Sweden as occupy-
ing a special place among modern societies is justifiable.

Specifically, I deal with the extraordinarily rapid, tranquil, and successful modernization of Sweden, the state and politics, the religious
situation, the egalitarian transformation of the schools, the universities
and intellectual life, relations between the sexes, the family, social
stratification, organizational life, and—from all of the foregoing—the
value system. I am fully aware that there is much of importance that I
have not considered. There is little here about the economy, popular
culture, social deviance, or on the well-developed system of welfare
legislation. This is perhaps a shortcoming, but I can at least mention
that the subject of Swedish welfare legislation has been dealt with in
comparative perspective by my colleague, Albert H. Rosenthal, in his
book entitled *The Social Programs of Sweden: A Search for Security in a
Free Society* (Minneapolis: University of Minnesota Press, 1967).

The pace of social change in Sweden as in America has been
enormously rapid in recent years. Because of this, certain sections of
the book are not always "up-to-date." This is perhaps most true of
the chapter on universities and intellectual life where change has been
spectacularly rapid in the past few years, just as in America. For the
most part, developments in Sweden after 1968 are not considered here.
In any case, this book is not meant to be a topical account of contemporary Sweden. It is, I hope, more fundamental and enduring than
that.

One observation about myself that I think has implications for this
book: I have a tendency to make what are essentially invidious com-

parisons between Swedish and American society. However, I believe (and hope) I am judicious in handling my material, even if there are some biases in the specific issues I have sometimes chosen to write about. Yet, I would expect a certain admiration for Sweden from any sensitive American from just looking at a few basic statistics. Sweden had an infant death rate of 12.6 per 1,000 live births in 1966; ours was 23. In the same year the average life expectancy at birth for Swedish males was 71.4 years; for American males it was 66.7 years. Swedes buy 54 newspapers per 100 people every day; we buy 32— and the average intellectual substance in the Swedish press is greater than in ours. The Swedish population reads about the same number of books per year on a per capita basis as does the college graduate population in America. A 1968 international poll found 17 percent of Swedes admitted to a belief in hell compared with 65 percent of Americans. In the 1968 elections, almost 90 percent of the eligible electorate turned out to vote; in America in the same year the figure was just over 60 percent. Over 95 percent of wage workers in Sweden belong to unions; in America the figure is between 50 percent and 60 percent.

This is indeed a society whose workings and institutions are deserving of much study by those interested in the good and rational society. I hope this book, besides being informative, will stimulate others to undertake more specific studies.

Albuquerque, New Mexico   RICHARD F. TOMASSON

Acknowledgments

I would like to thank Fru Catherine Djurklou, Executive Secretary of The United States Educational Commission in Sweden, for her support and encouragement during my two years in Sweden. She is everything she should be. I am indebted to Sten Johansson of Uppsala University and his wife Lena for commenting on the final draft of the manuscript. Sten, who knows so much about modern Sweden, answered hundreds of my questions both while I was in Sweden and afterwards. I learned Swedish, and a great deal more, from reading the four volumes of Herbert Tingsten's *Mitt Liv;* later I also learned a great deal from him. Dennis Wrong, my editor, has carefully read the entire manuscript and thinks it is not totally without merit. I also want to thank Gil Merkx, my colleague and friend at The University of New Mexico, also interested in things Swedish, who helped me in a number of diverse ways. Lynne Farber of Random House was a great support to me during the many months this book was in production. And last, and in some ways most important, I want to thank Dorothy Ballard Floyd for her good humor and expert typing of the manuscript.

Contents

sweden:
Prototype of Modern Society

I

Introduction

The Swedes are far less dominated by
their own national history than most
of the other countries of Europe.
—MARGARET COLE[1]

This book is an attempt to outline and explain the development, social
structure, and value system of contemporary Swedish society.[2] To a
great extent this will be done comparatively. The central theme of this
study is that Sweden has come to approximate the ideal type of the
modern industrial society to a greater extent than any other nation in
the world. In terms of such general factors as political and social stability, the integration of the society, the articulation of interest groups,
secularization, the diminution of class differences, role specialization
and segregation, the capacity to compromise, the attenuation of ideologies and the extent of consensus, and the creation and use of knowledge in shaping and controlling the environment, Sweden operates at
a level exceeded by no other modern society.

By the mid-1960s Sweden had become the society with the highest
standard of living in the world after the United States, as measured in
terms of per capita income.[3] Yet the living standards of those in the
bottom quarter are substantially higher in Sweden than they are in the
United States; the lower orders are more integrated into the society
(in other words, the dominant value system), and they are characterized by less social disorganization than is the case in the United States
or in most of the other advanced societies. In terms of most of the

diverse statistical measures of national well-being—of successful modernization—such as the infant death rate and life expectancy, newspaper circulation, membership in interest groups, or the percentage of homes electrified and having telephones and inside plumbing, Sweden is surpassed by no other society in the world.[4] In terms of modern values I would indeed argue with Seymour M. Lipset's contention in *The First New Nation* that the United States "more than any other modern non-Communist industrial nation, emphasizes achievement, egalitarianism, universalism, and specificity."[5] A better case, though perhaps emphasizing different factors, can be made for Sweden.

Geography, Population, and Language

In area Sweden is the third largest country in Western Europe exceeded in size by only France and Spain.[6] It is almost twice as large as Great Britain and larger than the state of California. From south to north the country stretches almost 1000 miles. Yet in terms of population Sweden is one of the small countries of Western Europe. In 1970 its population reached 8 million, about 10 percent less than the population of the state of Michigan in the same year, about one-seventh the population of the United Kingdom or West Germany, Italy or France, and about one twenty-fifth that of the United States. The population of Sweden is twice that of Norway, however, and almost twice that of both Finland and Denmark.

Sweden is located at about the same latitude as Alaska. The climate is temperate in the lower third of the elongated eastern half of the Scandinavian peninsula where three-fourths of the Swedish population lives. This third of the country and the whole east coast are relatively flat. Sweden is not nearly as urbanized as are most other highly industrialized countries. Only one out of five Swedes lives in a city with a population of over 100,000, and there are only three such cities—Stockholm, Gothenburg, and Malmö. Only two out of five live in cities of over 20,000. Industry is highly decentralized and much of it is located in small places.

Swedish is a North Germanic language that is closely related to Danish and Norwegian.[7] More than 9 million Danes, Norwegians, and Swedish Finns also understand Swedish. This does not include the more than 4 million Finnish-speaking Finns, whose native language is not even Indo-European, but for whom Swedish is the link with Scandinavia. On the whole, Swedish is closer to German than it is to

English, but, in terms of the number of cognates and word order, it is closer to English than to German. Of the non-Scandinavian Germanic languages, Swedish is most closely related to Frisian and Dutch.

Some Basic Variables in the Study of Total Societies

There are a number of fundamental variables—perhaps we can call them infravariables—that differentiate the developed societies from each other. These are characteristics whose implications reverberate throughout the whole social system.

The most obvious, perhaps, is the level of industrialization. Even among the fifteen or twenty so-called advanced societies, there are great differences in the extent of industrialization, which is a basic independent variable in the comparative analysis of national social systems because it so greatly determines, for example, the occupational structure, the strength of the labor movement, the level of living, and the pervasiveness of urban values and of bureaucratization. However, the relation of industrialization to these factors is not as simple as it may first appear. New Zealand is not highly industrialized, yet it has one of the highest standards of living in the world; England is more industrialized, but it does not have as high a standard of living as New Zealand; Italy is moderately industrialized, but a large proportion of Italians south of Naples live just above the subsistence level. By any criteria, however, Sweden is one of the most industrialized nations in the world. Fewer than one out of ten Swedes in the labor force is engaged in agriculture, which includes forestry. No small or medium-sized industrial society compares with Sweden in the diversity of her industry. Swedish industry manufactures two makes of automobiles, three makes of buses, jet airplanes, railroad cars and engines, and a great range of heavy industrial equipment. Indeed, Sweden is perhaps the only industrial society, aside from the largest, that has the capacity to be relatively self-sufficient, as was demonstrated during World War II.

A basic distinction among the modern societies is between those that grew out of more-or-less feudalistic societies—which includes most modern societies—and those, in Louis Hartz's phrase, that were "born free"—which includes the new societies that were settled by Europeans, such as the United States, Canada, Australia, New Zealand, and a few others.[8] A different pattern of modernization occurred in these born free, fragment societies as compared with the societies of Europe.

For the born free societies modernization was "mainly economic and technical."[9] It did not involve the great conflicts inherent in a hierarchical society adhering to traditional values. Sweden, however, perhaps deserves to be put in an intermediate category. Sweden and the other Scandinavian societies never had a feudal economy; the peasants were never repressed to the degree they were elsewhere in Europe. A sizable proportion of Swedish farmers in the Middle Ages and after owned their farms directly under the Crown. The transition to a modern society occurred in Sweden with less fundamental conflict than in England or in the Continental European societies.

The size of the population of a society has a number of implications for national social systems. For example, there is more intermingling of elites in small societies than in large ones. Among the advanced societies, a medium or small size frees the society somewhat from international power and prestige considerations and perhaps tends to focus political attention on domestic affairs. Small size further seems to inhibit the development of nationalism and to foster internationalism. A De Gaulle, even a Churchill, would be inconceivable in Sweden, Norway, or Switzerland. The Swedes, in fact, have sometimes felt that small countries are characterized by a moral superiority because of their commitment to international cooperation.[10] In the past when the Swedes spoke approvingly of the "small states" they meant the other Scandinavian countries, the Netherlands, and Switzerland—not, for example, Romania or Bulgaria. Though this snobbish provincialism is not now characteristic of Sweden, Swedes remain keenly aware of the fact that they are a relatively powerless quarter of 1 percent of the world, living at the most affluent level in an exceptionally stable and successful society.

Because of necessarily limited cultural resources, the smaller societies are particularly prone to external cultural influences. Sometimes they deliberately choose to be cultural satellites of major cultures, as Sweden was to Germany after the success of the latter in the Franco-Prussian War of 1870–1871.[11] During the period from around 1872 to 1910, in fact, much of what happened in Sweden echoed what had happened in Germany a few years earlier. This was particularly true in education, politics, and intellectual life. Since the early nineteenth century, the dominant external cultural influences on Sweden have come in turn from France, Germany, Great Britain, and the United States. Correspondingly, the first foreign language in the school system has been successively French, German, and English.

Another basic infravariable is the degree of homogeneity that exists in a society. Most advanced societies, however, have some fundamental regional, linguistic, religious, racial, or ethnic heterogeneity.[12] Perhaps all of the advanced national societies can be classified as heterogeneous except for the Scandinavian countries and Japan. The predominantly Catholic societies tend to have cleavages similar to those in France or Italy, where there are traditional-clerical and rationalist-anticlerical elements that seem to have structural consequences analogous to, but more severe than, Protestant-Catholic divisions. There is really no counterpart to this division of much structural importance in the predominantly Protestant societies; for example, severe conflicts over Church versus State control of education. A homogeneous society certainly finds it easier to achieve consensus and social integration than does a heterogeneous society that generally does so only after much struggle. Even after such struggle, the heterogeneous society often finds that the accommodative relation is rather delicate and sometimes results in a system of parallel institutions—a situation more typical of Dutch society than of any other modern nation.[13] In the Netherlands, accommodation has involved the maintenance of separate institutions for Protestants, Catholics, and Secularists. There are no minorities of any significance in Sweden. Catholics, Jews, Lapps, and the foreign-born together compose a mere 2 percent of the population. Ninety-eight percent of the population are at least nominal members of the Church of Sweden. Such homogeneity perhaps emphasizes cleavage around the basic variables of class and city-country divisions.

National social systems also vary in the extent to which they have elite and bureaucratic concentrations and in the relations between the center and periphery, the capital and the provinces. Among the western industrial societies, France represents the most extreme form of elite and bureaucratic centralization. Paris is like the center of a wheel with all spokes leading to it. The emerging national system of West Germany, with Berlin isolated from the rest of the country, is probably the best example of the opposite, elite and bureaucratic dispersion; this is truly a society without a center.[14] Bonn, the capital, is still only a provincial city; industry and commerce are somewhat concentrated in Frankfurt and Hamburg; cultural life is highly dispersed. Most of the dispersed systems, such as West Germany, the United States, Canada, and Switzerland, appear to have federal systems. While it seems that unitary states (those without any level of government between the county and national levels) generally have a greater focus on the center, this is less characteristic of Sweden than of, for example, England or France. In Sweden, government—and cultural activities to some extent—are centered in Stockholm, but industry and education are not. Even in terms of government, Sweden is fundamentally different from France in that while governance is at the national level, administration is largely at lower levels.

Another way in which national societies differ is in the patterns of interrelations of institutions and in the relative dominance, pervasiveness, or centrality of different institutions. Throughout the development of Sweden, the state and political institutions have been central. The state was integrated through the preëminent position of a national bureaucracy. As in all late modernizing countries, the state played a particularly important role in economic development. For centuries virtually all Swedes have been members of the State Church. The universities, for the most part, have prepared their graduates for government service. The traditional upper class consisted largely of the higher bureaucrats (most of whom were of the nobility), the clergy, and the professors and gymnasium teachers—civil servants all. Probably no American institution could be said to have had such a central role, certainly not the state. Comparable in Dutch society might be the religious institutions and the resulting *verzuiling*, or "pillarization" of society, with the tendency of Catholic, Protestant, and secular blocs to permeate other institutions.[15] In Italian society the extended family and the particularism that it engenders might be considered a central institution to which we would relate other institutions.

Of decisive importance in the comparative study of national societies is the timing (early or late) and pattern that modernization has taken.[16] We will turn to this topic following a brief discussion of some basic themes in Swedish history.

Some General Themes in Swedish History

What general themes, what persistent factors, and what crucial events (or their absence) have shaped the development of Swedish institutions and values? Let me suggest some of these.

Until the late nineteenth century Sweden had a rather insulated development, as she was both culturally and geographically on the periphery of Europe. The Romans never got to Sweden, and Christianity got there late. Prior to the early twentieth century, Sweden was behind the rest of Western Europe, including Denmark and Norway, in economic development. Modern agricultural practices were not adopted, and the centuries-old agricultural communities did not disappear until the second half of the nineteenth century. By Western European standards, therefore, Sweden is a new industrial society, but one that has modernized very rapidly and completely.

The entire modern history of Sweden is characterized by an absence of severe domestic altercations and by great institutional stability and continuity. The development of constitutionalism, the elimination of the privileges of the nobility and upper classes, and the growth of modern parliamentary government all evolved firmly between 1719 and 1921. The general course of events in Sweden is strikingly similar to that in England, although later and more rapid, and in marked contrast, for example, to the turbulent history of France.

Ever since Sweden emerged as a nation-state under Gustav Vasa in the sixteenth century, her history has been a clear-cut national one. The principal players have been the kings, the nobility, the independent farmers, occasionally the clergy, and increasingly in the nineteenth century the middle classes, followed by the industrial working classes at the very end of that century. For centuries there have been no religious, ethnic, linguistic, or provincial divisions to complicate this history or to hinder the development of a national consciousness and cultural homogeneity. As Herbert Tingsten has said, it is really a rather dull history.[17] One indicator of the high degree of cultural homogeneity that exists in contemporary Sweden is the similarity in the spoken language; the difference in the Swedish of the north and of Malmö in the south is slight, probably less than that between the English of Yorkshire and London, and certainly less than between the German of Hamburg and Munich.

Throughout Swedish history the independent peasantry have had more social and political freedom, have played a larger part in politics, and have had a more substantial status than their counterparts on the Continent or in England have had. The Scandinavian peasants, particularly in Sweden and Finland, were never stripped of their teutonic medieval rights as they were in Prussia.[18] The Swedish peasants have had a part in national government at least since the fifteenth century and were formally represented as the Fourth Estate in the Riksdag, or parliament, at its consolidation in 1617. Sweden, along with the other Scandinavian countries, never developed a feudal social organization because it never had the necessary condition of a feudal economy. The kings of Sweden often courted the peasants and frequently gave in to their demands in their continuing conflicts with the nobility. The peasants, in turn, were more often royalist than not. This is perhaps one of the sources of the general Swedish trust in the national government. Lockean and laissez-faire ideology have had little place in Swedish political development; indeed, the urban middle classes did not emerge as a major political force until the twentieth century.

The Swedish population is further removed from churchly tutelage and "the Christian tradition" than most other Western societies. The factors associated with maintaining and reinforcing the religiosity of a people have been largely absent from Swedish development. The Protestant Reformation occurred with scarcely a whimper. The wars and pogroms and their heritage that affected almost every Continental state between 1517 and 1648 never touched Sweden. There has been little history of conflict between church and state, no oppression by a conqueror of different religion, and none of the religious stimulation provided by a mixed Catholic and Protestant population. In addition, in the second half of the nineteenth century the Swedish Church played a particularly reactionary role in confronting modern ideas of equality and tolerance, liberalism and socialism.

The Modernization of Sweden

No society has undergone full modernization with greater rapidity, tranquility, and thoroughness than Sweden did. In the course of a generation, from the 1890s to about 1920, Sweden saw the rapid and simultaneous development of organized liberalism and socialism, of parliamentarianism and popular democracy, and the transformation to an industrial society. By 1930 the Swedish economy had achieved maturity according to the criteria of W. W. Rostow, that is (then), modern technology had been applied to most of the society's resources.[19] By the late 1930s the traditional ideologies of conservatism, liberalism, and socialism had become highly attenuated and were replaced by a far-reaching consensus politics which accepted democracy as an absolute principle, the necessity of collaboration and compromise, and a predominantly empirical approach to issues.[20] Substantively, there was general acceptance by all of the parties of the essentials of the modern social-service state. It was at this time that Sweden first captured the attention of the world for the effectiveness of her democratic politics in general and, in particular, her comparatively astounding success in overcoming the depression.[21] Marquis Child's *Sweden: The Middle Way*, which illustrated the successful workings of a welfare state, became a best seller in the United States in 1936.[22] And. from England in 1937, the Socialist New Fabian Research Bureau sent a delegation to Sweden to find out about Swedish politics and institutions of which so little was really known in the English-speaking world.[23]

The decade of the 1880s was the great turning point in modern Swedish history. Early in the decade, Sweden was an agricultural society with over two-thirds of the population living on farms[24]; later in the decade, a generation after Germany and at least a decade after Denmark, the society was launched on the path to becoming a modern industrial society. Even Norway, at this time, had a better-developed lumber industry, relatively more university graduates, a greater degree of urbanization, and a far more developed political party system than did Sweden.[25] The 1880s saw the actual formation and popular expansion of the major new movements that were to determine the directions that industrial Sweden was to take; examples of such movements were the Social Democratic party, the organization of labor, the free church movement, and the temperance movement with its emphasis on popular education. This was the decade when socialist and radical liberal ideas, rationalist and anticlerical thought swept over isolated Sweden with irreversible effects on the urban intellectuals and the students in the universities and, later, on the total society. All of these ideological forces came to Sweden late by the Western European timetable, but they have had particularly far-reaching effects, again by Western European standards. The ideological forces first came largely in literary form, stemming most directly from the writings and lecturing of Henrik Ibsen and Björnstjerne Björnson, both Norwegian, and Georg and Edvard Brandes, both Danes. Radicalism, of a middle-class and predominantly liberal sort, was well established in Norway and Denmark a decade before it came to Sweden, but when these new ideas came to Sweden, it was with greater intensity and persistence than in the rest of Scandinavia.

Those new forces were reflected in and encouraged by a "long overdue" literature of social protest that burst forth in this decade, which Alrik Gustafson has called "the Modern Breakthrough," and which includes the early works of August Strindberg, Gustaf af Geijerstam, and a dozen lesser-known writers.[26] This was a striking decade in ideological and class conflict. The conservative official classes and the large landowners defended the institutions of the old hierarchical society against the increasing political self-consciousness of the farmers, whose traditional prerogatives have always had to be reckoned with in the Scandinavian countries, and the new organized groups that were given birth by urbanization and industrialization. At this time there was an extraordinary similarity of purpose in literature and in social radicalism. Both called for the fundamental restructuring of the social order. Indeed, it was late in the day for the existence of a society in Northwestern Europe where only a quarter of the males had the right to vote, education in the common school was controlled by the Church and consisted largely of religion according to the beliefs of the Swedish State Church, and philosophy and intellectual life were dominated by a curious, bureaucratic, idealistic philosophy of the state put forth by the Uppsala Professor of Philosophy C. J. Boström (1797–1866) and his disciples. From a general European perspective, the 1880s in Sweden can be seen as the time of the belated arrival of the radical continental and English ideas of the 1860s and 1870s.[27]

The major pillars of the "official society" of the nineteenth-century society were the national bureaucracy, the church, and the universities. The civil servants, the clergy, and the professors were the dominant elements of the upper class in the traditional, bureaucratic Sweden. And, although the clergy and the professors were the most energetic articulators and apologists of the values of the old, agrarian society, their defense of these paternalistic and hierarchical values only aided the mobilization of the proponents of the values of modernization.

Yet the political heritage of the nineteenth to the twentieth century in Sweden was a stable and efficient centralized state bureaucracy that functioned with a high degree of autonomy. The state was governed by a small but responsible upper class who dominated the civil service and the Upper House of the Riksdag; the independent farmers were the major element in the theoretically equal Lower House, though they were deferential to the civil service and to the Upper House. In this traditional authoritarian state, parliamentarianism was not recognized and only a small minority had any involvement in politics; the monarch and civil service were seen as the legitimate and natural ruling power. Yet monarchical absolutism had been only sporadic in Sweden, as we shall see in the next chapter, and it was never as thoroughgoing as in most of Continental Europe.

There were also representative institutions that worked to compromise the interests of the major societal groups. As with England, political institutions developed slowly over a number of centuries without any major internal altercations, at least not after 1689; also, as with England, a certain measure of common rights had existed since medieval times. But unlike England and all of the continental countries, institutions in which even the farmers were represented had existed for centuries, even if they were sometimes disregarded in practice. A particularly important inheritance was the system of standing committees that became well developed in the nineteenth century for reconciling differences among the Four Estates (Nobility, Clergy, Burghers, and Farmers), a structure that was kept intact with the transformation to the present two-chamber system in 1866. Within these committees there was a strong traditional emphasis on achieving consensus, which counteracted the divisive effects of the political parties in the modern period. Thus, a mechanism for compromising the interests of different societal groups was well developed in Sweden even before the appearance of the organized lower-middle and working classes with their demands for the franchise and for equality. There was also a high level of literacy and popular education as well as a high degree of freedom of expression and freedom of the press, even though they appear to have been little used to criticize the existing social order until the last two decades of the century.

The relative tranquility that prevailed in Sweden can be interpreted as an expression of the legitimacy of the social and political order. Herbert Tingsten has suggested that as late as the 1880s "no other people with a comparable level of education seem to have shown such a low degree of political interest; only a minority of those who had the franchise for Lower House elections even voted."[28] Their tranquility also reflects the country's relative isolation and the late introduction of industrialization and urbanization into their lives. However, the size of the depressed classes—the agricultural proletariat and the small farm owners—did increase rapidly in this century, but these groups were able to emigrate to America without causing much political disturbance.

Within the Western European context I know of no fact that highlights the late political development of Sweden more sharply than that no nationally organized liberal party of the modern type existed in Sweden until 1902. However, all of the fundamental criteria proposed by social scientists for successful modernization were present in Sweden in the highest degree: a long-term political unification with a high degree of loyalty to the state, a tradition of political decision-making on a rational and secular basis, a well-developed national administration, an emphasis on performance rather than ascription in the governmental bureaucracy, and a high level of literacy in a single language.[29] And when the struggle for universal suffrage began, there was virtually no attempt by the state to hinder the organization, growth, and activities of the trade-union or socialist movements, as had occurred almost everywhere else in Europe, outside of Scandinavia and Switzerland.[30]

The central and sometimes bitter battle for universal suffrage beginning in the last decade of the nineteenth century shaped the traditions of both the Liberal and Social Democratic parties. The Liberal party largely represented the lower-middle classes, the urban intellectuals, and the religious nonconformists; the Social Democratic party represented the industrial working classes. The Swedish Liberals were primarily influenced by social reformist, democratic, and rationalist ideals, especially those of John Stuart Mill, and rather little influenced by laissez faire. The Liberals were also an underdog party, which enhanced their social-reformist and egalitarian tendencies. This orientation continues to be dominant, unlike in the Liberal parties of Continental Europe, which now defend business interests and can no longer be regarded as parties of the left.[31] For the Social Democrats, the overriding importance of the suffrage issue forced them to concentrate on practical problems and to keep their Marxist ideology in the background.

The victory of universal suffrage in Sweden, as in some other countries, was an achievement of both the Liberals and Socialists. Their mutual cooperation in the years prior to World War I appears to have been a *necessary* condition for the steady development of stable democracy and the diminution of class cleavages. Such cooperation occurred in Sweden, Norway, Denmark, Britain, and the Low Countries. It did not occur in Germany and Austria, France or Finland, Spain or Italy. The successful cooperation of the Social Democrats with the Liberals at all levels in the battle for the vote helped to mute their orthodox socialism and to enhance their pragmatism. One other influential factor in their success is that the Swedish Conservatives never voluntarily extended the vote to gain support against the Liberals, as the Conservatives had done in England, Germany, and Belgium.[32]

The dominant value system that has developed along with modernization and that has, in turn, reinforced it has been shaped by the double radical traditions of social democracy and social-reformist liberalism to a greater extent in Sweden and Scandinavia than in the other developed societies. Both traditions have been numerically stronger in Sweden than anywhere else in Western Europe, accounting for over two-thirds of the electorate for a number of decades. While the philosophical roots of the two movements are very different, both have been supportive of rationalist, egalitarian, secular, and empirical values. And it is the pervasiveness of these value orientations that has become so characteristic of Sweden in recent decades. A discussion of these values will be the subject of the final chapter of this book.

Sweden as Compared to Other Scandinavian Countries

From a distance there is great similarity in the social systems of all the Scandinavian countries, yet on a closer look, a welter of minor and major institutional differences can be seen. However, one will find a marked similarity between the institutions of Sweden and Finland and, to a lesser extent, between those of Denmark and Norway. The reasons for this are not difficult to find. From about the twelfth century until 1809, Finland was an integral part of Sweden, even though the overwhelming majority of the population was Finnish speaking. Until 1809 the two countries were officially named the Kingdom of Sweden-Finland, and from medieval times the Finns were represented in the Swedish Riksdag. After an unsuccessful war with Russia, Sweden ceded Finland to Russia—the greatest loss in Swedish history—and Finland was given the status of an autonomous Grand Duchy. However, the official culture, legal values, and most institutions were not affected by Russian rule during the formative nineteenth century, and influences from across the Baltic remained strong.

Norway, on the other hand, was part of Denmark for almost as long as Finland was part of Sweden, though the relationship was never as integral. Britain ceded Norway to Sweden in 1814 in retaliation against Denmark for her role in joining with Napoleon. However, Norway continued to be culturally dependent on Denmark far more than on Sweden during the period of the Swedish-Norwegian Union, which lasted until 1905. In recent decades, however, Norway has come increasingly to look to Sweden rather than to Denmark in many areas. Sweden has become the major innovator in a number of areas, the model for both Finland and Norway and to a lesser extent for Denmark.

Notes

1. Margaret Cole and Charles Smith (eds.), *Democratic Sweden* (London: Rout-ledge & Kegan Paul, 1938), p. 2.

2. The two most recent general histories of Sweden in English are Ingvar Andersson, *A History of Sweden*, Carolyn Hannay (tr.) (Stockholm: Natur och Kultur, 1955), and Stewart Oakley, *A Short History of Sweden* (New York: Frederick A. Praeger, 1966). For an economic history, see Eli F. Heckscher, *An Economic History of Sweden*, Göran Ohlin (tr.) (Cambridge: Harvard University Press, 1954). A recent and superior popular account of contemporary Sweden is Frederic Fleisher, *The New Sweden* (New York: David McKay, 1967). Other sources for specific topics will be found in the notes throughout this book.

3. The 1968 per capita income in Sweden was $3130 compared with $2489 for Denmark, $2264 for Norway, and $1547 for Finland. For a listing of 1968 per capita incomes throughout the world, see Agency for International Development, *Gross National Product*, Statistics and Reports Division, Office of Program & Policy Coordination, Agency for International Development, April 25, 1969, p. 14. (I exclude Kuwait from consideration here.)

4. The United States, however, surpasses Sweden in the relative number of personal automobiles, television sets, radios, and the like.

5. Seymour M. Lipset, *The First New Nation* (New York: Basic Books, 1963), pp. 213–214. In my opinion Lipset overstates the elitist character of Swedish society, which manifests itself, in any case, more as a respect for experts than for any well-defined upper class as it is in England. He is on very shaky ground comparatively when he states that "the values of the Swedish status system contain strong elements of ascription, elitism, particularism, and diffuseness." See pp. 235–236.

6. Three volumes with accounts of the geography of Sweden are: Andrew C. O'Dell, *The Scandinavian World* (London: Longmans, Green, 1957); W. R. Mead, *An Economic Geography of the Scandinavian States and Finland* (London: University of London Press, 1958); and Axel Sømme (ed.), *A Geography of Norden* (Oslo: J. W. Cappelens Forlag, 1960).

7. An account of the Swedish language is Gösta Bergman, *A Short History of the Swedish Language* (Stockholm: Swedish Institute for Cultural Relations, 1947).

8. See Louis Hartz, *The Liberal Tradition in America* (New York: Harcourt, Brace & World, 1955); see also *The Founding of New Societies* (New York: Harcourt, Brace & World, 1964).

9. See W. W. Rostow, *The Stages of Economic Growth* (Cambridge, England: Cambridge University Press, 1960), pp. 17–18.

10. See discussion on this in Herbert Tingsten, *The Debate on the Foreign Policy of Sweden, 1918–1939*, Joan Bulman (tr.) (London: Oxford University Press, 1949), pp. 303–304.

11. Andersson, *op. cit.*, pp. 349–350.

12. On the characteristics and effects of these cleavages, see Seymour M. Lipset and Stein Rokkan (eds.), *Party Systems and Voter Alignments* (Glencoe, Ill.: Free Press, 1967), and Robert A. Dahl (ed.), *Political Oppositions in Western Democracies* (New Haven: Yale University Press, 1966).

13. See Hans Daalder, "The Netherlands: Opposition in a Segmented Society," in Dahl, *ibid.*, pp. 188–236, and Johan Goudsblom, *Dutch Society* (New York: Random House, 1967).

14. See Richard L. Merritt, "West Berlin—Center or Periphery?" in Richard L. Merritt and Stein Rokkan (eds.), *Comparing Nations* (New Haven: Yale University Press, 1966), pp. 321–336.

15. Goudsblom, *op. cit.*, pp. 32–33, 50–51.

16. See C. E. Black, *The Dynamics of Modernization* (New York: Harper & Row, 1966).

17. Lecture by Herbert Tingsten, The University of New Mexico, October 21, 1967.

18. See Hans Rosenberg, *Bureaucracy, Aristocracy, and Autocracy: The Prussian Experience, 1660–1815* (Boston: Beacon Press, 1958), pp. 27–34.

19. Rostow, *op. cit.*, pp. 59–60, 62–63.

20. This is the central theme of Herbert Tingsten's monumental study of the ideological transformation of the Swedish Social Democrats. See Herbert Tingsten, *The Swedish Social Democrats*, Greta Frankel and Richard F. Tomasson (trs.), forthcoming. The original Swedish version is entitled *Den svenska socialdemokratiens idéutveckling*, 2 vols. (Stockholm: Tiden, 1941).

21. See Arthur Montgomery, *How Sweden Overcame the Depression, 1930–1933* (Stockholm: Bonniers, 1938), and the issue "Social Problems and Policies in Sweden" of *The Annals*, 197 (May 1938).

22. Marquis Childs, *Sweden: The Middle Way* (New Haven: Yale University Press, revised 1938, 1947), issued as a Yale Paperbound in 1961. A similarly admiring book was published in France in 1935 and translated into English in Sweden the following year: Serge de Chessin, *The Key to Sweden* (Stockholm: Fritzes, 1936).

23. Their findings were published in Cole and Smith, *op. cit.*

24. On the economic transformation of Sweden, see Chapter 6 of Heckscher, *op. cit.* For an excellent overview of the 1880s in Sweden, see Gunner Richardson, *Kulturkamp och klasskamp: ideologiska och sociala motsättningar i svensk skol- och kulturpolitik under 1880-talet* (Gothenburg: Akademiforlaget-Gumperts, 1963).

25. See Tingsten, *op. cit.*, Vol. 1, Ch. 1.

26. Alrik Gustafson, *A History of Swedish Literature* (Minneapolis: University of Minnesota Press, 1961), pp. 243–287.

27. See Carlton J. H. Hayes, *A Generation of Materialism, 1871–1900* (New York: Harper Torchbooks, 1963), Chs. 2, 4, 5.

28. See comparative discussion in Reinhard Bendix, *Nation-Building and Citizenship* (New York: Wiley, 1964), pp. 80-87.

29. Tingsten, *op. cit.*, Vol. 1, p. 15.

30. For example, see listing of criteria in Douglas H. Mendel, Jr., "Japan Today: Case Study of a Developing Nation," *Trans-action*, 3 (March–April 1966), 15–21, or in Black, *op. cit.*, passim.

31. In Italy, Belgium, West Germany, and elsewhere, the Liberals have become largely a party of business interests and are more generally conservative than the Christian parties. Reformist, social-welfare type Liberal parties seem to be limited to the Scandinavian countries and Britain.

32. See Stein Rokkan, "The Comparative Study of Political Participation: Notes Toward a Perspective on Current Research," in Austin Ranney (ed.), *Essays on the Behavioral Study of Politics* (Urbana, Ill.: University of Illinois Press, 1962), pp. 72–80, and David Harris, "European Liberalism and the State," *American Historical Review*, LX (April 1955), 501–526.

II

The State and Politics

In Sweden perhaps more than
anywhere else the technique of
compromise has been an essential
ingredient in the art of proposing
the terms on which men can live
together.
— DANKWART A. RUSTOW[1]

The development of the Swedish state and constitutional practice
parallels that of England more than any other European state.[2] Both
countries evolved free from foreign intervention over the centuries in
an orderly and tranquil fashion. Sweden has not been occupied by a
foreign power since 1523, when Gustav Vasa threw off Danish rule
and became king. The country has never had a civil war or a national
revolution and has not participated in a war since 1814.

Development of a Modern State

Sweden became a national state with a king and some degree of national consciousness as early as the thirteenth century with the establishment of the Folkung dynasty. It was a weak state, however, with
few resources. Medieval Sweden was very decentralized and consisted of a number of autonomous provinces that gave allegiance to the
king, although the king was elected and had little power. The king
traveled to each province to ask for the allegiance of the people, even
though each province retained its own legal code until the middle of
the fourteenth century.

National consciousness developed particularly during the fifteenth century when conflict developed between the Swedish separatists, mostly the peasants and lower nobility, and those who favored a Scandinavian union under Danish leadership, mainly the clergy and higher nobility who frequently owned land in the other Scandinavian countries. Indeed, one of the striking features of fifteenth-century Sweden was the political role played by the free, or taxpaying, peasants, who owned about half the land, and who were instrumental in calling national assemblies of representatives from all the provinces to protest the misery resulting from a long war with Denmark. In fact, the origin of the Riksdag is traditionally dated back to a national assembly called in 1435. While the peasants may not actually have been represented at this particular assembly, representatives of all Four Estates were in attendance at a number of national assemblies around this time. It was not until nation-building was well underway in the early seventeenth century, however, that the Riksdag—by now made up of separate chambers for each of the estates—became a regular part of the machinery of government, and the estate of the peasants became fully recognized. At this time, and until the dissolution of the four-chamber legislature in 1865, the estate of the nobility was dominant and the estate of the peasants was clearly subordinate to the other three. In the romantic history of the nineteenth century, the importance of the free peasants was much exaggerated, but their role and the absence of a feudal social structure distinguish Swedish history from that of England or the Continental countries.

The preeminent nation-builder in Swedish history was Gustav Vasa. At his death in 1560, Sweden was launched toward being an integrated modern nation-state. Gustav laid the foundation for a national bureaucracy, developed the national economy, and confiscated all of the church lands. He adopted Lutheranism, which greatly enhanced the process of nation-building, and he took over the leadership of the church, which was the most developed national institution at that time. The development of Sweden into a great power in the seventeenth century, with a population of only around a million people, is evidence of the high degree of national integration that had been achieved.

The Riksdag became a permanent power during the reign of Sweden's most esteemed king and the leader of the Swedish forces in the Thirty Years' War, Gustavus II Adolphus (1611–1632). During his reign his leadership was uncontested, but after his death long periods of regency followed under the minorities of Christina and Charles XI, during which power fell to the aristocracy. Throughout most of the seventeenth century, the Riksdag attempted to oppose the growing strength of the aristocracy. When Charles XI was crowned king in 1672, he entered into an alliance with the lower nobility and commoners, which led to a drastic confiscation of the tax-free lands belonging to the nobility, thereby destroying the supremacy of the aristocracy and greatly enhancing the assets of the royal treasury. During the reign of Charles XI, Sweden turned increasingly to royal absolutism, which culminated in the victories and then calamitous defeats and reverses of his son and Sweden's most aggressive king, Charles XII. After his death in 1718 and the loss of Sweden's Baltic empire—and the end of Sweden as a great power—there was a vigorous turn against Carolinian absolutism.

The subsequent period in Swedish history is known as the Age of Freedom (1718–1772), in which royal absolutism was reduced to a minimum, a great resurgence in the power of the Riksdag took place, and a protoparliamentary system developed, with a functioning two-party system consisting of "the Hats" and "the Caps." But this was also a period of growing corruption and antagonism between the nobility and the other Estates.

A coup by Gustavus III in 1772 brought this era of party rule to an end. The reign of Gustavus III ended in 1792, and his son Gustavus IV Adolphus' reign lasted until 1809, when he was dethroned. During their reigns, there was absolutism not unlike the epoch of Carolinian absolutism of a century earlier. Yet Gustavus III was an enlightenment king—a Swedish counterpart to Frederick the Great—who was much influenced by the French culture of his day.

This final period of royal absolutism lasted until 1809, when humiliating defeats in a war with Russia led to Gustavus IV Adolphus' deposition and the demand for a new form of government. The result was the Constitution of 1809, which struck an extraordinarily effective balance between monarchical and legislative absolutism. The following year, the Riksdag chose Jean Baptiste Bernadotte, Prince of Pontecorvo and one of Napoleon's marshals, King of Sweden. He took the name Charles XIV John, adopted the Lutheran faith, and immediately took over the rule of Sweden, not as a pawn of Napoleon, but to win the support of the Swedish people. The House of Bernadotte continues to rule Sweden to this day.

The Constitution

Swedish constitutional practice, like the British, has its roots in the Middle Ages and developed independent of outside influences until the early nineteenth century. Like the Constitution of the United States of America, the 1809 Constitution was shaped by Montesquieu's separation-of-powers doctrine. The present codified constitution of Sweden, however, consists of this document plus three other fundamental laws. These four are:[3]

(1) Instrument of Government (*Regeringsformen*, abbreviated *RF*), adopted in 1809, details the organization and functions of the executive and the Riksdag. The *RF* is a clear attempt at a compromise between the monarchical absolutism embodied in the Constitution of 1772 and the legislative dominance in the Constitution of 1720. It specifies that the Riksdag meet at least once every five years, that it can reject the budget, and that it can veto legislation with the same authority as the king. One unique and significant provision is that information from administrative officials must be obtained when preparing legislation. In practice, however, this has been extended to include all groups that might be affected by the legislation. The *RF* also grants fundamental civil liberties to all citizens and provides for the protection of individual citizens through the office of *ombudsman*, which is elected by the Riksdag to receive and investigate complaints against government bureaucrats. In spite of the later developments of parliamentarianism and popular democracy, the division of authority between the Riksdag and the executive branch of government remains essentially the same, except that the executive is now the Council of State and only symbolically the king. After the adoption of the *RF*, according to the late Elis Håstad, an authority on the Swedish Constitution, "a high standard of parliamentary etiquette, with its emphasis on objectivity, began to be built up. The Riksdag had been accorded a central place in the political life of the nation, and its deliberations were followed with enormous interest by the public."[4] Although only thirteen of the original 114 articles of the *RF* remain unchanged, it continues as the oldest written constitution in the world, after that of the United States.

(2) Riksdag Act (*Riksdagsordningen*, abbreviated *RO*) was adopted

in 1865 when the antiquated Four-Estate legislature was replaced by a modern bicameral one. This much-altered act specifies the functioning of the Riksdag and the system of national representation.

(3) The Act of Succession (*Successionsordningen*), adopted in 1810, prescribes how the Swedish Crown will be inherited by the male members of the Bernadotte family. Until 1544 Sweden was an elective monarchy. At this time Gustav Vasa introduced the principle of hereditary monarchy. Prior to the adoption of the Act of Succession, succession through the female line was permitted. Today, the Conservative party would like to reestablish female succession, as has been done in Denmark, in order to ensure the preservation of the monarchy. The only current heir to the Swedish throne is Crown Prince Carl Gustav, born in 1946, who has four sisters who are ineligible to inherit the Crown under the present law.

(4) The Freedom of the Press Act (*Tryckfrihetsforordningen*, abbreviated *TF*) was adopted in its present form in 1949 but many of its fundamental principles date back to legislation passed in 1766, 1810, and 1812. The modern version of this law grew out of certain very unpopular restrictions imposed on the press during World War II, when the Swedish government, fearful of German invasion, confiscated certain issues of newspapers in order not to offend the Nazis. The various Freedom of the Press Acts, in addition to stipulating freedom of the press, have contained unique regulations specifying that all official documents of state and local authorities be public.[5] The implications of this unique constitutional provision are enormous. It means, for example, that all documents relevant to any government decision, the promotion of a government official, or the choice of a professor or teacher are public. It literally means any citizen has the right to go into any government office and request any government document, and that the contents of any of these documents can be published in the press. Nothing can be regarded as secret unless specific legislation is passed exempting the documents from public scrutiny, as in cases of national defense or certain social-welfare documents. No other modern democracy, except Finland and Denmark who adopted the Swedish law after World War II, has this practice. Sweden's practice is, in fact, opposite from that of Great Britain, where the secrecy of public documents is regarded as absolutely essential for the practice of effective government. The Swedes, and many observers of Swedish

government, see this as one of the most remarkable features of the Swedish Constitution. Indeed, it is regarded by the Swedes as "an essential prerequisite for a free, uninhibited, enlightened, and objective public debate."[6]

To amend these fundamental laws requires a joint decision of the government and the Riksdag, and the Riksdag must pass the proposed change twice, with a general election intervening. But the Swedish Constitution includes much more than what has been enacted into law; it is also based on long-term practices which have a status analogous to common law. On the other hand, much that is incorporated into the fundamental laws is irrelevant to the practice of modern government and is just ignored.

In 1954 a government commission was appointed to update and rewrite the whole of the constitutional law to bring it into accordance with contemporary practice. In 1963 the Commission presented a draft of a new constitution providing for the adoption of a unicameral legislature, which, if there are no further disputes, will come into being on January 1, 1971. A similar reform was made in Denmark in 1953. While the Swedes are a highly legalistic people, there has been little opposition to the rational and radical modernization of the Constitution.

The Present Bicameral System

The Riksdag presently comprises two houses of equal status—the Lower House and the Upper House.[7] The Lower House is made up of 233 seats filled by Proportional Representation from twenty-eight electoral districts. The Upper House has 151 members elected indirectly by county councils and by the city councils of Stockholm and Gothenburg, which are not represented in the county councils. The term of office in the Lower House is four years; in the Upper House it is eight years, with one-eighth of the membership being elected each year. As a consequence of this system, the Upper House reflects changes in public opinion more slowly than does the Lower House and tends to preserve the power of the Social Democratic party, which has been in power for almost forty years. The government's reluctance to abolish the bicameral legislature stemmed largely from this, although it argued feebly that the indirect election of an Upper House preserved a communal relation with the national government.

The Swedish Riksdag is, to a greater extent than most parliaments, a microcosm of the larger society. A 1949 study found, for example, that 36.8 percent of the Riksdag membership were or had been members of trade unions, 13.7 percent were members of salaried employees' organizations, and 21.8 percent were members of the farmers' union.[8] Many of the Riksdag members are very passive and rarely speak. Indeed, there is relatively little debate in the Riksdag, and many speakers, even the most experienced, prefer to read what they have to say. Unlike the British Parliament and, to a lesser extent, the American Congress, the ability to debate or to make speeches does not distinguish a member, but committee work does.

A great proportion of the work of the Riksdag is done in committees. The Riksdag operates with a number of joint committees, all made up of members of the four major political parties. Other countries with bicameral legislatures, such as the United States and Britain, operate with one-house committees. In Sweden, however, reports from the joint committees are sent to both houses on the same day and are usually dealt with at the same time.

The importance of these committees is perhaps greater in the Swedish legislature than in any other. There is a great attempt to maximize the number of four-party motions and the high proportion of committee reports that are unanimous attests to the success of cooperation among members of the different parties in these committees. The extraordinary importance of these committees in shaping legislation is a strong factor in modifying the apparently dominant role of the Social Democrats, the only government party.

The Legislative Process

It is doubtful whether the legislative process of any modern government institutionalizes compromise, investigation, and consultation with interested parties to the degree that Sweden does.[9]

In Sweden it is often difficult to determine the origin of a new legislative proposal, but the initiative usually comes from the government, though it may come from a Riksdag member, an association, or a local authority. An early step in the passage of legislation is the appointment of a joint committee of investigation, which is sometimes assisted by outside experts, who often serve without formal membership on the commission. Nils Andrén summarizes the operation of such commissions as follows:

After a general debate about the nature and scope of the task the commis-

sion decides on the research necessary to provide it with all the important facts. When the research has been carried out the various problems can be taken up for closer study and debate. During this stage the commission reaches certain preliminary conclusions. Differences of opinion and interpretation are clearly established, and possible ways of compromise are discussed. When the whole has been covered, the debate and its results are summarized by the secretary in a memorandum which is studied by the members (but not available to the public or to anybody—with the possible exception of the minister and his undersecretary). The memorandum serves as a basis for the following deliberations of the commission which on the whole should lead to the final conclusions of the commission. Guided by these deliberations the secretary makes a final draft of the commission report. The chapters are amended and/or approved (as the case may be), and finally the whole report is approved.[10]

The Swedish commissions are extraordinarily thorough. Many of the commissions publish reports of their investigations that run to thousands of pages. For example, the Commission on Higher Education, appointed in 1955, published seven volumes between 1957 and 1963, totaling almost 3000 pages of dense text. The commissions also frequently operate very slowly. The commission appointed in 1954 to rewrite the Swedish Constitution did not publish its first report until 1963; the Commission on Church-State relations, appointed in 1958, published its first report five years later; one recent commission did not report until eighteen years after it was appointed. Over 100 commission reports are published annually in the government's official report series (*Statens Offentliga Utredningar*).

A goal of all royal commissions of investigation is to reach unanimous agreement and to avoid at almost all costs minority reports, since a unanimous report stands a better chance of serving as the basis for legislation. The next step is to invite various authorities and interested organizations to give their opinions on the report. The original report and all the advice and comments on it are then submitted to the appropriate ministry where all the material serves as the basis for drafting legislation. The ensuing proposition is frequently very comprehensive, often consisting of over a hundred pages. In some cases the proposed legislation is submitted to the Law Council "to give advice as to the technical side of the legislation and its general compatibility with the existing legal system,"[11] and the report is always published along with the bill.

The significance of this legislative process is summarized by Nils Andrén:

The process of legislation . . . should substantiate the view that Swedish government is really a government by discussion, in which all parties, entitled to a hearing by virtue of competence or genuine interest in the matter, have the duty or right to participate. It also indicates the Swedish technique of direct invitations to pressure groups to participate in this discussion. Instead of waiting for the strong organizations to apply pressure on the Government, the Government invites them to submit their views. It is, therefore, correct to say that they form a normal part of the working legislative machinery of the country. It is part of the process of reaching compromises and, if possible, agreement, which on the whole is a characteristic of the present Swedish pattern of government.[12]

As a consequence of this thorough preparation, most legislation is passed unanimously by both houses of the Riksdag, since all of the compromising is done in committee. It is no wonder that Swedish legislation so frequently provides a model for the other Scandinavian countries.

Decentralized Government

One of the striking features of Swedish government is the degree to which authority has been successfully decentralized; this has been accomplished both structurally and geographically.[13] Governmental administration is carried out largely by special-purpose administrative agencies headed by relatively autonomous boards.[14] The administrative authorities in Sweden (and Finland) are relatively free from supervision by the ministers of the various departments, as is conventional in modern democracies.

There are eleven departments in the Swedish government: Justice, Foreign Affairs, Defense, Social Welfare, Communications, Finance, Education and Ecclesiastical Affairs, Agriculture, Commerce, Interior, and Civil Service. Except for Foreign Affairs, they are all very small; nine of the eleven departments employ fewer than 100 persons including all clerical workers. The functions of these government departments are, as summarized by Albert H. Rosenthal:

(1) preparing and presenting the proposed laws and budget requests to the Riksdag; (2) issuing basic regulations and general rules for the conduct of the administrative boards; (3) making or recommending the higher ap-

pointments in the administration; and (4) receiving and acting on certain appeals from individuals which, according to tradition, are addressed to the king.[15]

Note that general administration is not one of the functions. The Department of Education and Ecclesiastical Affairs, for example, can illustrate how this form of organization differs from the conventional pattern in other societies. This department has an office in Stockholm with eighty or ninety employees, yet under its general jurisdiction are the Board of Education for the entire country, the Board of Vocational Education, the Office of the Chancellor of the Universities that coordinates virtually all higher education in Sweden, the Church of Sweden, the Public Records Office, and all libraries and museums. However, all of these large units operate relatively autonomously vis-à-vis the Minister of Education and Ecclesiastical Affairs.

The great bulk of administrative activities of the government is carried out by central administrative agencies, headed by a director-general, who, together with his bureau chiefs, generally constitute the board of directors of the agency. The administrative agencies are regulated by legislation passed by the Riksdag, and their accountability is ensured through the Riksdag's control of their budgets. While some government department generally has influence over them, they are highly independent of their ministries in their operations. In the early part of this century there were proposals to incorporate the administrative agencies into government departments because of their alleged independence from ministerial control, but nothing was done to curtail their independence. This form of decentralizing the authority and the responsibility of national administration has developed since the seventeenth century and, while it is practiced to some extent by all modern governments, the extent to which it characterizes Swedish (and Finnish) administration is quite unique.

Authority is also decentralized in Sweden through local governments.[16] Whereas the present legal structure of local government dates back only to 1862, its traditions go back to pre-Christian times. For centuries the owners of farms met in the villages to decide local issues. Local government plays an important role in the administration of the schools, social welfare, public health, and other areas. The most important local units are the *stad*, which corresponds to the American city, and the *kommun*, which corresponds to the American township or similar unit. There is also national-local administration, the most important form of which is the county administration. For many purposes of national administration Sweden is divided into twenty-four counties (*län*) plus the city of Stockholm, which is regarded as a county itself. The overall role of local government is probably not as extensive in Sweden as in England or the United States, but it is much greater than in France and somewhat greater than in most of the Continental European countries.

The Political Party System

The Swedish political party system consists of five parties. The Swedes divide them into the middle-class (*bourgeois*) and the socialist parties. The former are the Conservatives, the Liberals, and the Agrarians; the latter the Social Democrats and the Communists.[17] These five parties have dominated Swedish politics since the achievement of universal suffrage in the early 1920s. Table 2.1 shows the number of seats each party has had in the Lower House since 1940, which was the high point in the electoral success of the Swedish Social Democrats, who are by any criteria of strength and influence the most successful socialist or labor party in any Western democracy.

Sweden's political party system is similar to those of Denmark, Norway, and Britain.[18] All of these countries are culturally homogeneous, have predominantly Protestant backgrounds, and have

Table 2.1   Distribution of Seats in the Lower House of the Riksdag, 1940–1968.

	1940	1944	1948	1952	1956	1958*	1960	1964	1968
Middle-class parties									
Conservative	42	39	23	31	42	45	39	33	32
Agrarians (Center Party)	28	35	30	26	19	32	34	36**	39
Liberals	23	26	57	58	58	38	40	43	34
Socialist parties									
Social Democrats	134	115	112	110	106	111	114	113	125
Communists	3	15	8	5	6	5	5	8	3
Total	230	230	230	230	231	231	232	233	233

* An extra election was held in June 1958 after the government resigned.

** One member, elected by the Citizens League, was refused admission to the Center Party's Parliamentary group.

SOURCE: See *Statistisk Årsbok för Sverige* (Stockholm: Statistiska Centralbyrån) for appropriate years.

achieved a high degree of political consensus and stability. None has important Christian-confessional or regional parties to dampen the operation of class politics, and none has a large Communist party to dissipate the strength of their labor or socialist parties. The British system is least similar because it is predominantly a two-party system—a Conservative and a Labour party—with a Liberal party that is sometimes numerically important. Also Britain has no Agrarian party and the Communist party is microscopic.

The Swedish political party system has continued to be based on class and occupation to a greater extent than in most democracies, perhaps more than any other, but its reality has become more statistical than psychological.[19] Under conditions of political democracy and the general security provided by the welfare state, it is precisely economic and class interests that men are most willing to compromise about. Cleavages over religion, language, region, and ethnic group touch the core of men's existence in ways that economic and class-interest issues do not. While the former do not make consensus politics impossible, as the Low Countries and Switzerland show, they do lessen its scope and make consensus more difficult to achieve and maintain. Tensions caused by the language issue in Belgium, for example, or events that emphasize to Catholics the Protestant traditions of the House of Orange in the Netherlands make for a less robust and more sensitive kind of consensus politics than exists in Sweden.

The political parties of a modern state are both a microcosm of the values and attitudes of a people and the shapers and articulators of those values and attitudes. This correspondence must not be carried too far, however, for the political party system has many independent characteristics of its own. The following is a discussion of the political parties, their developments, their social bases, the attitudes and values they manifest, and their interrelations with each other. They are presented in terms of their strength over the past couple of decades, with particular attention to the Social Democrats, who have been the government party virtually continuously since the elections of 1932. And they have accomplished this in the framework of a five-party system. They are the preëminent example of Maurice Duverger's "dominant party."[20]

THE SOCIAL DEMOCRATS

What is particularly noteworthy in the development of the Social Democratic party (*Sveriges socialdemokratiska arbetarepartiet*) has been its political realism, the continuing ability of the leadership and rank and file to modify their ideas in order to allow the party to become larger and to assume greater power, even when the party suffered serious reversals, such as after World War II, during the late 1950s, and again in the middle 1960s.[21, 22] In terms of the perennial problem of modern political parties of "ideology versus pragmatism," the Swedish Social Democratic party lies far on the pragmatic side.

The whole structure of Swedish society and its tranquil development provided the preconditions necessary for the extraordinary success of Swedish Social Democracy. Its growth and ideological transformation were very rapid. In the 1880s and early 1890s the party was a numerically insignificant radical sect; after the election in the fall of 1914 it had become almost as large a party as the Conservative party and relatively one of the largest social democratic parties in Europe. After the 1917 elections it was clearly the largest party in the country. In the early years, the party adhered to orthodox Marxist views of the fundamental division of society into the bourgeoisie and proletariat, the inevitability of class struggle, the increasing impoverishment of the workers, the increasing concentration of wealth, and the necessary disappearance of capitalism and its replacement by the socialist utopia. All social evils, from drunkenness and prostitution to war and the inferior status of women, were seen as consequences of capitalism. The early leaders of the party were largely influenced by radical international socialist theory primarily from Germany; Swedish conditions were not the impetus, since industrialization had scarcely begun. Most of the early leaders had not read much more of Marx than *The Communist Manifesto*. Their thought was an amalgam of popular Marxism and Enlightenment rationalism. This early socialism was an ideology of protest of unattached young intellectuals and self-educated workers against the paternalistic and hierarchical social system in which they found themselves. It was late in the day for the existence of such a social order; every other country in Western Europe—even Germany—had progressed futher in expanding the franchise. The young radicals from this early period who lived into the the 1920s and 1930s—a number seem to have died young—went through the whole transformation from orthodox Marxism to nondoctrinaire moderation.

The party was nationally organized in 1889, though Social Democratic clubs and unions had already existed in a number of places. It was the first party in Sweden to organize outside of the Riksdag.

During the decade of the 1880s, radical socialist and liberal ideas gained in circulation and were spread by a number of writers; August Strindberg was the most famous of them. This was the decade when Sweden began to open the door wide to radical thought from Norway and Denmark, England and Germany, influences which quickly undermined the foundations of the old paternalistic order.

Almost from the start the orthodox Marxism of the Social Democrats began to crumble. At the first party congress in 1891 it was decided to support the Liberals in the new suffrage movement. In 1896 Hjalmar Branting was elected to the Riksdag with the aid of the Liberals as the first Social Democratic representative. From the beginning, he allied himself with the Liberals and proved himself a good committee worker as did the other Social Democrats who joined him several years later. In 1897 the party adopted its first official program based on the Erfurt Program of 1891. But unlike its German counterpart, which echoes *The Communist Manifesto* in its preamble, it specifically speaks of socialism developing "by degrees." Many of the specific social reforms demanded in the Swedish program, such as the eight-hour day and the prohibition of child labor, were also aims of the social-reformist Liberals. That the Swedish party was not strongly adverse to a policy of governmental collaboration with nonsocialist parties was evident as early as 1904, when the Swedish representatives at the international Socialist Congress in Amsterdam abstained from voting for Karl Kautsky's victorious proposal opposing socialist collaboration with bourgeois parties in coalition governments. Yet until World War I, the party was, in terms of its programmatic ideology and its general stance outside of the Riksdag, among the more Marxist of the Social Democratic parties, at least when compared with the moderate Belgian and Danish parties.

The period from 1895 through 1907—when universal suffrage in Lower House elections was first passed by the Riksdag—saw a rapid growth in electoral support, and party membership increased from 10,000 to 133,000. The central and overriding concern of the party in these years was the achievement of universal male suffrage in Lower House elections. But after this was accomplished there still remained the problem of equal suffrage in communal elections. Voting for members of the Upper House in county and municipal councils continued to be determined by sharp income and property qualifications that left power in the hands of the rich. Equal suffrage was first passed in 1918 by a coalition of Liberals and Social Democrats, who had entered the government in 1917, forming the first parliamentary government in Sweden to be generally recognized as such. The coalition fell apart in 1920, after which the Social Democrats formed the first wholly Socialist government achieved by peaceful means in the world. At this time the present division between the Social Democrats and the non-socialist parties came about; the Liberals opposed the economic radicalism of the Social Democrats.

The 1920s was a period of minority parliamentarianism with the Social Democrats forming three governments with a total tenure of about four years. Yet no attempt was made to realize any of the radical demands of the party's 1920 Program. The party increasingly functioned, both inside and outside the Riksdag, as one democratic party among others. German influences had become much less at this time and were partially replaced by the influence of the more pragmatic and less ideological English variety of socialism. The party began its long period of political dominance after the Lower House elections of 1932, since which time it has been the only party in the government or the senior partner in a coalition government, with the unimportant exception of the summer of 1936 when the Agrarians took over.

By the 1930s, after assuming the reins of government, the dissolution of orthodox socialism of a predominantly Marxist kind was evident; not even any *attempts* at active socialization were made. Corresponding developments in the other parties resulted in an "end of ideology" in Swedish politics, which has continued to develop to the present.

The Swedish Social Democratic party is the only European socialist or labor party ever to get a majority of the popular vote in general elections. They achieved this in the Lower House elections of 1940 and 1968 and in the Communal Elections of 1938, 1942, and 1962. More compelling, however, is the observation that the three non-socialist parties—the Conservatives, Liberals, and Agrarians—have not succeeded, except in 1956, in obtaining a majority of the mandates or of the popular vote in any Lower House election since 1934. The silent support of the Communists has provided the Social Democrats with a functional majority in the Lower House of the Riksdag most of the time when they lacked an actual majority, and the Upper House, soon to be abolished, has had a Social Democratic majority since 1941. No European political party in this century has had such long-term governmental dominance as has the Swedish Social Democrats.

It was in 1940 that the Social Democrats reached the peak of their popular support by electing 134 of the 230 mandates in the Lower House, a larger majority than has ever been achieved by any social democratic or labor party anywhere, and a majority that has never since been approached in Sweden. This was the result of the stunning achievements of the Social Democratic government in applying the "new economics" in the 1930s, the introduction of a coalition government of the four major parties under the Social Democrats in the previous year, and the marked worsening of the international situation with both Norway and Denmark occupied by the Nazis.

The coalition government under the Social Democratic Prime Minister Per-Albin Hansson continued during the war years with power centralized in the cabinet. After peace was achieved in Europe, the wartime coalition was dissolved, and the Socialists formed a new government, with only half of the Lower House but a majority in the Upper House.

The 1944 program of the Social Democrats was made more radical and, after the forming of the new Socialist government in 1945, the party turned to the left, which expanded the cleavage with the nonsocialist parties. As elsewhere, both world wars strengthened the left in Sweden. World War II increased the prestige of the Soviet Union and communism; everywhere in Western Europe the Communist vote jumped. In the communal elections of 1946 the Swedish Communists got 11.2 percent of the vote, the highest ever; the Social Democratic vote fell to 44.1 percent, the lowest since 1934. In the 1948 general elections, the Communist vote fell sharply, and the Liberals more than doubled their number of seats in the Lower House, largely at the expense of the Conservatives. After this election, the Social Democrats changed course and moved back to moderation; little has been said about socialization since.

At this time the position of the government was not as secure as it had been, though it could still rely on a declining majority in joint votes with the Upper House.

After the 1948 election, the Social Democrats approached the Agrarians to enter the government to provide a secure majority in the Lower House. They were rebuffed, but did accept an invitation three years later. This second "red-green" coalition lasted until 1957 when the Agrarians stated they could no longer remain in the government; this resulted in an extraordinary extra election and the formation of a minority Socialist government. The immediate reason for the resignation of the Agrarians was their inability to accept the government proposal for a universal and compulsory supplementary pension plan similar to that provided for Swedish civil servants. Furthermore, a continuing decrease in the proportion of farmers and workers in the society had resulted in declines in both the Agrarian and Social-Democratic vote; the coalition was becoming restive.[23]

The Social Democrats engineered with this pension plan one of the most advanced pieces of welfare legislation anywhere, which reversed the downward trend in the Social Democratic vote of the 1950s and broadened the attractiveness of the party.[24] The strategy of the Social Democrats was to appeal to the interests of employees—both white-collar and manual workers. Their success resulted in a great reversal for the Liberals in the extra election of 1958. After the government proposal was passed in May 1959, however, the Liberals quickly supported the proposal; they are continually torn in their support for social welfare measures and their desire to maintain a united front with the Conservatives and Agrarians. The Conservatives and Agrarians reluctantly supported the legislation after the 1960 election. In this election the Social Democrats succeeded in becoming the leading party among the white-collar workers. In the 1964 election they obtained more votes from white-collar workers than the Conservatives and Liberals combined.[25] The party's hold is tenuous here, yet more and more this is the group which will determine the future fortunes of the Social Democrats.

One necessary condition for the success of the Swedish Social Democrats has been the high degree of industrialization that came about in the first three decades of this century. By the 1930s the only European country with a substantially larger industrial working class was Britain. In the Scandinavian countries, and perhaps most of all in Sweden, there has always been a very high level of support in the working class for the socialist left. In recent elections for which survey data exist less than 20 percent of industrial workers who vote support nonsocialist parties.[26] By contrast, for example, a third or more of British and West German workers vote for nonsocialist parties.[27] In Sweden there are no religious, ethnic, or regional parties to dampen the operation of class politics as exist everywhere else in Western Europe with the exceptions of Britain, Denmark, and Iceland.[28] Throughout Continental Europe, the presence of Christian parties that have competed with the socialists for the votes of the workers has greatly limited the potential strength of the Social Democrats. Outside of Britain and Scandinavia, with their predominantly secular political systems, no Western European socialist party other than the Austrian and the West German (but not until 1969) has ever succeeded in obtaining as much as 40 percent of the vote and a similar percentage of the mandates in a national election.[29] The general pattern in Belgium and the Netherlands, in West Germany and Austria is for the Christian party to be the largest party and for the Social Democrats to play second fiddle. Nor has there ever been a Conservative working-class tradition in Sweden, such as exists in Britain.[30] When Swedish workers vote nonsocialist, they most frequently vote Liberal; barely 2 or 3 percent vote Conservative. On the other side, the Communists and Left-Socialists have never been strong enough to seriously dissipate the strength of the Social Democrats. There have been a number of eruptions from the Left through the 1930s—although there have been none since—but they never had much appeal, and the dissidents generally returned to the Social Democratic fold.

Another key to the strength of the Swedish Social Democrats is the relationship between the Social Democratic party and the trade-union movement, which has always been close and supportive. Most of the organizations that came together to form the Swedish Social Democratic party were trade unions, yet none of the official leadership of the party has come from the unions, and in fact few trade-union officials have ever served in the government. The trade-union movement and the Social Democratic party grew up together, yet each has kept its own identity and organizational autonomy. There is no union representation as such at the congresses of the Social Democratic party. The relations that exist between them at the national level are informal and nonofficial.[31] Since 1909 there has been no statement in the rules of The Swedish Confederation of Trade Unions (*Landsorganisation*, abbreviated *LO*) about any cooperative relationship with the party. However, such cooperation clearly exists and always has from the top level down, especially at election time when many trade-union functionaries are active campaign workers.

There appears to be a high correlation between the level of development of the political and the trade-union aspects of the labor movement.[32] In Scandinavia and Britain both have been highly developed, whereas in France and Italy neither has been developed. The rapid success of the Swedish Social Democrats in the years prior to World War I was, in fact, largely a result of the success of the solidly Social Democratic trade-union movement in organizing and politicizing the workers. Robert Michels claimed that Sweden even at this early date

(1915) had a higher percentage of its workers in the trade-union movement than any other country had.[33]

LO members are collectively enrolled as members of the Social Democratic local organization if the majority of the members in a local so vote. Prior to World War I, about 80 percent of the membership of the Social Democratic party was collectively joined to the party,[34] although the membership declined to about 60 percent in 1945, where it has remained. LO has provided financial support to the Social Democratic press, most of which has not been self-supporting, has officially supported the party in its journals, and has actively campaigned for and financially supported the election of Social Democrats. At the top there is an informal council of the party and LO leaders that meets regularly. To symbolize their supporting relationship, the present chairman of LO, Arne Geijer, sits as a Social Democratic representative in the Upper House.

LO remains the only major interest group in Swedish society that has not adhered to an official policy of political neutrality through the years. The cooperative movement, farm organizations, employer organizations, and white-collar unions have all come to adopt such a policy, even if their policies sometimes parallel those of one of the political parties. This supporting relationship together with the institution of collective membership has been a source of irritation to nonsocialists in Sweden just as it has been in Britain and Norway, the only other countries where it exists. In recent years, however, some intellectuals within the Social Democratic party have voiced opposition to the institution of union locals collectively joining Social Democratic party locals.[35]

Comparatively speaking, one might say that the Swedish (and, to a somewhat lesser extent, the Norwegian) Social Democrats have had the benefits of a strong trade-union movement without the disadvantages. The trade-union movement brought the workers to a high level of support for the party, yet it never suffered from the onus of the British Labour party, in which the party was seen as only the political arm of the trade-union movement—which indeed the Labour party was during the early decades of its existence. And, on the other hand, the party has never had the opposition or indifference of the trade unions, as was the case in Germany prior to World War I. Nor has there ever been the independence between party and union that characterizes the United States and France.

While there is now great similarity in the moderate social-reform-ism of all the Scandinavian Social Democratic parties, their ideological histories have been strikingly different. The Danish movement, even though it was Marxist, was gradualist and accommodating from the start.[36] In contrast to Sweden, craft unionism was well established in Denmark before the advent of social democracy in the 1870s. The early leaders of the party were largely skilled workers who saw the political movement as a means of enhancing union power. The slow and steady growth of industrialism and urbanism in Denmark prevented the growth of the masses of uprooted workers that occurred in Sweden and Norway; it seems that rapid industrialization in agrarian societies and the cultural discontinuities it engenders are conducive to radical politics.

Until around 1915, the Norwegian Labor party held to a moderate socialist line similar to that which prevailed in Denmark.[37] The Socialists cooperated with the Liberals to such an extent, in fact, that they functioned virtually as one party vis-à-vis the Conservatives. However, a rapid industrialization after 1905 resulted in a large number of displaced farm owners and workers who helped form a left wing. Sweden underwent a similar period of rapid growth in the years prior to World War I, but the proportion of rootless laborers was not as large as Norway's, and they were unable to turn the party in a radical direction, as they did in Norway. The strong radical opposition that developed within the Norwegian Labor party was influenced by syndicalist thought, the activities of the I.W.W. in the United States, and the Russian Revolution. At the 1918 Congress the Left Wing leaders were elected to the top offices in the Norwegian party. In 1919 the party accepted the severe conditions of the "Moscow theses" and joined the Soviet-dominated Comintern. The Norwegian Labor party thereby became the most radical socialist party in Western Europe. The moderates broke away in 1921 and formed the Social Democratic party. The Norwegian Labor party left the Comintern in 1923, rejoined the Social Democrats in 1927, and began to move in the direction of moderation and compromise. The program adopted in 1933 still adhered to a Marxist line and manifested an ambivalence about democracy, but when the Social Democrats began their thirty years in the government in 1935, they behaved democratically and moderately.[38] Not until after World War II, however, did the party program eschew Marxism and speak of serving all groups within society. In the party program adopted in 1949, there is not a trace of discussion about class struggle, socialist transformation, and the like.

A number of factors distinguish the development of social democracy in these three Scandinavian countries from their counterparts elsewhere, in spite of their different histories. In Sweden, Denmark, and Norway, the labor movement developed in an environment of freedom to organize and agitate. The relations between the political and trade-union movements have been close and mutually supportive. These countries have had particularly strong radical-liberal elements which were democratic and with which the Social Democrats were able to cooperate in the early years. In Sweden and Norway, but not in Denmark, the Social Democrats were later able to establish supportive and cooperative relations with the Agrarians—in Sweden in the 1930s and 1950s and in Norway in the 1930s. Almost everywhere outside of Scandinavia this most culturally conservative of the major societal groups has merged its interests with urban conservatives. This is a fundamental structural difference between the Scandinavian party systems and those of Britain and Continental Europe. The inability of the urban conservatives to fuse politically with agrarian interests explains the weakness of the conservative parties in all the Scandinavian countries.[39] In addition, it is only in these three countries that the Social Democratic parties have clearly become the dominant parties and have remained so for a number of decades.

The development of Swedish Social Democracy can serve as a model of the process of the dissolution of socialist ideology that has occurred in all of the Western European Social Democratic parties. It is also a prime example of a class party able to transcend the boundaries of its original support to include new categories of voters; it has moved from being primarily a party directed to workers to one directed to employees. The whole course of the Swedish Social Democratic movement has been exceptionally continuous, clear, and smooth; but this must be seen as only one aspect of the tranquility of the whole process of modernization that has occurred in Sweden. For these reasons, in addition to having been the most successful of all similar political movements, the Swedish Social Democrats hold a position of particular importance among modern political parties.

THE LIBERALS

No Swedish political party is or has been so diverse in its composition as the Liberal party (*Folkpartiet*). Liberalism has had an appeal to intellectuals, businessmen, the lower-middle classes, farmers, and workers. In 1964 almost one-third of the voters who were classified as big businessmen, managers, and professionals voted Liberal, as did one-third of those classified as small businessmen, one-quarter of those classified as white-collar workers, one out of eight farmers, and one out of twelve workers.[40] From 1948 through 1968, with the exception of the period 1958 to 1960, it has been the largest of the three non-socialist parties, but with a highly fluctuating vote that ranged from more than one-half to less than one-third that of the Social Democrats. It has been the largest Liberal party in Scandinavia and, relatively, one of the largest in Europe, even with less than one-fifth of the vote.[41]

The party's roots are in nineteenth-century ideas of individual freedom, tolerance, popular democracy, social reform, and individualism.[42] Liberalism is the conventional name for these diverse ideas, which are all rooted in philosophical individualism. The specific ideological influences on Swedish liberalism were: American experience, particularly as described by Alexis de Tocqueville; English political thought of the middle decades of the nineteenth century, mainly the doctrines stemming from Jeremy Bentham and Walter Bagehot; and later—and most important—the doctrines of John Stuart Mill. Of equal importance was evangelical Protestantism with its free-church and temperance movements. From one point of view, the Swedish Liberals can be viewed as the principal adherents of English and American, and, to some extent, French, ideas and experience during the nineteenth and early twentieth centuries. In the decades prior to 1914, the Conservatives and Socialists, each in their own ways, were predominantly oriented toward Germany and held to primarily nonindividualistic theories of the relationship between man and society. The Conservatives were exponents of nationalistic and organic views of society, which were shaped by nineteenth-century German philosophy and official culture;[43] the Social Democrats by Marxist class theory. From another point of view, Swedish Liberalism can be seen as a doctrine of opposition against the politically dominant, large landowners and official classes by the independent farmers and emerging middle classes. From the 1890s, after protectionism left the center of the political stage, the dominant concern of the Swedish Liberals crystallized around achieving universal manhood suffrage. It was at this time that they entered into cooperative relations with the Social Democrats.

Liberalism has centered in free-church groups, temperance groups, cultural radicals (urban intellectuals), social reformers, and nonconservative farmers since around the turn of the twentieth century, when an attempt to form a permanent Riksdag party was successful.[44]

The free-church and temperance movements gained increasing strength in Sweden from the 1860s, influenced by England and, particularly, by America. The free churches were also generally in favor of total abstinence, but a number of the temperance organizations declared themselves nonsectarian in matters of religion. These ideas found their greatest strength in the lower-middle classes of the towns (*småfolk*) but later spread to the working classes.[45]

Cultural radicalism is an element in both the Liberal and Social Democratic traditions, but it has been relatively more important among the Liberals, even though "cultural radicals" are a small minority even here. It traces its origins back to the founding of the Verdandi Debating Society at Uppsala University in 1882, which was founded to promote rationalist criticism of the beliefs of the Swedish State Church, conventional morality, and traditional institutions in general. This stream of liberalism was particularly influenced by foreign sources. As Hans-Krister Rönblom put it, "these were Norwegian, Danish and French, and even English, but above all not American."[46] Urban radicalism and the rationalist criticism of society of a predominantly literary sort were well established in the other Scandinavian countries a decade before they came to Sweden, and they quickly became a strong force in journalistic and intellectual circles. Annie Besant, Charles Bradlaugh, and the Rationalist Press Association represented the English version of cultural radicalism of the latter decades of the nineteenth century.[47] The influence of the extremely rationalist liberalism has been subsequently much greater in Sweden than in England, and it is not regarded as eccentric. The influence of this tradition is particularly notable in a number of the larger Liberal and Social Democratic newspapers, a tradition which has little counterpart in the English or American press, and it is a more important element in the major Swedish press than in the other Scandinavian countries.[48] *Dagens Nyheter*, the most important liberal paper in Sweden that adheres to this tradition, according to its own statement, "aims to be an organ for opinion formation in a liberal and radical spirit, a newspaper which takes up the burning problems, pushing aside the fetters of catchwords and thought clichés, and prepares the way for a better society, without unreflective respect for established opinions and institutions."[49] This tradition is, however, strongest among the left student organizations in the universities.

Another stream in Swedish Liberalism was of an economic sort favorable to free trade, but with a strong social reformist bent. Economic liberalism in Sweden was influenced by French economic thought in the 1850s, but it never assumed the Social Darwinist form that it did in England or the United States. There were never many adherents of laissez-faire liberalism in nineteenth-century Sweden. The social-reform liberals supported protective legislation for women and children in industrial work and other kinds of social reform. Like the Conservatives, they were much influenced by Bismarck's social legislation in Germany in the 1880s, but the writings of John Stuart Mill, more than any other source, can be said to represent their views. The Liberals—and perhaps all articulate elements of the Swedish population—reacted against the dismal consequences of industrialization in England.[50]

Nonconservative farmers, particularly those in the north of Sweden who opposed the activities of the large lumber companies, are another element in Swedish Liberalism. The rural liberal tradition, reinforced by a free-church tradition, remains stronger in the northern province of Västerbotten than anywhere else,[51] but there is also marked Liberal-party strength on the west coast, particularly in the second largest city of Gothenburg. The same pattern is true of Bergen and the west coast of Norway. This pattern is probably partly related to close contact with England and long distance of these areas from their capitals.[52]

Representatives from these groupings in the Lower House of the Riksdag came together in 1900 to form the Liberal party (then called the *Liberala samlingspartiet*) under the leadership of the moderates who have generally led the party. Two years later a national organization was formed to support the election of candidates of liberal persuasion. These groups were able to unite by their overriding concern with achieving universal suffrage. The strength of this single aim also enabled them to cooperate with the Social Democrats in electing candidates and, finally, in forming a coalition government with them in 1917. Similar patterns of mutual help existed between the Liberals and Socialists in *all* Western European countries that moved in the direction of stable democracy.

However, this cooperation did not survive in Sweden after the goal of universal suffrage was reached in both houses in 1919; the Liberals could not tolerate the economic radicalism of the Social Democrats, and they have never been able to collaborate with the Social Democrats since. Furthermore, the diverse elements in the party could no longer hold together after the burning issue which had united them was removed. Between 1923 and 1933 the party was split over the issue of prohibition (also influenced by America), with the majority Ekman Liberals favoring it and a minority, made up primarily of cultural radicals and non-free church members (*Löfgrenites*), opposing it. The support for both factions declined during the decade of their separation in spite of the fact that the Prohibitionists formed two governments during this period of minority parliamentarianism. They were called weighmaster (*vågmästare*) governments because they were unstable center governments precariously balancing the Conservatives and Social Democrats against each other in order to remain in power. The fortunes of the reunited Liberals, now named the *Folkpartiet*, remained at a low ebb in the elections between 1934 and 1944, obtaining around 12 or 13 percent of the vote. Their situation improved greatly in the years after World War II; they reached 24.4 percent of the vote in 1952. This was probably the combined result of a postwar reassertion of socialist aims by the Social Democrats, an effective propaganda program that emphasized the incompatibility of socialism and democracy, and the identification of socialism with the aggressive policies of Stalinist Russia after the war. The party suffered a major setback in the 1958 communal elections, obtaining only 15.6 percent of the vote, after having opposed the government's proposal for the compulsory supplementary pension plan, which was finally passed in 1959. In the elections of the early 1960s they made a slight comeback, but they had serious reverses in the 1968 elections.

Of the four major parties, the Liberals are perhaps the most ideological in their approach to the electorate. The diversity of their support encourages the party to appeal to the entire electorate. Much of their election propaganda is directed to the voter as consumer and general citizen. In a less uncertain manner than the Conservatives and in a more universalistic manner than the Agrarians, they advocate expanding social-welfare legislation.[53] In fact, one of their principal means of attacking the Social Democratic government with which they have so much in common is the argument that welfare is inadequate for a number of groups in the population such as the old, the handicapped, and the part-time students. They have repeatedly charged the government with poor planning that has led to a "queue society" in which one must wait years for an apartment and months for a needed operation. They also charge that the government has been deficient in aid to the developing countries. They oppose expanding governmental bureaucracy and increased centralization and favor less regulation of the economy. The Liberals, along with the Conservatives, are most friendly to the Common Market. They tend to be closer to the Conservatives than to the Social Democrats in their opposition to economic leveling through highly progressive taxation.

Since 1911 the electoral record of the Liberals has been the most erratic of the four major parties, reflecting their absence of ties to clear-cut class or occupational groupings and the low degree of organization of the party. While it is predominantly a middle-class party, it is also "the second largest labor party," receiving the vote of one out of twelve workers. The size of the party membership in relation to their share of the vote has been appreciably lower than that of the other major parties. According to national interview studies of the electorate, Liberal voters in 1956 and 1960 were more likely to have voted for other parties than the voters for the other major parties. Also, they were less likely in both the 1956 and 1960 elections to be "convinced" adherents of their party than the members of the other parties. The unstable character of the Liberal vote is also characteristic of Norway (*Venstre* party), Denmark (*Radical Venstre* party), and, most of all, Britain.[54] A large proportion of liberal voters are probably subject to cross-pressures from the right and left, and the ups and downs of the Liberal vote can perhaps be seen as a kind of barometer of the satisfaction of the not so strongly politically committed of the society to the politics of both the Conservatives and the Socialists.

By most criteria the Swedish Liberals are clearly a party of the left, in that on most issues they are closer to the Social Democrats than to the Conservatives. Swedish usage recognizes this in the expression *borgerliga vänstern*, which may be translated as the "bourgeois left" or "nonsocialist left," to refer to an important segment of the party. The party has generally favored the expansion of welfare and egalitarian legislation and has always maintained a broad appeal. That the Liberals are closer to the Social Democrats than are the Agrarians or Conservatives is only inadequately corroborated by the finding that 16 percent of Liberal voters in 1960 had voted for the Social Democrats in 1956 as compared with 12 percent of the Agrarian voters and 5 percent of the Conservative voters.[55] How left the Swedish Liberal party really is can be seen when it is compared with Continental parties that regard or call themselves "liberal" but that are conservative parties from a Swedish point of view. The Liberal parties of Belgium and Switzerland, Austria and Italy, for example, now largely reflect business interests.[56]

THE CONSERVATIVES

Like the Social Democrats, the Conservatives have made major re-adjustments to their changing environment. They did not give up their hostility to the emerging industrial society until the 1880s, and did not come to terms with popular democracy and parliamentarianism until after World War I, with the defeat of Germany and the achievement of universal suffrage in both houses of the Riksdag.[57] Their acceptance of democracy was probably as late as anywhere in Northwestern Europe except Germany, but it was complete and deepgoing.

In spite of the fact that some segments of the upper class in Sweden —the nobility, the clergy, the military, upper-level civil servants— maintained a German orientation during the interwar years, the Conservatives remained steadfastly loyal to democratic principles throughout the 1930s when Fascism and antidemocratic thought permeated Europe. Arvid Lindman and the other leaders of the Conservative party refused the demands of the Conservative youth for a more positive orientation toward the Nazis, and in 1934 the party's youth organization declared its independence and formed a new organization called the Young Swedes (*Ungsvenskarna*). Three members of the Riksdag resigned from the Conservative party in that year to support the demands of the youth organization and to form a new National party. None was reelected in 1936. Neither this group nor two outright Nazi groups were ever able to elect a single candidate to the Riksdag. Only two well-known Conservatives in the intellectual and scholarly community were publicly Nazi sympathizers in the 1930s, the literary critic Fredrik Böök and the world famous explorer Sven Hedin.[58] No European conservative party was more resolutely antifascist during this period than was the Swedish Conservative party. Not since the 1930s has there been any identifiable political group remotely comparable to the "radical right" either as it exists in France or in the United States.

The Swedish Conservatives have little continuity with their elitist and nondemocratic pre-World War I heritage other than a stronger commitment to national defense, the monarchy, the state church, and to more elitist values than the other parties. Even though there is a division within the party between a more-conservative minority and a less-conservative majority ("dark blues" versus "light blues"), the party must be classified as a moderate and nonideological conservative party rather similar to its English counterpart. The far more successful

English Tories have become a model for their Swedish counterparts. For example, the Conservative election posters in 1964 reflected the main theme stressed in the English posters in the 1959 and 1964 general elections, showing happy and prosperous family scenes in the attempt to appeal to the interests of young small property owners.[59]

The Conservative party is supported by fewer than one out of six Swedes. The support for the Conservatives is high in upper-status groups; among 1960 and 1964 voters more than half of the upper-level managers, civil servants, and professionals supported the party, whereas only about one out of seven small enterprisers, farmers, and white-collar workers voted Conservative, and only about 3 percent of the workers supported the party.[60] Unlike the situation that exists in Britain, the proportion of workers who support the Conservatives is almost negligible. To a great extent the party represents the financial and status interests of the upper classes and the old middle classes.

In 1896 more-or-less conservative candidates for the Riksdag received around 67 percent of the vote in the Lower House elections. That was the year the first Social Democrat was elected to the Riksdag and in a time when only one-quarter of the adult males had the franchise.[61] The percentage of Conservative votes rapidly declined as the right to vote was expanded, falling to 24.7 percent by the election of 1917, six years after the first election in which nearly all adult men had the right to vote in Lower House elections. The fortunes of the Conservatives improved a few percentage points in the 1920s, largely at the expense of the divided Liberals, but after 1930 there were two decades of almost uninterrupted decline; the Conservative share of the vote reached an all-time low of 12.3 percent in both 1948 and 1950. Their vote increased to 20.4 percent in the communal election of 1958, after which a steady decline set in, dropping to less than 14 percent in the Lower House elections of both 1964 and 1968. During the past three decades, except for the time around 1958, the Swedish Conservatives have consistently been weaker than their counterparts in Denmark and Norway.

While the Conservatives clearly have accepted the basic reforms of the welfare state, there are a number of relatively minor retreats they would favor and, unlike the Agrarians and Liberals, they are hesitant to expand it. They are also more distant from the Social Democrats than are the Agrarians and the Liberals. The Conservative party has opposed raising child allowances and has advocated the abolition of an allowance for the first child, similar to the Norwegian system. They have opposed educational allowances for students over twenty-one (mostly university students). In general, they have tended to favor tax reductions for children and educational expenses rather than a system of universal grants. No party is as vigorous in its support of national defense as the Conservatives. They have favored a four-year rather than a three-year gymnasium and the retention of the allegedly invidious university matriculation examination (*studentexamen*). Unlike the other parties, they have emphasized quality in education rather than making it more egalitarian, though they have favored the expansion of education and research in general. They have also favored a less progressive taxation system and the abolition of rent controls. Unlike the other nonsocialist parties, they have continued to oppose the government administration of the general pension fund (ATP fund) as a form of hidden socialism that gives the government an allegedly dangerous control over the economy. The party program makes strong appeals to Christian and traditional values, and unlike any of the other parties, it explicitly defends the interests of the State Church.[62]

While the Conservatives are good compromisers, like all the parties in the Riksdag, their views on the minority of issues that are controversial have little influence because of their small size and the fact that they generally have difficulty in forming a united front with the Liberals and Agrarians.

THE AGRARIANS

One of the most distinguishing characteristics of the political systems of Sweden, Norway, Finland, and Iceland is the existence and strength of Agrarian parties. In Denmark, the Social Liberal party (*Venstre*), the second largest party, gets a large proportion of the vote of farmers and is sometimes considered an Agrarian party,[63] but it also gets a sizable vote from middle-class urban groups and is therefore not parallel to the farmer parties in the other Scandinavian countries.[64] While such parties are not unique to Scandinavia—they are also found in Switzerland, Australia, Canada, and sometimes in the United States, Belgium, and Germany—their high degree of effective organization is.[65] Like the Social Democrats, the Agrarians have a high ratio of party members relative to their share of the vote. The presence of Agrarian parties renders the relationship between occupation and voting behavior closer in northern Scandinavia than in other countries that have a high degree of class voting, such as

Britain and Denmark. The Agrarians appeal primarily to independent farmers, about two-thirds of whom supported the Agrarian party in 1964. The big farmers, however, are more likely to vote for the Conservatives than the Agrarians. Only about one-fifth of the agricultural workers who voted, however, supported the Agrarians; the majority voted for the Social Democrats.[66]

The party was formed in 1913 by farm organizations and succeeded in electing representatives to the Riksdag in 1917. Swedish farmers have a long and unique tradition of organized political activity in the Peasant Estate from the Middle Ages to 1865 and in the Lower House of the Riksdag as the Ruralist party (Lantmannapartiet) for the remainder of the century.[67] Like the Social Democrats, and unlike the other parties, the modern Agrarians became a national party before they succeeded in obtaining a place in the Riksdag. According to Nils Andrén, the party was established "on the conviction that the fast declining agricultural population, in order to hold its own, must follow the example of industrial workers and form a solid front against other organized groups."[68] In 1957 the party changed its name from Farmers' party (Bondepartiet) to Center party (Centerpartiet) to broaden its appeal, particularly to nonagricultural small enterprisers, who comprise the most politically diverse of the major occupational groupings; almost one out of five nonagricultural small enterprisers supported the party in 1960 and 1964, but the party gets a very small vote in the cities, averaging less than 3 percent in the three largest cities.

The Agrarians are more clearly an interest-group party than any of the other parties. In their history they have been able to cooperate, in turn, with the Conservatives, the Social Democrats, and the Liberals. During the 1920s they supported the Conservatives when they were in office. In the periods 1936 to 1939 and 1951 to 1957, they were junior partners in coalition governments with the Social Democrats. They entered into a supporting relation with them as early as 1933 by voting for the government's unemployment policies, which were of greatest direct benefit to industrial workers, in return for consideration of the interests of the farmers, particularly in maintaining a standard of living comparable to urban industrial workers. In recent years, but particularly after the 1964 elections, they have entered into much-publicized cooperation with the Liberals.

Their capacity for tactical maneuverability is indicated by their party program.[69] It is less than half as long as that of the other major parties and somewhat shorter than that of the Communists, and, in contrast to these, it makes few proposals not directly related to the specific interests of farmers and small enterprisers. The theme of the party program is concern with the effects of industrialization. It warns of the danger of "financial concentration, private or government" that can lead to "the misuse of power," and it favors localization and decentralization of governmental administration and of economic life. While the Conservative and Liberal programs contain these ideas, they also contain views on a broad array of subjects, and they are not the central concerns they are in the Agrarian program. The Agrarian program also takes a stronger position than does the Conservative program on the role of Christianity in society. It states explicitly, as does the Conservative program, that society should be built on a Christian foundation, but when dealing with education it goes further and states that Christianity "shall be presented so as to give a positive position to the Christian life view." These ideas differ from those in the Liberal program which adheres to values stemming from "Christianity and humanism," the Social Democratic and Communist programs say nothing on the subject. In general, the emphasis on other traditional values in the Agrarian program is greater than in the Conservative program, which does not hold that work in the home should be valued as much as work outside, that mothers should be encouraged to remain in the home and to take care of their children until they are grown, and that the roots of Swedish democracy are in the rural society (*bondesamhället*).

Yet along with the traditional, moralistic, and antibureaucratic ethos that permeates the party goes a positive view toward a broad range of welfare legislation. They have favored the expansion of child and educational allowances with particular enthusiasm.

While the party is able to enter into cooperative relations with other parties because of its lack of commitment on many issues, the fact that it represents such a narrow segment of the population tends to make such alliances fragile. This would appear to be particularly true of their present alliance with the Liberals, who must, because of their diversity, make the broadest appeal. Such an appeal is most effective to the voter as consumer, who is the major antagonist of the farmer. The high level traditional-moral orientation combined with a great facility for political maneuverability makes the Agrarian party the most similar to American political parties.

THE COMMUNISTS

The Communist parties of Western Europe fall into two categories of strength, those that are large and important and those that are small and relatively unimportant. France, Italy, Finland, and Iceland fall in the first category; Sweden and the other Western European countries fall in the second category.

The Swedish Communist party (present name *vänsterpartiet kommunisterna*) was established in 1921 after separating from the Left Socialists, who had broken away from the Social Democrats in 1917, the leadership of which had given them an ultimatum to cease plans for a general strike to thwart an anticipated Swedish participation in World War I, which they refused to accept. The majority of the Left Socialists who became the Communist party accepted the conditions for membership in the Communist International, the so-called Moscow theses, whereas a minority retained the original name but returned to the Social Democratic fold in 1923. Up to the late 1930s, several splits occurred within the Communist party with the dissidents usually returning to the Social Democrats.

Table 2.2 indicates the substantial and continual movement both ways between the Communist and Social Democratic parties. From 1921 to 1936 when the socialist proportion of the vote was rapidly increasing, there was no apparent tendency for the Communist and Social Democratic vote to vary inversely from one election to the next. But in thirteen of the sixteen interelection periods between 1936 and 1968, the vote for the Communists and Social Democrats varied inversely. For example, between 1964 and 1966 the Communists had their second largest percentage increase since 1944 (1.2 points) and the Social Democrats had their greatest loss (5.1 points). Between 1942 and 1944 the Social Democratic vote declined 3.6 points, whereas the Communist vote increased 4.5 points. In elections between 1950 and 1968 the Communist vote varied between 2.8 and 6.4 percent of the total vote.

The systems of proportional representation that have been in effect in Sweden, however, have discriminated against small parties and have made their representation in the Riksdag only one-half to two-thirds of their share of the popular vote. The greatest success of the party was in 1946 when positive feelings toward Communism and the Soviet Union were strong throughout Western Europe. In that year they received 11.2 percent of the total vote, but the percentage dropped to 6.3 in the 1948 election, which was held after the Communist coup in Czechoslovakia and the Berlin blockade. The Communist vote

Table 2.2   Relation Between Social Democratic and Communist Vote from Election to Election, 1921 to 1936 and 1936 to 1968 (Excluding Extra Lower House Election in 1958).

	Number of interelection periods	
	Social Democratic and Communist Vote Varied Inversely Between Elections	Social Democratic and Communist Vote Varied in Same Direction Between Elections
1921–1936	3	5
1936–1968	13	3

SOURCE: Calculated from official election statistics.

dropped to an all-time low of 2.8 percent in 1968, partly because of the Russian invasion of Czechoslovakia a few weeks before the election, and partly out of the fear that the Social Democrats might lose. For the most part, they feared a bourgeois government more than they supported the Social Democrats.

Unlike the Anglo-American countries, particularly the United States, there is comparatively little economic, social, or legal discrimination against Communists. Several of the leading Communists are teachers in the universities. However, a certain distance is kept between members of the four major parties and the Communists in the Riksdag, and some official discrimination prevails.[70] In political discourse the phrase "the four democratic parties" is frequently used, which pointedly excludes the Communists much to the annoyance of Carl-Henrik Hermansson, the attractive and intellectual chairman of the party since 1964. The leader of the Communist party has always been excluded from the formal role of advising the king, and the party was excluded from the wartime coalition government. But the Communists are given equal time with the other four parties on radio and television during the election campaigns. And proposals in the Riksdag to make the party illegal all have come to nothing.

Sharp conflicts have existed within the party between those who have supported the views of the Soviet Union, those who have supported the views of China, and those who have wanted to be independent from both. In any case, the dominant view now is that the party should be wholly independent from all external allegiances. And, in recent years (but less since the invasion of Czechoslovakia) the Communist party has had an attractiveness to some radical intellectuals and left-wing Social Democrats.

The party program claims that socialism has been the goal of the working-class movement, that it remains the goal of the party, and that only socialism can adequately develop the productive powers of Swedish society.[71] The Communists want to transform Swedish society along the lines of the scientific socialism of Marx and Lenin. The early radical Social Democrats August Palm, Axel Danielsson, and the young Hjalmar Branting are mentioned in their program and in their election propaganda as the pioneers of socialism in Sweden, and they regard themselves as the inheritors of the radical tradition that the Social Democrats have given up. They favor neutrality (as do all the parties) and closer relations with the Eastern bloc, and they oppose United States military bases in Europe and the military alliances led by the United States. They make strong expressions of solidarity with the populations of the developing countries. Much emphasis is placed on the rule of "monopoly capitalism" in Sweden and the dominating role of "fifteen families"—most notably the Wallenbergs.[72] Their election propaganda, however, emphasizes a number of specific issues, including stopping price and tax increases, a forty-hour week, higher child allowances, raising pensions, an extension of welfare to the retired, lowering rents, and increasing the building of housing in place of other less essential building. The party maintains that it is democratic, that it favors all the traditional freedoms, and that there is no conflict between it and Christianity.

Swedish communism is primarily made up of urban communism, and there is little "backwoods communism," to use Erik Allardt's apt distinction for analyzing Finnish communism.[73] Sven Rydenfeldt made a pioneer study of communism in Sweden[74] in which he did not make a distinction analogous to Allardt's for Finland. Rydenfeldt's theory is that communism thrives where alienation from society, social and geographic isolation, and rootlessness are high, such as among Swedish lumber workers, which agrees generally with Allardt's findings of the conditions related to backwoods communism in north and east Finland. But, according to Allardt, urban communism is fundamentally different. Whereas urban communists may also be isolated from national institutions, they are more ideologically sensitive, more active in organizations, and less economically insecure than backwoods communists. In Sweden, urban communism is mainly centered in Stockholm and Gothenburg and in a number of small industrial cities in northern and central Sweden that have strong radical traditions. Backwoods communism is most typically found in rural Norrbotten,

Sweden's northernmost, poorest, and most unevenly developed province.

The Parties and Consensus Politics

Following is a brief outline of what the major recent issues and developments in Swedish politics have been and where the parties have stood on those issues.

Neutrality and National Defense. There has been a high level of consensus in Sweden over the issue of neutrality, which all of the parties favor.[75] Yet, in the late 1940s *Dagens Nyheter* was a vocal proponent of a small minority, mainly in the nonsocialist parties, who advocated Sweden's joining NATO. The official position of the Social Democratic government was for the establishment of a Northern Defense Pact to expand Swedish neutrality to include Denmark and Norway. In 1949, however, both those countries joined NATO, leaving Sweden to continue her neutrality alone. Since that time there has been a high level of consensus on a policy of formal neutrality, but also on a strong national defense.

During the late 1950s the traditional stances of the parties emerged over the issue of whether Sweden should become a nuclear power. The Social Democrats, in line with their pacifist heritage, were opposed to any involvement with nuclear weapons. The Conservatives, also true to their heritage of strong emphasis on national defense, supported Sweden's becoming a nuclear power. The Agrarians also supported nuclear weapons, but with more qualifications than the Conservatives. The Liberals, as on so many issues, were divided. *Dagens Nyheter* and a few other Liberal newspapers, opposed the noninvolvement policy of the government, whereas other Liberal elements supported the government. The issue subsided by the mid-sixties.

The consequence of these policies of neutralism and noninvolvement with nuclear weapons has been to prevent the kind of eruption to the Left that occurred in the other small Western European countries after the easing of the Cold War tensions in the late 1950s. In 1958 a Pacifist Socialist People's party came into being in the Netherlands, which has since dissipated the strength of the Social Democrats. In Norway a Socialist People's party that was formed in 1961 elected two mandates and held the balance of power in the Parliament (*storting*) until 1965. The defeat of the Labor government in 1965 was a direct consequence of the dissipation of 6 percent of the total vote that went to this Left-wing party. In Denmark a similar party came into being, after breaking away from the Communist rather than the Social Democratic party, and it has been very successful in appealing to Left-wing Social Democrats and radical Liberals. The Swedish Social Democrats seem to be well-protected from this sort of factionalism on the Left, however, at least as long as the status quo continues on these issues.

While Sweden adheres to a line of formal neutrality, there is no question of the fundamentally pro-Western attitudes of the overwhelming majority of Swedes. Yet they are becoming increasingly sympathetic to developments in the Eastern socialist societies. There has been a remarkable upsurge in anti-Americanism as a result of the Vietnamese war, though it is not a highly generalized anti-Americanism. Although in 1963 Gunnar Myrdal could write "that the only two countries in Europe without a trace of anti-Americanism, either in the post-war era or today, are Sweden and Switzerland,"[76] three years later anti-Americanism had become endemic, particularly among student political groups and in the press. In a public opinion poll taken in February 1967, a majority of respondents of all ages in all parties, with the exception of older Conservatives, opposed American policy in Vietnam.[77] In fact, only 8 percent supported the American position.[78] Most of the major student political organizations, except among the Conservatives, have come out in favor of the FLN. In February 1968 Olof Palme, since October 1969 Prime Minister, marched in an anti-Vietnam War parade in which the North Vietnamese ambassador to the Soviet Union also marched. In January 1969 Sweden established full diplomatic relations with North Vietnam, the first Western European nation to do so, and in September 1969 promised forty million dollars in aid to North Vietnam. Since 1966, in fact, it has been very difficult for any member of the American Embassy or any "official" American to give a public lecture without causing a demonstration, which is indeed unusual in Sweden. Yet in the summer of 1968, the government and the press were equally vigorous in their condemnation of the Russian invasion of Czechoslovakia.

Economic Policy and Taxation. Not only is there consensus among the parties in Sweden on the need to control inflation, the maintenance of full employment, and the government's role in stabilizing the business cycle, but there is also consensus on the specific techniques for achieving these goals. About half of Sweden's manufactured goods are exported, a substantial proportion of which are highly priced quality goods. Any marked inflation would be particularly damaging to business and industrial interests, providing a kind of restraint that is almost absent from the American economy and not so compelling for the larger Western economies. The government's success in maintaining full employment has made for a rational labor-market policy that has strong support from both employers and labor—a cooperation difficult to comprehend for visiting trade-unionists from Britain.[79] The ingenious methods pioneered in Sweden for controlling the business cycle have been extraordinarily successful and are strongly supported by business and industry. The Swedish economist Erik Lundberg has demonstrated that the Swedish economy has been more stable in terms of variations in the rate of economic growth and in the level of unemployment than the economy of any other highly industrialized society from the early 1950s through the early 1960s.[80] This, together with the jealously preserved independence of collective bargaining from government interference, are areas in which the level of consensus is probably greater than anywhere else.

There is no consensus of this kind on issues of taxation, however. The Social Democrats favor an egalitarian taxation, and the Liberals, Agrarians, and Conservatives, together, oppose a highly progressive system of taxation. Taxation in Sweden is more progressive than in Denmark yet less so than in Norway.

Welfare. There is a high level of consensus on the principle of the welfare state. The Liberals are virtually at one with the Social Democrats about this. In a less uncertain way than the Conservatives and in a more universalistic way than the Agrarians, they support expanding welfare legislation. However, legislation is so thoroughly worked out and compromised in committee that much of it is passed unanimously. The nonsocialist parties frequently oppose the government on the grounds that welfare legislation is inadequate for certain groups in the population, such as farmers, part-time students, the handicapped, older people, and so forth. The Conservatives accept the great bulk of social legislation passed over the past third of a century, but, as was previously mentioned they have generally opposed the raising of the child allowances, have advocated the abolition of the allowance for the first child, have opposed educational allowances for students over twenty-one, and have favored the repeal of rent control.

Education and Religion. One of the most thoroughgoing achievements in the past two decades in Sweden has been the radical trans-

formation of the school system. On this issue there was no fundamental division between the middle-class parties and the Social
Democrats, and the whole program was a compromise in which the
Liberals and the Agrarians supported the school reform as much as the
Social Democrats did. The Conservatives also went along with the
reform, but with somewhat less enthusiasm. The school reform
began in the early 1950s with the establishment on a trial basis of
the nine-year common school, and it continued with a restructuring of
secondary education in the 1960s. Changes in the structure of higher
education began in the 1950s, but will be the object of greater changes
in the 1970s. Sweden has achieved what is structurally the most egalitarian school system in Western Europe with the support of all of the
parties; this will be discussed in some detail in the chapter on the
schools.

Since the 1950s there has been an increase in criticism of religion
and the Church, which had declined in the 1930s. In 1951 the Religious Freedom Act was passed, which realized old Social Democratic
demands, providing for, among other items, the right to leave the
State Church without joining another congregation (which had also
long been favored by the Church), removal of religious tests for holding office, and the establishment of "objective" teaching of religion in
the schools. Both the Liberals and Social Democrats were in accord
on this issue. In the 1950s there was also a tug of war between the
government and the Church (and within the Church) over the question of the ordination of women.[81] The government won, and wom-
en are now ordained. There was also a marked increase in criticism
of the relation of church and state, which resulted in the appointment
of a governmental committee in 1958 to investigate the possibilities
and desirability of changing it. These reports were published in the
1960s, but no action will take place before the 1970s.

Stability Versus Vitality

According to Herbert Tingsten, the enormous stability of Swedish
democracy has led to a certain loss of vitality. He has gone so far as to
proclaim that there has been a disappearance of all the old ideologies
and the "growth of the fund of common purpose and the shrinkage
of the margin for conflicts, particularly fundamental conflicts," and
he explains that:

The great controversies have . . . been liquidated in all instances. As a result the symbolic words and the stereotypes have changed or disappeared. All parties emphasize their patriotism, their feeling for democracy, their progressiveness and their striving for social reform. Liberalism in the old sense is dead, both among the Conservatives and in the Liberal Party; Social Democrat thinking has lost nearly all its traits of doctrinaire Marxism, and the label of socialism on a specific proposal or a specific reform has hardly any other meaning than the fact that the proposal or reform in question is regarded as attractive. The actual words "socialism" or "liberalism" are tending to become more honorifics, useful in connection with elections and political festivities.[82]

The loss of vitality is a result of the growth of consensus and of a consequent "movement from politics to administration, from principles to technique."

How valid this view of Swedish democracy is has been a persistent subject of debate in Sweden for a number of years.[83] However, few would argue with the contention that the stability of Swedish democracy and the extent to which it operates by compromise and consensus is exceeded by no other modern democracy.

Notes

1. Dankwart A. Rustow, *The Politics of Compromise* (Princeton: Princeton University Press, 1955), pp. 230–231.
2. Among studies in English that deal with the development of modern Sweden are Nils Herlitz, *Sweden: A Modern Democracy on Ancient Foundations* (Minneapolis: University of Minnesota Press, 1939); Ingvar Andersson, *A History of Sweden*, Carolyn Hannay (tr.) (Stockholm: Natur och Kultur, 1955); Dankwart A. Rustow, *The Politics of Compromise* (Princeton: Princeton University Press, 1955); Elis Håstad, *The Parliament of Sweden* (London: The Hansard Society for Parliamentary Government, 1957); Douglas V. Verney, *Parliamentary Reform in Sweden, 1866–1921* (Oxford: Clarendon Press, 1957); Nils Andrén, *Modern Swedish Government* (Stockholm: Almqvist & Wiksell, 1961); Stewart Oakley, *A Short History of Sweden*

(New York: Frederick A. Praeger, 1966); and Nils Stjernqvist, "Sweden: Stability or Deadlock?" in Robert A. Dahl (ed.), *Political Oppositions in Western Democracies* (New Haven: Yale University Press, 1966); Gideon Sjoberg, M. Donald Hancock, and Orion White, Jr., *Politics in the Post-Welfare State: A Comparison of the United States and Sweden* (Bloomington, Ind.: Carnegie Seminar of the Department of Government at Indiana University, 1967); M. Donald Hancock, *Sweden: A Multiparty System in Transition?* (Denver: Social Science Foundation and Graduate School of International Studies, University of Denver, 1968); D. W. Brogan and Douglas V. Verney, *Political Patterns in Today's World*, 2nd ed. (New York: Harcourt Brace & World, 1968); and Kurt Samuelsson, *From Great Power to Welfare State* (London: Allen & Unwin, 1968). A volume that deals with all the Scandinavian countries, but has a great deal on development, is J. A. Lauwerys (ed.), *Scandinavian Democracy* (Copenhagen: Universitets-Bogtrykkari, 1958).

3. ————, *The Constitution of Sweden*, Sarah V. Thorelli (tr.) (Stockholm: Royal Ministry for Foreign Affairs, 1954), with an introduction by Elis Håstad.

4. *Ibid.*, p. 9.

5. See Nils Herlitz, "Publicity of Official Documents in Sweden," *Public Law* (Spring 1958), pp. 50–69.

6. *The Constitution of Sweden*, *op. cit.*, p. 9.

7. For discussion of the Riksdag and its functioning, see Håstad, *op. cit.*, pp. 51–159, and Andrén, *op. cit.*, pp. 22–98.

8. Andrén, *op. cit.*, p. 57.

9. On the legislative process, see Rustow, *op. cit.*, pp. 173–196, and Andrén, *op. cit.*, pp. 156–165.

10. Andrén, *op. cit.*, p. 161.

11. Andrén, *op. cit.*, p. 163.

12. Andrén, *op. cit.*, pp. 164–165.

13. This phrase was used by Albert H. Rosenthal, *The Social Programs of Sweden* (Minneapolis: University of Minnesota Press, 1967), p. 99.

14. For a discussion of these administrative agencies, see Douglas V. Verney, *Public Enterprise in Sweden* (Liverpool, England: Liverpool University Press, 1959), and Andrén, *op. cit.*, pp. 109–148.

15. Rosenthal, *op. cit.*, p. 100.

16. On local government, see Andrén, *op. cit.*, pp. 122–123, 181–204.

17. For discussions of the Swedish political party system in general, see Rustow, *op. cit.;* Verney, *Parliamentary Reform in Sweden, 1866–1921, op. cit.;* Andrén, *op. cit.*, pp. 22–37; Stjernqvist, *op. cit.;* and Hancock, *op. cit.* See Note 2 for full citations.

18. For a general discussion of the political parties in all of the Scandinavian countries, see Nils Andrén, *Government and Politics in the Nordic Countries* (Stockholm: Almqvist & Wiksell, 1964); see also the essay by Seymour M. Lipset and Stein Rokkan, "Cleavage Structures, Party Systems, and Voter Alignments," in Lipset and Rokkan *Party Systems and Voter Alignments*, (New York: Free Press, 1967), pp. 1–64.

19. A similar phrase is used by Dahl, *op. cit.*, p. 369.

20. Maurice Duverger, *Political Parties*, Barbara and Robert North (trs.) (London: University Paperbacks, 1964), pp. 307–312, 410, 417–418.

21. This discussion of the Swedish Social Democrats is from Richard F. Tomasson, "The Extraordinary Success of the Swedish Social Democrats," *Journal of Politics*, 31 (August 1969), 772–798. This article looks at the Swedish Social Democrats in cross-national perspective.

22. The Russian invasion of Czechoslovakia a few weeks before the 1968 Lower House elections was certainly an important factor in the great Social Democratic success. This was particularly responsible for the decline in the Communist vote from 6.4 percent in the 1966 communal elections to 2.8 percent in the 1968 elections.

23. Manual workers declined from 58.2 percent of the labor force in 1940 to 51.3 percent in 1960 and have continued to decline through the 1960s.

24. Pensions will be provided at age sixty-seven equivalent to two-thirds of an individual's income during his best fifteen years with generous upper limits. See the English summary of Björn Molin's Gothenburg University dissertation on the politics of the pension question: Björn Molin, "Swedish Party Politics: A Case Study," in *Scandinavian Political Studies* (New York: Columbia University Press, 1966), pp. 1, 45–58; this is a yearbook published by the Political Science Associations in Denmark, Finland, Norway, and Sweden.

25. Sveriges Officiella Statistik, *Riksdagsmannavalen åren 1959–1960* (Stockholm: Statistiska Centralbyrån, 1961), Vol. II, p. 56, and Sveriges Officiella Statistik, *Riksdagsmannavalen åren 1961–1964* (Stockholm: Statistiska Centralbryån, 1965), Vol. II, p. 93.

26. Bo Särlvik, "Political Stability and Change in the Swedish Electorate," *Scandinavian Political Studies*, Vol. 1, pp. 188–222. See also the election reports published by the Swedish Central Bureau of Statistics. Sweden has the most detailed official election statistics of any country in the world.

27. For a discussion of class and voting in Britain, see J. Blondel, *Voters, Parties, and Leaders* (London: Penguin Books, 1963), pp. 56–68; Robert R. Alford, *Party and Society* (Chicago: Rand McNally, 1963); and Robert T. McKenzie and Allen Silver, "The Delicate Experiment: Industrialism, Conservatism, and Working-Class Tories in England," in *Party Systems and Voter Alignments*, Seymour M. Lipset and Stein Rokkan (eds.) (New York: Free Press, 1967), pp. 115–125. For Germany, see Richard F. Hamilton, "Affluence and the Worker: The West German Case," *American Journal of Sociology*, 71 (September 1965), 144–152, esp. 151; and Juan J. Linz, "Cleavage and Consensus in West German Politics: The Early Fifties," in Lipset and Rokkan, *op. cit.*, pp. 283–321.

28. Norway has a small Christian People's party, the only confessional party ever represented in a Scandinavian parliament. Finland has a Swedish People's party, which is the party of most Swedish speaking Finns. A Christian confessional party (*KDS*) was formed in Sweden in 1964, but has not yet succeeded in electing any candidates.

29. See election statistics in Sigmund Neumann (ed.), *Modern Political Parties* (Chicago: University of Chicago Press, 1956), passim; Dahl, *op. cit.*, pp. 405–435; and the statistical yearbooks for the various European countries.

30. On the working-class Tories, see Robert T. McKenzie and Allan Silver, "The Delicate Experiment: Industrialism, Conservatism, and Working-Class Tories in England," in Lipset and Rokkan, *op.cit.*, pp. 115–125.

31. T. L. Johnston, *Collective Bargaining in Sweden* (London: Allen & Unwin, 1962), pp. 23–44.

32. See Walter Galenson's short book, *Trade Union Democracy in Western Europe* (Berkeley and Los Angeles, University of California Press, 1961).

33. *Political Parties* (New York: Collier Books, 1962, 1915 edition), p. 322.

34. *Ibid.*, p. 28.

35. On April 11, 1965, *Stockholms Tidningen*, until its demise in April 1966 the most influential Social Democratic paper in Sweden, proposed in an editorial that collective membership of *LO* members to party locals be abolished.

36. For a comparative discussion of the development of the labor movement in Denmark, Norway, and Sweden, see Walter Galenson, "Scandinavia," in *Comparative Labor Movements*, Walter Galenson (ed.) (New York: Prentice-Hall, 1952), pp. 104–172; see also Walter Galenson, *The Danish System of Labor Relations* (Cambridge: Harvard University Press, 1952), pp. 1–27; and Kenneth E. Miller, *Government and Politics in Denmark* (Boston: Houghton Mifflin, 1968), pp. 61–70.

37. There is probably more written in English on Norwegian politics than on the politics of any of the other Scandinavian countries. See, for example, Henry Valen and Daniel Katz, *Political Parties in Norway* (Oslo: Universitatsforlaget, 1964), pp. 12–99; Walter Galenson, *Labor in Norway* (Cambridge: Harvard University Press, 1949), pp. 1–77; Stein Rokkan, "Norway: Numerical Democracy and Corporate Pluralism" in Dahl, *op. cit.*, pp. 70–115; and Harry Eckstein, *Division and Cohesion in Democracy, A Study of Norway* (Princeton: Princeton University Press, 1966).

38. Herbert Tingsten, *Fran Idéer till Idyll* (Stockholm: Pan/Norstedts, 1967), pp. 185–187.

39. Stein Rokkan has pointed this out in "Electoral Mobilization, Party Competition, and National Integration," in Joseph La Palombara and Myron Weiner (eds.), *Political Parties and Political Development* (Princeton: Princeton University Press, 1966), pp. 241–265, esp. 256–265.

40. Estimates based on data in *Riksdagsmannavalen åren 1961–1964*, *op. cit.*, Vol. II, p. 93.

41. The Danish Liberals have obtained less than 6 percent of the vote in recent elections, in Norway around 7 to 8 percent, in Finland around 6 percent, and in Britain the strength of the party increased from 2.7 percent in 1955 to 11.2 percent in 1964.

42. For a discussion of the ideological background of the Liberal party, see Hans-Krister Rönblom, *Frisinnade landsföreningen* (Stockholm: 1929), pp. 11–43.

43. For a detailed discussion of Swedish conservatism prior to World War I, see Nils Elvander, *Harald Hjärne och konservatism: konservative idédebatt i Sverige* (Stockholm: Almqvist & Wiksell, 1961).

44. A discussion of each of these groupings appears in Rönblom, *op. cit.*, pp. 11–43.

45. For a discussion of the temperance movement in Sweden, see the chapter entitled "The Temperance Question" in Herbert Tingsten, *The Swedish*

Social Democrats, Greta Frankel and Richard F. Tomasson (trs.), forth-coming.

46. Rönblom, *op. cit.*, p. 31.
47. See David Thomson, *England in the Nineteenth Century* (Middlesex: Pelican Books, 1950), pp. 177, 227. There were fifty Republican clubs in England around 1870–1871. For an account of one of the most well known of the English cultural radicals, see Arthur H. Nethercot, *The First Five Lives of Annie Besant* (Chicago: University of Chicago Press, 1960).
48. The Liberal press in both Copenhagen (*Politiken* and *Ekstrabladet*) and Oslo (*Dagbladet*) is much weaker than the Conservative press. Just the opposite situation prevails in Stockholm.
49. This statement of purpose was printed in large letters in *Dagens Nyheter*, December 23, 1964, p. 3.
50. Verney, *Parliamentary Reform in Sweden, 1866–1921, op. cit.*, p. 98.
51. In the 1960 election the Liberals got 24.3 percent of the vote, while the Agrarians got only 6.7 percent, which is a large difference for a predomi-nantly rural province.
52. See Stein Rokkan, "Geography, Religion, and Social Class: Crosscutting Cleavages in Norwegian Politics," in Lipset and Rokkan, *op. cit.*, pp. 367–444. The cleavages discussed in this brilliant essay, except for social class, are less apparent in Sweden than in Norway, and language is not at all a basis of cleavage in Sweden.
53. Compare the different party programs in Hans Wieslander, *De politiska partiernas program* (Stockholm: Prisma, 1964).
54. The Liberal vote has declined sharply and erratically in Norway and Den-mark since 1930. In Britain the Liberal vote has fluctuated enormously since 1918.
55. Särlvik, *op. cit.*, p. 193.
56. For a discussion of the Belgian Liberals, see Felix E. Oppenheim, "Belgium: Party Cleavage and Compromise," in Neumann, *op. cit.*, pp. 178–180. For a discussion of the postwar German Liberals (*FDP*), see Richard Hiscocks, *Democracy in Western Germany* (London: Oxford University Press, 1957), pp. 97–102.
57. Elvander, *op. cit.*, pp. 480–489.
58. Alrik Gustafsson, *A History of Swedish Literature* (Minneapolis: University of Minnesota Press, 1961), pp. 354–355. Tingsten has stated about his col-leagues in the Humanities faculty at the University of Stockholm in the period 1935 to 1945: "As far as I know, there was no one sympathetic with Nazism or, in any case, none gave the impression of such sympathy." Her-bert Tingsten, *Mitt liv: mellan trettio och femtio* (Stockholm: P. A. Norstedt, 1962), Vol. II, p. 196.
59. See pictures in D. E. Butler and Richard Rose, *The British General Election of 1959* (London: Macmillan, 1960).
60. *Riksdagsmannavalen åren 1959–1960, op. cit.*, p. 56; and *Riksdagsmannavalen åren, 1961–1964, op. cit.*, p. 93.
61. This is only an estimate based on the fact that 156 of the 230 Riksdagsmen elected in 1896 were Conservatives. See Sten Carlsson and Jerker Rosén, *Svensk Historia* (Stockholm: Bonniers, 1961), Vol. II, p. 595.

62. See 1956 Conservative program in Wieslander, op. cit., pp. 37–64.
63. Dankwart A. Rustow classifies the Social Liberals as an Agrarian party. See "Scandinavia: Working Multiparty Systems," in Neumann, op. cit., pp. 169–193.
64. Denmark: An Official Handbook (Copenhagen: Royal Danish Ministry of Foreign Affairs, 1964), pp. 181–182.
65. For some comments on Agrarians parties, see Maurice Duverger, Political Parties, Barbara and Robert North (trs.) (London: University Paperbacks, 1964), pp. 6–7, 203–205, 233–239.
66. Riksdagsmannavalen åren 1961–1964, op. cit., p. 93.
67. The Lantmannapartiet, however, is the ancestor of the modern Conservative party.
68. Andrén, Modern Swedish Government, op. cit., p. 28.
69. See 1959 Agrarian program in Wieslander, op. cit., pp. 65–78.
70. Håstad, op. cit., p. 158.
71. See 1961 program of the Communist party in Wieslander, op. cit., pp. 133–149; see also Axel Jansson, Vad vill kommunisterna? (Stockholm: Sveriges kommunistiska parti, 1963).
72. See C. H. Hermansson, Monopol och storfinans (Stockholm: Arbetarkulturs förlag, 1962), pp. 306–347.
73. Erik Allardt, "Social Sources of Finnish Communism: Traditional and Emerging Radicalism," International Journal of Comparative Sociology, V (March 1964), 49–74.
74. Sven Rydenfeldt, Kommunismen i Sverige (Lund: Gleerupska Universitetsbokhandeln, 1954).
75. Herbert Tingsten, "Issues in Swedish Foreign Policy," Foreign Affairs, 37 (April 1959), 474–485.
76. Gunnar Myrdal, Challenge to Affluence (New York: Vintage Books, 1965), p. 126.
77. SIFO (Svenska Institutet for Opinionsundersökningar), Stockholm; from a letter from Sten Johansson dated September 2, 1967.
78. Gunnar Myrdal, "The Vietnam War and the Political and Moral Isolation of America," New University Thought, 5 (May–June 1967), 4.
79. Andrew Shonfield, Modern Capitalism (London: Oxford University Press, 1966), p. 199.
80. From a lecture by Erik Lundberg, University of Illinois, Chicago, October 1965.
81. See English summary in Carl Arvid Hessler, Statskyrkodebatten (Stockholm: Almqvist & Wiksell, 1964), pp. 433–451.
82. "Stability and Vitality in Swedish Democracy," Political Quarterly, XXIV (April–June 1955), 24–33.
83. Two recent Swedish criticisms of this view are Kurt Samuelsson, Är ideologierna döda? (Stockholm: Aldus/Bonniers, 1966), and Leif Lewin, Planhushällningsdebatten (Stockholm: Almqvist & Wiksell, 1967), with an English summary, pp. 523–541. Tingsten answers his critics in Strid kring idyllen (Stockholm: P. A. Norstedt, 1966).

III

The Religious Situation

A pious Swede is often ashamed
of admitting his allegiance to
God, while a rationalist Swede
is not a bit ashamed of admitting
his allegiance to Reason.
—HANS L. ZETTERBERG[1]

Sweden is a highly secularized society when compared with most
Western societies. Indeed, the Swedes themselves conceive of their
society as being particularly secular. In terms of church attendance and
the extent of traditional Christian belief, Sweden is probably more
secular than the socialist societies of Eastern Europe, in which the state
pursues a more-or-less active antireligious line. Four or 5 percent of
the population attends church on an average Sunday.[2] In Stockholm it
is around 2 percent. The number of the clergy in the 1960s was no
greater than it was two centuries ago when the population was less
than one-quarter what it is today. The mass media, with the exception
of radio, which regularly broadcasts religious services, devote little
attention to religion and the Church, at least when compared with a
society like the United States. And, a number of important Liberal
and Social Democratic newspapers show negative attitudes toward
the State Church, its relation to the state, and its activities. In addition, the school system is the only one in Western Europe that has
established, as it did in 1951, a universal policy of "objective" teaching
of religion at all levels.

Yet there is little popular hostility toward the Church and the
clergy. The majority of Swedes (72 percent) claim they would volun-

tarily join the Church if it were disestablished, which appears likely to occur in the 1970s. The overwhelming majority of Swedes (around 9 out of 10) continue to be baptized, confirmed, married, and buried by the Church. The most fitting term for the most common attitude toward the Church and traditional religious belief in contemporary Sweden is *indifference*. In the conclusion to a standard two-volume Swedish history text, the contemporary religious situation is summarized by Sten Carlsson as follows:

The Church and Christianity have a much weaker hold on souls than in agrarian Sweden. The catechism has practically disappeared, the Bible and the Psalm Book are studied less than before. The Sermon on the Mount's message of love is respected in principle, but, for the rest, the Christian norms mean quite little. Many citizens do not come in contact with the Church other than in connection with baptism, confirmation, marriage, and burial. Active conscious atheism is, however, not very widespread; the majority's attitude toward the Church and Christianity oscillates between a lukewarm benevolence and pure indifference. Knowledge of the Bible and religious questions has declined considerably.[3]

In a lecture on Swedish democracy at the University of Manchester some years ago, Herbert Tingsten commented that "active faith is regarded in our exceptionally secularized community as being nearly as strange as active atheism."[4] One of the strongest contrasts observed by Swedish university students in the United States is the much greater role that churches and religious activity play in the United States as compared with Sweden.[5]

Modern Christian thought and research play a small part in Swedish cultural and intellectual life as compared with Anglo-American and Continental countries. Geo Widengren, Professor of the History of Religion at Uppsala University, has stated with some bitterness that "theological research and its achievements do not attract much attention in modern Swedish intellectual life outside theological circles—except when it is criticized."[6] Lars Gustafsson, the editor of the Swedish literary magazine *Bonniers Litterära Magasin*, has pointed to the isolation of Christian thought that has come to prevail in Sweden:

The debate on religion may to a certain extent be said to have ceased since the beginning of the 1950s, and in the debate on new moral norms in "the vacuum after Christianity" the Christian contributions have unfortunately been very sparse. One might say, with some degree of correctness, that the representatives of Christianity during the last decade have not played any influential part in the Swedish debate on ideas, but have preferred a position of observation with their comments limited to the specifically Christian sector of the newspapers and periodicals.[7]

An American scholar-cleric, Deane William Ferm, who went to Sweden to study the "relationship and relevance" of the Church of Sweden to the much-publicized Swedish sexual mores, wrote a caustic article in the *Christian Century* in which he condemned the isolation of Swedish theology from the life of the society. He said that the church

will stick out her neck only on matters that please grandma but will not offend the power structures of society. Her general approach to social problems is still of the "trust in God, follow Jesus, let us pray" variety. Few people listen, because there is nothing to hear. Swedish society today is unashamedly and irrevocably pragmatically oriented. But the church continues to grind out the same old authoritarian tunes of four centuries ago.[8]

The isolation of religious thought and activities from other institutional areas in modern Sweden is not a recent phenomenon. Anticlericalism and agnosticism have been the predominant stance in the intellectual community and in much of the press, if not among the general population, since the transition of Sweden into a modern society began in the 1880s and 1890s. Opposition to the official position of the State Church played an important role in the ideology of the Social Democrats, who were also hostile to religion itself, and of the Liberals during their formative years prior to World War I. Sweden offers a particularly clear-cut case of church and official religion being solidly wedded to the institutions and values of a traditional society at the time when modern notions of popular democracy and egalitarianism, liberalism and socialism began to capture the imagination of the mass of the people.

The late 1960s, however, has seen a decline in outright antireligiousness in the intellectual community. Among young theology students and young active Christians generally there has been a remarkable upsurge of radicalism, even going so far as active communication with young Marxists and interest in Marxism. The young radicals were especially active at the 1968 Uppsala conference of the World Lutheran Federation.

All industrialized societies can be regarded as more-or-less secular, at least when viewed in historical perspective. The scope of the sacred and the pervasiveness of traditional religious belief have declined everywhere with modernization. Yet, there is striking variation among the developed societies in the extent to which they are secular, in how and to what extent traditional religion is a part of the modern society. For example, compare Swedish with Dutch society.[9]

In this chapter we will look at the major aspects of the contemporary religious situation in Sweden from a comparative viewpoint and then suggest some explanations for the particularly high degree of secularization that has accompanied modernization. First, however, we will discuss the historical role of religion and the Church in Sweden—including the events of the Reformation, their consequences, and how the Church and religion initially met the challenge of modernization.

Historical Development

The Swedes were one of the last peoples in Europe to be Christianized, followed only by the Finns, the Hungarians, and some of the peoples of Eastern Europe.[10] The first Christian missionary, a Frankish monk named Anskar, did not arrive in Sweden until 829 or 830, and the complete triumph of Christianity took three centuries. Yet as late as the close of the sixteenth century, "considerable remnants" of paganism existed.[11] An established Catholic Church existed in Sweden for only four centuries before the Reformation of the sixteenth century, but the Swedish (and Scandinavian) variety of Catholicism was radically different from that of central and southern Europe. The supremacy of the Pope was continually disputed, and the clergy, then as later, were elected by the people. Celibacy of the clergy was not the custom. The Church, unlike the state and commerce, was very much a national organization with its own institutions. Yet during this period, as elsewhere in Europe, it became the strongest and richest power in the land.

The Church was an ally to the establishment of monarchy in Sweden. By mid-thirteenth century, Sweden had become a national state with a king and some degree of national consciousness. But the state was weak and had few resources. Just prior to the Reformation, the church owned 21.0 percent of all the land and the crown owned only 5.5 percent.[12] Besides the presence of a rich and powerful Church, an autonomous nation-state was prevented by the strong commercial hegemony exerted in Sweden by the Germans and the Danes. Hostility to the Danish monarchy, which led the so-called

Union of Kalmar (1397–1523), and continued warfare with the Danes enhanced Swedish nationalism throughout the fifteenth century. In perhaps no other European country was the Reformation more of an aid to furthering a national monarchy and a strong centralized government than in Sweden. And the arrangements that came into being at this time have determined the basic relation between church and state and the official role of the Church of Sweden to the present.

In 1523 Gustav Vasa was elected King of Sweden after leading a patriotic revolt against Denmark. Though he was neither a particularly learned nor a particularly religious man, he was an enormously effective administrator, and no Swedish monarch "even remotely compares with him in economic understanding." [13] His overriding aim was the creation of a strong, centralized, and secure nation-state. And it did not take him long to see the great advantages of the doctrines of Martin Luther in carrying out his purposes. In 1544, the Riksdag declared Sweden to be an Evangelical Lutheran State for the first time, after a slow, step-by-step break with Rome.

Gustav's immediate aims after becoming king were to strengthen the financial position of the state—he was intensely concerned with the "liberation" of Sweden from German merchants—and to reduce the economic position of the church. In 1527, he gained the consent of the Riksdag to reduce the land holdings of the church, but he went much further and confiscated most church treasures. Whereas this did not formally abolish the authority of the Pope, it represents the first step that led to the complete replacement of the king for the Pope and canon law as the leading authority of the church. At his death in 1560, the crown's holdings had increased from 5.5 to 28.2 percent of the land, and the church's lands had been totally confiscated.[14] The 1527 Riksdag, which represents the first step of the Reformation in Sweden, also proclaimed that the Word of God should "be preached pure"—a support to Lutheran doctrine, but not strong enough to disturb non-Lutherans.

A second basic step in the progress of the Swedish Reformation was Gustav's confirmation of the election of Laurentius Petri as Archbishop of Sweden in 1531, an office that had been vacant since 1521, when Archbishop Gustav Trolle, whose sympathies were with Denmark, fled the country. Laurentius had been trained in Germany at Wittenberg University, where Luther had taught, and was a leading reformist in the church. His election marked the special authority of Lutheran views over the whole Swedish church.

In 1536, a Church Assembly was called by Laurentius in which the Reformation was furthered in a number of ways. The Swedish Mass and Manual became obligatory throughout Sweden, and the clergy were officially given the right to marry. An autonomous national church had in fact appeared, but no official declaration had been made. The New Testament had already been translated into Swedish, and the whole Bible appeared in Swedish translation in 1541. The basic changes of the Swedish Reformation had, therefore, been made at the official level, but many decades passed before Sweden was considered to have a unified Evangelical Lutheran Church.

The Reformation occurred in Sweden with little fundamental change from the medieval church; the liturgy, vestments of the clergy, and fundamental organization of the medieval church have been retained in general form to the present. There was almost no iconoclasm in sixteenth-century Sweden, and a great tolerance for paintings and images in the churches continued. The canonical hours and a large number of ceremonies and holidays, which had been abolished in Germany and the other Scandinavian countries, were kept in Sweden. Many of the religious holidays are the same as in Catholic parts of Europe. The Church can lay claim to an unbroken apostolic succession; though it has never been treated as important, it does indicate the tranquil character of the Swedish Reformation.

Gustav increasingly came into conflict with Laurentius Petri and his brother Olavus, the shapers of the Swedish Reformation, when he attempted to claim all ecclesiastical authority for himself. The Petris were adherents of the views of Philipp Melanchthon, a German Protestant reformer (1497–1560), who believed in the separate authority of the spiritual and temporal spheres, but both under God. Their views were ultimately triumphant, and their influence on the Swedish Church is difficult to overestimate. There was the maintenance of continuity with the medieval church—with its emphasis on liturgy, the ordained place of the episcopacy, and opposition to all subjective and individualistic religion—and they gave the Church of Sweden a code of law and independence from the state. After the death of Gustav, the church reasserted its authority and autonomy, which it has since kept most of the time, and the monarch was no longer the head of the church. In the adoption in 1571 of Laurentius's Swedish Church Ordinance, which was based, as the Church historian Robert Murray has put it, "wholly" on the thought of Melanchthon, this was made apparent. According to Murray:

The Church emerges clearly autonomous, though in a cooperative relationship with the State. The bishops are to be chosen by laymen as well as clergy, but the final decision rests with the king [now the government]. Each parish is self-governed, and the parishioners play an important role in its administration. . . . In many respects the Church of Sweden acquired in Laurentius Petri's Church Ordinance the character it still possesses.[15]

This was clearly a different pattern from that of Germany, where the church was dominated by the monarch. One seventeenth-century Swedish bishop, Johannes Rudbeckius, said of the difference, "In Germany since the Reformation, it has gone badly with religion, for the province has patterned itself after the ruler. But we, praise God, have hitherto managed well. If the magistrate has wanted to do what he ought not to do, the clergy had held the magistrate in check; the magistrate has also kept the clergy in mind during these one hundred years." [16]

As was the case in England and Denmark, the Reformation occurred in Sweden through a decision of the king. It was, at least at first, a revolt from Rome by the monarch for wholly political and economic reasons, without even an excuse of general corruption or of the selling of indulgences, neither of which were common in Sweden. The Reformation occurred quite clearly from the top down. In Calvinist lands—the Netherlands, Switzerland, and Scotland—the Reformation was to a large extent a popular mass movement. Even in Germany a popular leader emerged in Luther who rallied support among the people.

And, as in England, the transformation to Protestantism occurred slowly. Indeed the situation in sixteenth-century Sweden was strikingly similar to that of England, in that both populations were divided into Lutheran, Catholic, and Reformist elements through much of the century. Also, as in England, the monarchs were of different religious persuasions. In Sweden, unlike in the provisions of the Peace of Augsburg for Germany, the people did not follow the monarch in questions of religion. When the Augsburg Confession was adopted as the official doctrinal position of the Church of Sweden at the Uppsala Church Council of 1593, the Catholic Sigismund was king. It was not until the reign of Gustavus Adolphus (1611–1632), the great leader of the Swedish army in the Thirty Years' War, that Sweden had a monarch who personified the orthodoxy of the Swedish State Church.

In 1544, the Riksdag declared the Evangelical-Lutheran religion to be the official religion of the state, saying that anyone who opposed its doctrines would be "banished and regarded as a heretic and heathen." At that time, there was a concerted attempt to establish orthodoxy throughout the religiously divided country.[17] Not only were there religious divisions within, there were the forces of the Counterreformation from without. Catholic attitudes and feeling remained in certain groups of the population, particularly the peasants and manual workers, until well into the sixteenth century. There was much unrest in the provinces over the new doctrines, which sometimes turned into open rebellion in the early years of the Reformation.

In 1593, the Church Council reasserted Lutheranism as the official religion, no longer using such vague expressions as "God's pure and solitary word," but adding the Augsburg Confession to the ancient creeds as the only true interpretation of the Scriptures. In the words of the Council, "Now Sweden is become one man, and we have all one Lord and God."[18] The meeting of the Church Council marked the beginning of a period of extensive emphasis on orthodoxy, both for itself and for its instrumental purpose in maintaining a strong and unified state. This concept dominated Swedish religious and political thought until into the eighteenth century, and it continued to be dominant in somewhat abated form in official and religious thought until after the mid-nineteenth century. Vestiges of it remained in the law until the passage of the Religious Freedom Law of 1951, up to which time all cabinet ministers and civil servants had ⸢ be members of the Church of Sweden.

The seventeenth century saw the culmination of the unified religious state, where the "state and the Church had become one and the same." The 1604 Riksdag passed a statute stating that anyone who leaves "our Christian faith" shall forfeit "his goods to his closest kinsman and be banished from the kingdom, so that he may not have an opportunity to disgorge his poison." In 1634 in the first written Swedish Constitution, the thesis on the religious unity of the state reached its full development. It stated:

As unity in religion and the right worship are the strongest foundations for a lawful, cooperative, and lasting kingdom, so shall hereafter all kings, as well as all civil servants and subjects in the kingdom, first and foremost, stand by God's pure and clear word, as proclaimed in the Prophetic and Apostolic writings, in the universal Christian symbols, Luther's catechism, and the unaltered Augsburg Confession accepted and resolved in the Uppsala concilio, in addition to former decisions and assurances decreed by the state.

With this, the conception of the unified religious state was incorporated into the fundamental law of the land. Similar formulations are contained in all successive constitutions up to that of 1809, in contrast to seventeenth-century England and Holland, where norms of religious tolerance began to develop. But few people died for the cause of orthodoxy in Sweden, and when religious conviction conflicted with political advantage, as in tolerating dissident foreign businessmen the law was overlooked. Yet after the defection of Queen Christina to Catholicism and her exodus from Sweden in 1655, the emphasis on orthodoxy became even greater, resulting in the removal of several bishops from office for reasons of dogma.

In the eighteenth century, two forces entered Sweden that led to the breakdown of the orthodoxy in the church: Pietism, a movement that stressed personal piety over religious formality and orthodoxy, and the skepticism and rationalism of the Enlightenment. Lutheranism, particularly in its Swedish form, was always a low-temperature religion with strong doctrinal and intellectual concerns, and it has shown persistent disdain for all the various forms of Protestant enthusiasm and subjectivism. Because of this together with the belief in the need for orthodoxy to maintain a strong national state, Pietism, with its criticism of the official church and its emphasis on subjective religious experience, was vigorously opposed, sometimes in extreme forms. Pietism had spread in Germany in the last quarter of the seventeenth century and began to make progress in Sweden in the early decades of the eighteenth century. Pietists quickly became the object of much repressive legislation. The most far-reaching was a government edict of 1726 forbidding all assembly for worship, public or private, except for family prayers, without the presence of a parish clergyman. The penalty for violation was fines, imprisonment, or banishment from the country. However, this law was not strictly enforced, and it was repealed in 1858 in the name of religious freedom; there had even been opposition to it from within the church because it hindered religious activity.

The influences of the Enlightenment had great effects in weakening the position of the church and orthodox religion in Sweden; by the early nineteenth century, the church had become rationalistic and quite secular. The influences were enhanced by the turning against absolutism that occurred after the death of Charles XII in 1718 and the arrival of a period of protoparliamentarianism, known as the Age of Freedom (1718–1771). This period saw the introduction of legislation allowing certain foreigners to build and worship in their own churches. With the coup de'état of Gustavus III in 1771, Sweden had a full-fledged Enlightenment king, a Swedish counterpart to Frederick the Great. In 1781 he gave foreign Christians the right to form their own congregations, to build their own churches, and to have their children trained by their own clergy. The next year similar rights were given to Jews. But, for the remaining Swedes, the compulsions to attend church, to take communion, and a number of prohibitions on their religious activities remained intact.

However, the consequences of these exceptions were realized in paragraph sixteen of the current 1809 Constitution, which prescribes that:

The conscience of no one is to be compelled nor is compulsion to be allowed, but everyone is to be protected in the free exercise of his religion insofar as he thereby does not disturb society's tranquility or bring about general indignation.

But, in effect, this provision only removed the state's right to force people to attend church and to take communion. Until well into the nineteenth century, it was still regarded as self-evident that all who were members of the Swedish state were also members of the Swedish State Church. One could leave the Church only by leaving the country.

Along with their conservatism and orthodoxy, a great deal of freedom developed within the Swedish Church. The clergy was an educated one, and it placed a great emphasis on scholarship. By Calvinist standards, there was an absence of both puritanism and narrow moralistic concerns. Their orthodoxy frequently seems to have been of an official and compartmentalized sort, and there is an impression from the eighteenth century on that the Swedish clergy were not always so pious. The clergy traditionally functioned as teachers, doctors, and parish politicians, and they had the duty of taking care of the population registers, acting, in effect, as Anglo-American county clerks, a function they have carried on to the present. Many of them tilled their own farms, and a number made contributions to agricultural science. The more well-situated among them were learned men who led an upper-class style of life. With all of their activities, it is not surprising, as Sten Carlsson has suggested, that the care of souls was "often of secondary importance." [19]

At the highest levels, the Swedish Church had become highly

secularized by the first half of the nineteenth century. Becoming a bishop was considered a natural outcome for leading cultural figures. Until mid-century, in fact, appointments to high ecclesiastical office in Sweden were determined primarily by scholarly and cultural attainment; piety and orthodoxy were not of major importance. Esaias Tegnér (1782–1846), a professor and the most popular poet of his time, was made Bishop of Växjö in 1824. He was a leading figure in the Romantic school in Swedish letters, who idealized the pre-Christian early Scandinavian past. After his appointment as bishop, he wrote to a friend, "A pagan I am and shall remain." [20] The other dominant Romantic of this time, Erik Gustaf Geijer (1783–1847), also a professor, though more orthodox than Tegnér but also without any training in theology, was offered a bishopric, but refused it.

Since around the 1840s, a general return to greater orthodoxy and social conservatism occurred in the Church, in reaction to the advanced secularism that had arisen. This tightening-up was well advanced at the time when liberal and, later, socialist ideas were spreading. Up to the mid-1880s, and to some extent even later, the church held to reactionary ideologies that rationalized and defended the existing benevolent and hierarchical order against, at first, liberalism and natural rights doctrines and, later, socialism. A leading student of state-church relations in Sweden, Carl Arvid Hessler, has summarized the views of an important segment of the Church in the 1860s when the idealistic *Weltanshauung* was at its height:

It is not at all the case . . . as the liberals sought to delude themselves and others into believing, that one's religious convictions were only a concern between his conscience and God. . . . The conscience is not divine, it is by nature egoistic and it is for this reason corrupted by sin. The individual person does not have the capacity to comprehend the divine revelation. The power was given to the Church. It is not the case as people sometimes make it out to be that the Church is an association of individual members. The Church is an organism with Christ himself at the head. All life in this organism came from Christ through the Word and the sacraments. Because of this the Church has its tremendous authority. And the task which the Church was entrusted is now to be the teacher of the people. . . . The divine will was made apparent through the Church, and one is to take this will into his own conscience. [21]

Religion and the Church are seen as basic supports of the state. But the religion could only be one religion, not religion in general. The churchmen saw the state as a personality, "existing in a unity between the national idea and the individual's consciousness." It was necessary for Sweden, in order to actualize her national idea, to adhere to and to protect the Lutheran doctrine, "the one true and right faith." This was the ideology, perhaps somewhat exaggerated, of the Swedish Church when modern notions of religious freedom and tolerance, equality and popular democracy became popular.

A period of two or three decades of intense value conflict ensued, in which the Church provided the major support for the values of the traditional society. The Social Democrats and some of the Liberals held hostile views toward the Church and religion, which were, in turn, further aggravated. Up to the beginning of the twentieth century "as far as is known no State Church clergy or any person involved in the activities of the Church joined the Social Democratic party. . . ." [22] The same could undoubtedly be said concerning the Liberal party. Not until the first decade of this century were there the slimmest beginnings of a rapprochement between the Church and the Social Democrats and the other popular movements, including the unions, the free churches, and the temperance societies. In 1914 with the appointment of Nathan Söderblum Sweden got an archbishop who repudiated the diminishing social reaction in the Church and emphasized the need of the Church to be politically tolerant and not to be bound to any economic or social system. The fact that the Church committed itself so completely to the values of the old order during the early period of modernization is a crucial factor in the development of the far-reaching secularization that has occurred in the industrial working class and the educated middle class in Sweden.

Changes in the Relation of Church and State

In the more than a century and a half since the 1809 Constitution was adopted, three areas of development in the relation of church and state have occurred: (1) the legal development of freedom of religion, (2) the institution of a Church Assembly to deal with matters of internal concern to the Church instead of the Riksdag, and (3) the transfer to the civil community of a number of the responsibilities regarding education and local government previously under the jurisdiction of the clergy and the Church.[23]

With respect to the legal development of freedom of religion, the first proposal to allow members to resign from the State Church was presented in the Riksdag in 1824. It came to nothing, but in 1856 the government again proposed that the right to leave the Church be legalized, and a law to that effect, containing a number of stipulations urged by the clergy, was passed in 1860. It was now possible for a person to leave the State Church, but only if the person entered a Christian congregation approved by the state. The applicant had to be at least eighteen years old, and he had to apply to the local parish office, where the clergy were to attempt to dissuade the potential dissenter from leaving the Church. In 1873 this law was replaced by another that lessened the more compulsive aspects of the 1860 law, but it was still required that the dissenter state the approved Christian sect he would enter. The main agitation at this early period for the right to leave the Church came from members of the free churches, which were growing rapidly. By the late 1850s there were almost 100 Baptist congregations in Sweden. But few dissenters, then or now, ever left the Church. One reason for this has been the desire to continue to exert influence in the Church through voting in parish elections. In 1929 even the Swedish bishops recommended that the right to freely leave the State Church be established, but it was not until the passage of the Religious Freedom Law in 1951 that it became possible to leave the Swedish Church without entering another religious congregation. The Religious Freedom Law also removed the requirement that all members of the government must be members of the Church of Sweden. In the years since 1952, when the law first went into effect, only around 40,000 Swedes have left the Church, even though by doing so they can save paying 40 percent of the money assessed through the Church tax; they must still pay 60 percent for the secular duties carried on by the Church.

Yet the right to leave the Church without joining another congregation has generally been of secondary importance to Social Democrats and radical Liberals in their battle for freedom of religion. Of primary importance has been the separation of church and state. From the early 1930s to the end of World War II this was not much of an issue because of the urgencies of economic problems and the threatening world situation. Since World War II, however, the forces favoring disestablishment have resumed their old demand. The opponents of the State Church argue in the press that a democracy should not give a privileged position to any particular religion. Those in favor of the Church argue that Swedes have full religious freedom and that the traditional link with the state has a number of advantages. In 1958 the government appointed a commission to make an intensive study of the implications and consequences of different relationships between church and state. What action will finally be taken remains to be seen in the 1970s.

The clergy no longer had formal representation in the Riksdag after the liberal parliamentary reform of 1866. In exchange for losing their general legislative role, a Church Assembly was established by the Riksdag with the authority to veto government decisions in the areas of Church law and the prerogatives of the clergy, in addition to giving the Church and clergy greater authority over their internal affairs. Since legislation passed in 1949, the Church Assembly consists of a majority of laymen; of a membership of one hundred, fifty-seven are laymen, forty-three are clergy. The Swedish Church presently has a greater degree of autonomy from the government than does the state church in either Norway or Denmark, but not as much as in Finland.[24]

Legislation passed in 1862 took many of the secular functions of the Church and clergy and put them under the jurisdiction of the civil community. Subsequent legislation over the past century has totally removed the clergy from any involvement in education, including the teaching of religion in the schools, and from social welfare, and it has sharpened the distinction between what is ecclesiastical and what is civil. The exception to this is that the parish clergy continue to have jurisdiction over the registration of vital events and the maintenance of the population registers.

The Free Churches

Between 4 and 5 percent of the Swedish population are members of the free churches, nearly all of whom continue to maintain their membership in the State Church.[25] This is a higher percentage than in the other Scandinavian countries, though smaller than in Britain. All of the free churches have traditionally placed an emphasis on evangelism, individual salvation, strict morality, being a community of believers, and freedom of religion. The early growth and development of the free churches was shaped by English and American influences from the mid-nineteenth century in the form of missionaries and returning emigrants. The older free churches—the Methodists, the Baptists, and the Mission Covenant Church—no longer adhere to a fundamentalist line and are probably more theologically liberal than their American counterparts.[26] The Pentecostals and a number of other sects, however, adhere to fundamentalist theologies and conservative morality and tend to reject many of the secular values of the greater society. These latter groups are the backbone of a Christian confessional party (*KDS*), which came into being in 1964 and which has yet to elect its first representative. Predominantly, the members of the older and higher-status free churches continue to support the Liberals.

Those who belong to the free churches typically manifest a much greater religiosity than those who belong only to the State Church. Yet their membership has been declining constantly for a number of decades. Berndt Gustafsson has projected this decline into the future and suggests that by 1990 the free churches will have one-third less membership than they did in 1967.[27] The membership of the free churches consists disproportionately of older women; 60 percent of the 1967 membership were women over fifty. Most of those who join the free churches are from the homes of free-church believers, few are outsiders.

The opposition between the free churches and the State Church has declined in recent decades in the face of the common threat of advanced secularism. In contrast to the United States and even Britain, there is little support for traditional religious belief or church attendance in the general culture.

Some Aspects of Religiosity

Following is a discussion of four aspects—participation, beliefs, attitudes, and influences—of the secular-religious continuum in Sweden.

Participation. All Swedes—except a fraction of 1 percent who have resigned from the Church, some 33,000 Catholics, and around 15,000 Jews—are formal members of the Church of Sweden, comprising more than 98 percent of the population. Four or 5 percent of these also belong to the various free churches.

Attendance at Sunday mass at the State Church declined from 17 percent on an average Sunday in 1900 to 3.0 percent in 1950, but by 1962 the percentage increased to 3.3 percent.[28] However, those who belong to the free churches are more likely to attend Sunday services and the overall figure, therefore, comes to perhaps 5 percent general church attendance for an average Sunday. Finland and Denmark have equally low patterns of Sunday church attendance;[29] in fact, attendance is probably lower in these three countries than in any other Western society.[30] In Norway attendance is somewhat higher than elsewhere in Scandinavia.[31] Average Sunday attendance in Great Britain as reported by survey research is around 15 percent,[32] and average attendance in the United States declined from 49 to 43 percent between 1958 and 1968.[33]

Table 3.1 gives official Church of Sweden statistics on attendance at Sunday mass for each of the thirteen dioceses in Sweden for the period 1953–1963. It shows the overall average attendance to be 3.1 percent. Note the variations in attendance in the different dioceses; for example, the low of 1.1 percent occurring in the urban diocese of Stockholm to the high of 6.3 percent in the diocese of Luleå, which is the most northern, most rural, and most unevenly developed area in Sweden. A substantially higher overall figure for church attendance has been reported by Berndt Gustafsson, from survey research data.[34] He reports that 27 percent of a 1955 sample of the population aged eighteen and over had attended a church service of some kind in the previous month. A 1960 study reported a figure of 23 percent to have attended a "church or chapel" in the previous month,[35] and a 1968 study reported 9 percent to have attended church in the previous week.[36] Even though these figures tend to include attendance at

Table 3.1 Average Percentage of Sunday Church Attendance, Church of Sweden, by Diocese, 1953–1963.

DIOCESE	Period	Percentage
Skara	1953–1958	5.1
Karlstad	1953–1958	3.1
Luleå	1953–1958	6.3
Växjö	1953–1958	4.7
Ärkestiftet	1953–1959	2.7
Visby	1954–1959	5.4
Linköping	1954–1960	3.2
Västerås	1955–1960	2.1
Strängnäs	1956–1961	2.1
Lund	1956–1962	2.3
Göteborg	1957–1962	4.3
Stockholm	1957–1962	1.1
Härnösand	1958–1963	2.5
Entire country		3.1

SOURCE: Statistical Office, Church of Sweden (Stockholm: Diakonistyrelsen, Statistiska Kontoret, May 26, 1964) mimeo.

Table 3.2 Baptisms, Confirmations, Marriages, and Burials Conducted by the Church of Sweden and by Other Religious and Civil Auspices, 1953–1963.

| | *(Percentages, ND means no data)* | | | | |
	Church of Sweden	Free Church	Catholic	Jewish	Civil
Baptisms	89.1	ND	ND	ND	ND
Confirmations	87.6	ND	ND	ND	ND
Marriages	91.8	1.7	.3	.04	6.1
Burials	96.4	3.4		.14	.08

SOURCE: Statistical Office, Church of Sweden (Stockholm: Diakonistyrelsen, Statistiska Kontoret, May 26, 1964) mimeo.

ceremonies such as baptisms, weddings, and burials, the great majority of which are conducted under church auspices, as can be seen in Table 3.2, they seem rather high when compared with the official church statistics. Attendance is considerably higher than regular Sunday attendance, however, on Christmas and Easter Sunday and nearly all Swedes continue to be baptized, confirmed, married, and buried by the Church.

Survey research data show that Church attendance is greater among rural people, women, and the old than among urban people, men, and the young.[37] The interesting relationship between social class and church attendance is shown in Table 3.3, which indicates the percentage by status group of those who attended a religious service at least two times in the previous month. While the percentages are from survey research and are inflated, the differentials revealed are what

Table 3.3 Active Participants in the Church of Sweden and the Free Churches, by Social Class, 1955–1956 (Percentages).

Attended Church at Least 2 Times in Previous Month	Church of Sweden	Free Church	Total
Social Group I (professionals, executives, university graduates)	10	2	12
Social Group II (white-collar workers, small businessmen, etc.)	10	8	18
Social Group III (workers)	6	7	13

Note: N = 2579.

SOURCE: Berndt Gustafsson, *Kristen i 50-talets Sverige* (Stockholm: Svenska Kyrkans Diakonistyrelsens Bokförlag, 1958), p. 30.

would be expected. The working class and the highest-status category participate to a lesser extent in organized religion than those of intermediate status. And, there are marked differences by social category in participation in the Church of Sweden and in the free churches; the working class is the least likely to participate in the Church of Sweden, whereas the highest-status category is the least likely to participate in the free churches.

Beliefs. The majority of Swedes believe in God, if not in an orthodox Christian manner, at least in a deist conception of a god who "oversees the world." Yet, this "belief in God" does not approach that of the United States where more than 95 percent consistently report such belief.[38] A 1956 study, shown in Table 3.4, found 52 percent of men aged eighteen to fifty-five and 72 percent of women in the same age category to at least believe in such a God. When the same people were asked whether they believed in a God who intervenes in their own lives, the percentage declined to 37 percent for men and 57 percent for women. When asked whether they believe that believers will go to heaven, the percentages dropped again, to 22 percent for men and 36 percent for women. When asked if they try to be real Christians, only 26 percent of the men and 36 percent of the women answered in the affirmative. In Sweden the connotation of a "Christian" is not of one who behaves in a morally approved way, as it so often is in the Anglo-American countries, but rather one who is of the community of believers.

A 1968 Gallup poll study of belief in God in a number of Western countries showed Sweden at the bottom of the list.[39] The percentages of people who answered affirmatively for the twelve countries are: 98, United States; 96, Greece; 89, Uruguay (cities); 85, Austria; 84, Switzerland; 83, Finland; 81, West Germany; 79, Netherlands; 77, Britain; 73, France; 73, Norway; and 60, Sweden. Note that the gap

Table 3.4   Religious Beliefs of Swedish Men and Women, Aged 18–55, 1956.

PERCENTAGE WHO	Men	Women
"believe in a God who oversees the world"	52	72
"believe in a God who intervenes in my own life"	37	57
"believe that believers will go to heaven"	22	35
"try to be a real Christian"	26	36

NOTE: N = about 1000 men 18–55; about 1000 women 18–55.

SOURCE: Svenska Institutet för Opinionsundersökningar (*SIFO*), (Stockholm, April 13, 1956) mimeo.

Table 3.5 **Answers to the Question: "Do You Try to Be a Real Christian?" by Age, Entire Population, 1955–1956 (Percentages).**

	Yes	Uncertain Don't know	No	N
12–15	35	41	24	(289)
16–17	20	36	44	(91)
18–25	18	20	62	(320)
26–35	24	27	49	(366)
36–45	31	27	42	(375)
46–55	38	24	38	(356)
56–	70	19	11	(641)

SOURCE: Gustafsson, *op. cit.*, p. 27.

here between Sweden and the next lowest countries, France and Norway, is thirteen points.

The issue of whether one tries "to be a real Christian" is probably a good indicator of an individual's relationship to orthodox Christian belief. Table 3.5 shows a remarkable age variation in answer to this question, indicating that 35 percent try to be real Christians at ages twelve to fifteen, but between eighteen and twenty-five only 18 percent do, and 70 percent of those fifty-six and over do. Even in the absence of similar data from other societies, these figures certainly indicate a low acceptance of orthodox Christian belief. Especially notable is the figure of only 18 percent between age eighteen and age twenty-five,[40] answering in the affirmative; for males it is only 15 percent. While there is evidence that religiosity increases with age, the variation is so great here that a marked decline in religious belief over past decades is indicated.[41]

A 1968 study of the attitudes of over 2000 Swedish youths aged twelve through twenty-four revealed that almost half of the youths unequivocally deny the existence of a deity.[42] In secular Stockholm only 12 percent answered "Yes, absolutely" to the question "Do you believe there is a God?," 24 percent were uncertain, and 63 percent answered negatively. Note in Table 3.6 that university students and young workers believe least. Table 3.6 is also broken down into categories showing the age, geographical areas, and educational and working statuses of the respondents.

A sizable minority of Swedes believe in a life after death, though fewer than in most Western societies. In the 1968 international Gallup poll previously referred to 38 percent of a national sample of Swedes

Table 3.6   Answers of 2120 Swedish Youth, Aged 12–24, to the Question "Do You Believe There Is a God?" 1968 (Percentages).

	Total	Males	Females
Yes, absolutely	22	17	28
Maybe, uncertain	31	30	33
No, there is not	46	53	39

	Age					
	12–13	14–15	16–17	18–19	20–21	22–24
Yes, absolutely	25	21	27	18	25	20
Maybe, uncertain	38	40	25	25	26	32
No, there is not	36	38	47	57	48	48

	Residence			
	Stockholm	Gothenberg and Malmö	Remaining Cities	Rural
Yes, absolutely	12	25	21	30
Maybe, uncertain	24	28	32	36
No, there is not	63	46	46	35

	Those in School			
	Presecondary	Vocational	Gymnasium	Higher Education
Yes, absolutely	23	24	22	13
Maybe, uncertain	39	29	24	28
No, there is not	37	47	54	59

	Those who work		
	Middle class	Worker	Housewife
Yes, absolutely	26	17	32
Maybe, uncertain	30	31	28
No, there is not	43	53	39

SOURCE: *Dagens Nyheter* April 7, 1968. Survey done by *SIFO*.

answered in the affirmative, which represents a decline from 49 percent in 1948. The percentage in Sweden of those who believe in life after death can be compared with eleven other Western countries: 73, United States; 57, Greece; 55, Finland; 54, Norway; 50, Netherlands; 50, Switzerland; 42, Uruguay (cities); 41, West Germany; 38, Britain; 38, Austria; 38, Sweden; and 35, France.

The percentage of Swedes who stated a belief in hell in this same international study is lower than in any of the other countries: 65, United States; 62, Greece; 44, Uruguay (cities); 36, Norway; 29, Finland; 28, Netherlands; 26, Austria; 25, Switzerland; 25, West Germany; 23, Britain; 22, France; and 17, Sweden.

Similar percentages of those who believe in the devil are: 67, Greece; 60, United States; 45, Uruguay (cities); 38, Norway; 29, Netherlands; 26, Finland; 25, Switzerland; 25, West Germany; 23, Austria; 21, Britain; 21, Sweden; and 17, France.

In 1964, a cross section of Swedes aged sixteen and over were asked whether they "pray to God." [43] The results show that 13 percent pray "daily," 13 percent pray "quite often," 27 percent pray "more rarely," and 46 percent "never" pray. By contrast, only 8 percent of a 1953 American sample claimed that they never prayed.[44]

An important observation about religious belief in Sweden is the absence of much opinion that sees religion as the sole basis of morality. The same 1964 sample when asked about prayer chose the following alternatives regarding the relation between religion and morality:

16 percent   "There is no other basis for morality than religion."

27 percent   "For me personally religion is the only basis for morality, but I still believe that men can find another basis for moral behavior."

41 percent   "Morality does not need to be based on religion."

16 percent   "Do not agree with any of the above statements." [45]

In the United States, on the other hand, religion is conventionally viewed not only as the basis of morality, but as the basis of both the "American way of life" and democracy.[46] Similarly in England, which is more comparable with Sweden in having an established church, morality and democracy are conventionally viewed as being rooted in religion. The substantially enhanced role for Christian education in England, which is contained in the Education Act of 1944, was facilitated by "the association of the Christian religion with the cause of democracy. . . ." [47] Basic to those who framed the law was the conviction that "education must have a religious base. . . ." [48] Essentially, religious education in English schools is Christian-confessional training, and it is inextricably intertwined with moral teaching. The following statement from a 1963 report of the Central Advisory Council for Education (England), for example, recommends that "(r)eligious education has a part to play in helping boys and girls to find a firm basis for sexual morality based on chastity before marriage and fidelity within it."[49]

Christian education as a school subject in Sweden, on the other hand, must, by law, be "objective" and must not propagandize for any particular religion or view of morality. While this is often not adhered to in practice, a substantial majority of Swedes accept this "objective" view, as indicated in this 1964 study. The sample chose the various alternatives on Christian education as follows:

25 percent   "Christian education should not only give students knowledge but also influence them toward the Christian faith."

66 percent   "Christian education should only give students knowledge about religion, but should not attempt to influence them in questions of faith."

4 percent   "Any special Christian education is not needed in the schools."

4 percent   "None of these agree with my opinion."

1 percent   No answer.[50]

Attitudes. In spite of the relatively low level of both church attendance and orthodox Christian belief, Swedes are not unfriendly to religion in general. In one study from 1961, 82 percent of a national sample agreed that "men in our time need religion."[51] In 1962 a Swedish weekly *Vecko-Journalen* sponsored a study of what Swedes regard as important problems. To a question about the need to have a "greater interest in religion," 30 percent said that it was "very important," 42 percent said it was "quite important," 24 percent believed it was "not at all important," and 4 percent were undecided.[52]

In addition, most Swedes are not disturbed by the relation between the Church and the State. In 1957 a national sample was asked how they would vote if there were a referendum on the separation of Church and State. Eighteen percent said they would vote for it, 51 percent said they would vote against it, and 31 percent were undecided.[53] Some pious people, particularly high-church Lutherans, favor the separation arguing that the Church would then be free from government pressures and would be able to become a community of believers. On the other hand, others favor the present relation because it does make the church subject to some controls by the government, particularly in the appointment of clergy and the control of the budget. The role that the government played in exerting influence on the Church Assembly in the 1950s in forcing through the right of women to be ordained, so bitterly opposed by high-church opinion, is an example of the kind of pressure the State can exert on the Church by threatening to use its power of appointment to accomplish certain ends.[54]

Both inside and outside the Church, there are a number of conflicting ideas about what the most desirable relationship between State and Church should be and how it might be realized.[55] Indeed, for a number of years it has been clear that there is intense factionalism within the church over these and related issues. The great majority of Swedes indicate that they would request church membership if it were no longer automatic, which shows predominantly positive feelings toward the services performed by the Church. A 1958 study of the population over age fifteen found that if the church should be disestablished 72 percent would join, 19 percent would not join, and 9 percent were undecided as to what they would do.[56] In 1961 a sample of the population was asked how well they thought the State Churches and the State Church clergy were performing their duties. Their verdict was that they were doing tolerably well; 25 percent said "very well," 53 percent said "fairly well," 9 percent said "not especially well," 3 percent said "poorly," and 10 percent did not say.[57]

Swedes evaluate the clergy somewhat differently than Americans do. A comparative study of eight occupations was conducted to determine the comparative prestige, usefulness to society, and intellectual ability of these occupations, using a sample of Swedish and American university students.[58] There were no differences in relative prestige ranking, but the Swedes ranked the clergy significantly lower in "usefulness to society" than did the Americans—lower than dentists or business executives—but, on the other hand, the Swedes ranked them relatively higher in intellectual ability than did the Americans. This latter evaluation can be explained by the academic status of the State Church clergy, in that the clergy are all graduates of the same prestigious universities that other professionals graduate from, and they have the status of *akademiker*, whereas the majority of the American clergy are the products of little-known denominational institutions.

Influence. It is difficult to precisely assess the influence of religion and the clergy on any modern society. Yet even after only a superficial study of contemporary Sweden, it is clear that influences from religious sources are minimal. The Church has no illusions about the magnitude of her influence. In fact, the Swedish contributor to a recent symposium on Christian social ethics, sponsored by the World Council of Churches, aptly titled his contribution "Where the Church No Longer Shapes the Common Life." [59]

The clergy and the Church are neutral in political questions. It is almost inconceivable for a clergyman to officially support any political party or position, even though there are fewer sanctions against the participation of a clergyman as a private individual in partisan politics than in many other societies. The Church has had little influence on public policy of any kind in recent decades. It is even difficult for the Church to speak out on questions of morality, particularly when it takes a conservative position, without being subject to a barrage of criticism. For example, when the bishops in 1964 deplored the "privatizing" of sexual life and reasserted their 1951 view that pre-marital intercourse was sinful, they received sharp criticism in a number of Liberal and Social Democratic papers. "What do the Bishops Know about Love?" was the headline of a critical editorial in the Stockholm paper *Aftonbladet*.[60]

Religious beliefs or affiliations are irrelevant in politics, except to the extent that some of the candidates on the Liberal party lists are chosen for their free-church affiliations. No confessional party has ever been able to elect a representative to the Riksdag. And, members of the government or political leaders virtually never invoke God or religious sanction in any context. Gunnar Heckscher, the leader of the Conservative party (1961–1964), even conceded to being an atheist during a television interview in the early 1960s, though he claimed to be sympathetic to the Christian tradition.[61] Even though the Conservative party is the party of those most strongly involved in the Church of Sweden, Heckscher's proclamation caused him no difficulties.

Various studies have shown predictable findings, such as that the more religious engage in less premarital sexual behavior and are generally more attitudinally conservative than the less religious.[62] It is also clear that those with a strong involvement in the State Church tend disproportionately to support the Conservative party, whereas those strongly committed to the free churches tend to support the Liberal party or the small confessional party (*KDS*).

There is a "strong, living, and genuine" religiosity in a small minority of Swedes in the State Church and among a greater proportion of free-church members.[63] This minority acts as a pressure group in the political parties and wields a disproportionate influence. In fact, there is even a "Christian group" that meets regularly in the Riksdag. Both the Conservative and Center parties have strongly worded statements in their party programs favoring Christianity, and the Liberals have a statement in their program supporting the ethical values put forth by Christianity and humanism. The Social Democratic and Communist programs, however, make no references at all to Christianity. Still, the great majority of Swedish Christians, are, according to Herbert Tingsten:

Christians-in-name-only (namnkristna), *indeed, even the phrase Christians-in-name-only seems almost too strong when used to designate total indifference bounded by approval of tradition and convention. They say they believe in God, yet do not accept the doctrines that distinguish Christianity. They want to keep education in Christianity [in the schools], yet do not go to Church. Baptism, confirmation, marriage, and burial—these are the contacts these people have, not with religion (for there is no reason to have such contact!), but only with the Church. The holy sacraments provide a setting for festive occasions. A necessity for this state-of-affairs is that they do not listen, do not understand, or at least do not pay any attention to what is said. They inquire as little into the meaning of these things as they ponder electricity on a journey by tram. This we all know, and this we all say—but convention is so well established that it is considered a trifle unbecoming to say so publicly.*[64]

An Explanation

The high degree of secularism that prevails in Sweden can perhaps be explained by several factors:

(1) A long-term religious homogeneity has prevented religion from becoming a focal point of social differentiation. This is contrary to the religious situation in the United States or the Netherlands or even England with its more historically important free-church population and its sizable Catholic minority. Religious diversity seems to increase the saliency of religion. However, as in the homogeneously Catholic countries, though to a lesser extent, differentiation between the religious and nonreligious sectors of the population is sometimes apparent, such as in politics.

(2) During the crucial period of early modernization, particularly the last two decades of the nineteenth century, the Church solidly aligned itself with the old order and its traditional values, thereby

alienating those segments of the society that were oriented toward modern values. Related to this is the observation that State Church Lutheranism, with its emphasis on absolutistic doctrinal authoritarianism and its essentially medieval view of society, was inherently less amenable to modern values of egalitarianism and tolerance than was Calvinism and the more individualistic forms of Protestantism. In this respect, Sweden offers a close parallel to Lutheran Germany prior to World War I.

(3) Empirical and positivist value orientations and a pragmatic attitude toward norms and values (called "nihilism of values" in Sweden) predominant in Swedish society. This is partly the consequence of the relatively late, intense, and extraordinarily successful and rapid modernization that thoroughly discredited the traditionalist and idealistic values of nineteenth-century society. The dominant value orientations of contemporary Sweden appear to support agnosticism and nonbelief in terms of traditional religion and of pragmatism in terms of conventional morality. The pervasiveness of these modern values, particularly in the articulate segments of Swedish society, is exemplified in Lars Gustafsson's assertion that in the whole contemporary discussion of issues in Sweden "nihilism of values is a *leitmotif*" [65] or the observation of Herbert Tingsten—a central figure in modern Swedish life—that "most of my friends and colleagues in scholarship and journalism could be called nihilists." [66]

Notes

1. Hans L. Zetterberg, "Sweden—A Land of Tomorrow?" in Ingemar Wizelius (ed.), *Sweden in the Sixties*, Rudy Feichtner (tr.) (Stockholm: Almqvist & Wiksell, 1967), p. 15.
2. Sources for the data in the first two paragraphs will be found in the references to the more detailed discussion in this chapter.
3. Sten Carlsson and Jerker Rosén, *Svensk historia: II, Tiden efter 1718* (Stockholm: Svenska Bokförlaget, 1961), p. 739.
4. Herbert Tingsten, "Stability and Vitality in Swedish Democracy," *Political Quarterly*, XXIV (April–June 1955), pp. 140–151.

5. See Franklin D. Scott, *The American Experience of Swedish Students* (Minneapolis: University of Minnesota Press, 1956), pp. 38, 83–85, and William H. Sewell and Oluf M. Davidson, *Scandinavian Students on an American Campus* (Minneapolis: University of Minnesota Press, 1961), pp. 43–45.

6. Uppsala Studentkår, *The Intellectual Face of Sweden* (Uppsala: Uppsala Studentkår, 1964), p. 95.

7. Lars Gustafsson, *The Public Dialogue in Sweden: Current Issues of Social, Esthetic and Moral Debate*, Claude Stephenson (tr.) (Stockholm: P. A. Norstedt, 1964), pp. 34–35.

8. Deane William Ferm, "Sex, Sin and Salvation in Sweden," *Christian Century*, LXXXIII (September 21, 1966), 1142–1146; see also letters qualifying Ferm's views under the rubric "Sweden: Not Quite That Bad," LXXXIII (November 2, 1966), 1343–1345, and his article "The Role of the Church in Modern Sweden," *American Scandinavian Review*, LV (Winter 1967–1968), 360–370.

9. See Johan Goudsblom, *Dutch Society* (New York: Random House, 1967), esp. pp. 50–57.

10. There is only one detailed history of religion and the Church in Sweden written in English that is good, even though it is very out of date; it is John Wordsworth, *The National Church of Sweden* (London: A. R. Mowbray, 1911). See also the short but more up-to-date account by Robert Murray, *A Brief History of the Church of Sweden* (Stockholm: Diakonistyrelsens Bokförlag, 1961). On the Reformation and early seventeenth century see *The New Cambridge Modern History* (Cambridge: Cambridge University Press, 1958), Vol. II, pp. 146–153; Michael Roberts, *Gustavus Adolphus: A History of Sweden, 1611–1632* (London: Longmans, Green, 1953), Vol. I, pp. 350–427. Conrad J. T. Bergendoff, *Olavus Petri and the Ecclesiastical Transformation in Sweden* (New York: Macmillan, 1928). An account in French of the Swedish Reformation is Jean G. H. Hoffman, *La réforme en Suède* (Neuchatel, Switzerland: Delachaux and Niestle, 1945). An English summary of the history of church-State relations in Sweden from the 1850s is to be found in Carl Arvid Hessler, *Statskyrkodebatten* (Stockholm: Almqvist and Wiksell, 1964), pp. 433–451.

11. Roberts, *op. cit.*, p. 377.

12. Eli F. Heckscher, *An Economic History of Sweden*, Göran Ohlin (tr.) (Cambridge: Harvard University Press, 1954), p. 67.

13. *Ibid.*, p. 68.

14. *Ibid.*, p. 67.

15. Murray, *op. cit.*, p. 33.

16. Quoted and translated by Edgar M. Carlson, *The Reinterpretation of Luther* (Philadelphia: Westminster Press, 1948), p. 24.

17. Unless otherwise noted, the quotations in this and the following paragraph are from Per-Olov Ahrén, "Stat och kyrka i Sverige. Historisk översikt," in *Statens Offentliga Utredningar*, 1964:16 (1958 Års utredning Kryka-Stat: IV *Historisk Oversikt*), pp. vii–liii.

18. Quoted by Murray, *op. cit.*, p. 36.

19. Carlsson and Rosén, *op. cit.*, p. 71.

20. Quoted by Alrik Gustafson, *A History of Swedish Literature* (Minneapolis: University of Minnesota Press, 1961), p. 184.

21. Hessler, *op. cit.*, p. 11.

22. Herbert Tingsten, *Den svenska socialdemodratiens idéutveckling* (Stockholm: Tidens förlag, 1941), Vol. II, p. 294.

23. These three categories are used in the discussion by Ahrén, *op. cit.*, p. xliii.

24. This is the opinion of Research Docent Arne Palmqvist of the Theology Faculty of Uppsala University, an authority on church organization.

25. For a history of the free churches and an account of their place in contemporary Swedish society, see Erik Nyhlen, *Svensk frikyrka* (Stockholm: Bokförlaget Prisma, 1964).

26. An opinion of Professor Georg Karlsson, Institute of Sociology, Umeå University.

27. Reported in an article on the free churches by Rune Johansson, *Dagens Nyheter*, October 23, 1967, pp. 1, 12.

28. Berndt Gustafsson, "Det religiösa livet," in Edmund Dahlström (ed.), *Svensk samhällsstruktur i sociologisk belysning*, third ed. (Stockholm: Scandinavian University Books, 1965), p. 346.

29. Paavo Seppänen of the Sociology Institute, University of Helsinki, claims from his research that Finnish Church attendance is about 4 percent. In his opinion, it is about the same in Denmark.

30. See comparative discussion on church atendance in Michael P. Fogarty, *Christian Democracy in Western Europe* (London: Routledge & Kegan Paul, 1957), pp. 345–357; see also the Swedish reference in footnote 31.

31. The north and east of Norway are probably similar in church attendance to the rest of Scandinavia, but in the south and west religious activity is appreciably greater; see Stein Rokkan and Henry Valen, "Regional Contrasts in Norwegian Politics," in Erik Allardt and Yrjö Littunen (eds.), *Cleavages, Ideologies and Party Systems* (Helsinki: The Academic Bookstore, 1964), pp. 162–238. In 1960 an international study of religious behavior in a number of countries reported 32 percent of the Norwegians questioned had visited a "church or chapel" in the previous month as compared with 23 percent of the Swedes. Sweden was the lowest of the eight countries for which data were presented, and Norway was next to the lowest; see *Svenska Institutet för Opinionsundersökningar (SIFO)* (Stockholm: December 6, 1960) (N not given, mimeo.).

32. See Michael Argyle, *Religious Behaviour* (London: Routledge & Kegan Paul, 1958), pp. 5–7.

33. See Hazel Gaudet Erskine, "The Polls: Church Attendance," *Public Opinion Quarterly*, XXVIII (Winter 1964), 671–680.

34. Berndt Gustafsson, *Kristen i 50-talets Sverige* (Stockholm: Svenska Kyrkans Diakonistyrelsens Bokförlag, 1958), p. 27.

35. *Svenska Institutet för Opinionsundersökningar* (SIFO) (Stockholm: December 6, 1960).

36. *New York Times*, December 22, 1968, Part 1, p. 39.

37. See, for example, B. Gustafsson, *op.cit.*, passim.

38. See, for example, *New York Times*, *op. cit.*, p. 39.

39. *New York Times*, December 26, 1968, p. 21. The data in the subsequent two paragraphs are from this source.

40. B. Gustafsson, *op. cit.*, p. 23.

41. See M. Argyle, *op. cit.*, pp. 58–70.

42. *Dagens Nyheter*, April 7, 1968, pp. 1, 40. Survey done by *SIFO*.

43. These percentages were calculated from data (N = 1142) in Table 5 (p. 281) of Jörgen Westerståhl, "Samkristna skolnämndens namninsamlingsaktion," *Statsvetenskaplig tidskrift*, 67 (1964), 277–290.

44. See "Americans and Prayer," *Catholic Digest*, 18 (November 1953), 53–56.

45. Westerståhl, *op. cit.*, p. 287 (N = 1166).

46. See the argument in Will Herberg, *Protestant, Catholic, Jew*, rev. ed. (Garden City, N.Y.: Doubleday Anchor, 1960), esp. pp. 254–272.

47. W. Roy Niblett, "The Religious Education Clauses of the 1944 Act: Aims, Hopes and Fulfillment," in A. G. Wedderspoon (ed.), *Religious Education, 1944–1984* (London: Allen & Unwin, 1966), p. 20.

48. *Ibid.*, p. 22.

49. Ministry of Education, *Half Our Future* (London: Her Majesty's Stationery Office, 1963), p. 58.

50. Westerståhl, *op. cit.*, p. 286 (N = 1166).

51. *SIFO*, *op. cit.*, June 30, 1961 (N = about 1000, mimeo).

52. *Vecko-Journalen*, August 24, 1962, 23–25; 32.

53. *SIFO*, *op. cit.*, February 21, 1957 (N not given, mimeo).

54. For a summary in English of this struggle, see Hessler, *Statskyrkodebatten*, *op. cit.*, pp. 433–451.

55. For a detailed account of different conceptions of the church, see Arne Palmqvist, "De aktuella kyrkobegreppen i Sverige," *Statens Offentliga Utredningar*, 1964:16, pp. 1–324.

56. *SIFO*, *op.cit.*, December 5, 1958 (N = 750, mimeo).

57. *SIFO*, *op. cit.*, June 30, 1961 (N not given, mimeo).

58. Edward C. McDonagh, Sven Wermlund, and John F. Crowther, "Relative Professional Status as Perceived by American and Swedish University Students," *Social Forces*, 38 (October 1958), 65–69.

59. See Harry Aronson's contribution in John C. Bennett (ed.), *Christian Social Ethics in a Changing World* (New York: Association Press, 1966), pp. 253–265.

60. *Aftonbladet*, September 27, 1964, p. 2.

61. Sten Johansson of the Institute of Sociology, Uppsala University, supplied this information.

62. See B. Gustafsson, *op. cit.*, passim.

63. Herbert Tingsten, "Svensk Kristendom," *Dagens Nyheter*, July 21, 1949, p. 2; reprinted in C. A. Wachtmeister (ed.), *Ateistens handbok* (Verdandi Debatt XV: Bokförlaget Prisma, 1964), pp. 13–15.

64. *Ibid.*, p. 14.

65. L. Gustafsson, *op. cit.*, p. 11.

66. Herbert Tingsten, *Mitt liv: Tio år, 1953–1963* (Stockholm: P. A. Norstedt, 1964), Vol. IV, p. 356.

IV

The Schools

One might ask why these rather drastic
changes [in the schools] have taken place
in Sweden and not in countries such as
England, France, or the Federal Republic
of Germany.
—Torsten Husén *and* Gunnar Boalt[1]

The transformation of the Swedish school system from the primary
schools through the universities, which has been developing since the
early 1950s, has been the most extensive in any Western European
country.[2] Sweden is also providing the model for similar changes that
are now occurring in Norway, Finland, and perhaps in other countries.

In addition to the problems arising out of a quintupling of enrollments in the secondary schools and universities that has occurred since
the late 1940s, the usual European double-track system of primary
education has been abolished and a number of major reforms have
been legislated to realize what the Swedes call the "democratization
of the schools." Soon the system whereby the youths who are to go
on to academic secondary education (and later to the universities) are
funneled out of the primary school into academic schools will be
eliminated from all communities in Sweden. This has been the traditional pattern in every European country, and in fact, most countries
still begin the process at age ten or eleven, leaving the great majority
of children to continue their education through age fourteen to sixteen without the "brighter" and more academically oriented middle
and upper-class youth.

The new Swedish primary school is a single-track comprehensive or common school (*grundskola*),[3] which gives an obligatory nine-year course for all youths from age seven to age sixteen.[4] (It is only in Scandinavia and in the Eastern European countries that children wait until age seven to begin school.) Some differentiation begins in the seventh year (at age thirteen) when some pupils choose German or French as a second foreign language and others do not; English is compulsory for all from the third grade. These choices are, however, entirely those of the student and his parents, with provisions for changing one's mind in subsequent years. All youth in public instruction, the overwhelming majority, will be enrolled in such a school by the early 1970s. Among Western European nations only Sweden and Norway—which has a unique tradition of seven years of common schooling that goes back to 1889 and is developing a nine-year common school based on legislation passed in 1959—have done away with this most basic structural support of a class-linked educational system.[5] Finland will be next; legislation passed in 1965 provides for a nine-year comprehensive school.

These changes do not mean that cultural background and social class no longer remain major factors in determining the educational futures of Swedish youth, but only that early streaming has been removed from the system. Probably the best single measure of the extent to which an educational system is class-linked is the proportion of working-class and farm youth that is represented in the universities. Sweden, Norway, and Finland—together with Great Britain—appear to be substantially above the countries of Continental Europe in this respect.[6] They may, indeed, be above the United States, if the comparison is limited to academically selective colleges and universities.

The Common School

In spite of the late industrialization of the Scandinavian countries, they were in advance of the American states and all of the other countries of Northwestern Europe, with the important exception of Prussia and some of the other German states, in legislating compulsory primary education. Denmark established compulsory primary education in 1814, followed by Norway in 1827, and finally by Sweden in 1842.[7] England, by contrast, did not do so until the legislation of 1876 and 1880,[8] and France did not do so until 1882.[9] In 1852 Massachusetts was the first of the American states to pass such legislation, and Mississippi was the last in 1918, with a large number of states doing so in the 1870s and 1880s.[10]

All of the Lutheran monarchies of Europe took seriously Luther's emphasis on the state's duty to establish schools to teach the common people to read the Bible. Popular education (as opposed to academic education) under the auspices of the State Church goes back to the seventeenth century in Sweden and in the other Scandinavian countries. In post-Reformation England, on the other hand, in contrast to the rest of Protestant Europe (including Calvinist Scotland), education was regarded as a wholly private responsibility. This difference in tradition partly explains the length of time it took for popular education to become universally established in England and the absence of much national involvement in nonacademic secondary education until the historic Educational Act of 1944.

The established tradition of popular education, the presence of a free peasantry, and certain structural factors aided Sweden in building up a relatively substantial system of primary education in the nineteenth century. Sweden had become a highly centralized state prior to that time. There was virtually no opposition to the state's assumption of responsibility for primary education, because the church was an integral part of the state apparatus. Everywhere in Europe, the church, whether Protestant or Catholic, demanded and maintained control of education. Opposition to such control was only occasionally voiced until the last two decades of the century. However, in France compulsory primary education was slow in developing because the church opposed state-supervised education and the rationalist elements would not tolerate education under the church.[11] This division has remained a dominant theme in the history of primary education in France. This division came late to Sweden, not really arriving until this century, but by the 1950s the struggle had been decisively won by the state and the forces that favored secularization of the schools. In 1950 legislation was passed, stipulating that the teaching of religion at all levels was to be "objective" and that religions other than Lutheranism were to be studied. And, with the passing of the Religious Freedom Act in 1951, teachers of religion no longer needed to be members of the Evangelical Lutheran Church.

Unlike Britain or the United States, but similar to Germany, individualist and laissez-faire philosophy—an ideology that sought to limit the authority and jurisdiction of the state—had little currency in nineteenth-century Sweden. Organic theories of the state and society prevailed.[12] The middle classes, who were the dominant carriers of an anti-state and local-control ideology, did not become a major political force until the twentieth century. In the 1880s, for example, in the vigorous educational debate over what form primary education would take, there was consensus that education at all levels should be governed by the state, and even at this late date there was not much opposition to its supervision by the Church.[13] The educational debate in the Riksdag revolved around questions of what was to be taught and how the system was to be structured.

From one point of view, since the nineteenth century Sweden has only been transformed from an agricultural-bureaucratic to an industrial-bureaucratic state. Her developed and effective state apparatus has been a major factor in restructuring educational institutions, making for less continuity with the past than, for example, the United States or Britain have. This is most evident in primary education, to a much lesser extent of the universities. To use William Graham Sumner's apt terms, Swedish educational institutions tend to be "enacted" institutions, whereas Anglo-American ones tend to be "crescive," that is, they have developed through time without much overall direction.

At first there might appear to be great similarity between the Swedish system of education and the French, since they are both highly centralized. There are, however, some crucial differences. De Tocqueville makes a useful distinction between centralization of *government* and centralization of *administration*.[14] To a great extent, the Swedish educational system can be said to be centrally governed as evidenced by the fact that educational policy is centrally determined for the entire nation, but the administration is not highly centralized, at least when compared with France or the Soviet Union. In Sweden, county and municipal school committees do not determine curriculum or policy, but they do hire *grundskola* teachers, build schools, and generally administer the local school systems. The French system, on the other hand, is both centrally governed and centrally administered with a minimal degree of local involvement. A British student of comparative school systems has described the French educational system as operating "with almost complete disregard for local feelings, local conditions and the wishes of parents."[15] The United States is, of course, the outstanding example of the opposite, having a low degree of central governance even at the state level.

A second important difference between Sweden and France is in the mode of centralized governance. The Swedish Minister of Education, unlike his French counterpart, obtains most of his authority from specific legislation passed by the Riksdag, though the legislation is largely written by his department. Furthermore, he does not directly govern the agencies under his jurisdiction, such as the Board of Education, and the Office of the Chancellor of the Universities, which are headed by directors and are highly autonomous. In France, on the other hand, the Minister of Education has enormous authority by virtue of his office and is checked only by the National Assembly.[16] He can establish policy that is binding on all schools until such time as the National Assembly chooses to countermand them, which does not happen often.

The single-track school system, which is universal in principle in the United States though largely vitiated by de facto ethnic and class segregation in urban and suburban areas, has been a goal of progressive and radical forces in Europe since at least the early part of the nineteenth century.[17] It is an egalitarian idea whose origin is in the Enlightenment. Conservatives, mainly the Church and the official classes, the aristocracy and the bourgeoisie, have traditionally supported a dual system of education in which those who are to be academically trained are to be given segregated education.[18] This separation has been defended as necessary for obtaining a well-trained elite, and it has been maintained that there is great utility, if not necessity, in beginning at an early age. Only a minority of youth were believed to be suited for and capable of benefiting from an academic education. And conservatives could generally point to a system of academically excellent schools to support their position. Certainly the gymnasia of Germany and Switzerland, the Netherlands and Scandinavia, were far more rigorously academic institutions than the unselective American high school, in spite of their authoritarian and not very intellectual character. In the past the gymnasia were probably even more academically substantial than the great majority of American colleges.[19]

The progressives who have favored the idea of a common school have generally not been very concerned with the specifically educative functions of the schools, but have emphasized rather their social functions. They have found the dual system a means of perpetuating class distinctions, as a way of maintaining the power position of the official and upper classes, and as an obstacle to the upward mobility opportunities of the lower classes.

Yet early Marxism as a vehicle for social protest tended to lessen the perceived importance of educational structures as supports of class privilege. They were regarded as of minor importance compared with economic and political institutions. Sweden provides an excellent example of this. The leading Marxist Social Democrats in Sweden from the 1880s and 1890s and after—Hjalmar Branting, Axel Danielsson, and August Palm—gave ideological support to the idea of a common school as part of their concern with the achievement of equality, but it was fundamentally an unimportant issue to them.[20] They held that the education problem could only be solved after a thoroughgoing transformation of society. "The hunger problem" came first.

The liberal reformists of the time, on the other hand, who drew their philosophy largely from the "new humanism" of Esaias Tegnér, Erik Gustaf Geijer, and C. J. L. Almqvist of a half century earlier, saw the education of individuals as the principal means of transforming society. This native tradition—and not that of the socialists—was the early source of the strong support for the abolition of the double-track school system.

In the 1920s in Vienna, where the Social Democrats had a strong majority, the first comprehensive school system in Europe was established.[21] It was an eight-year secular school with some ability differentiation in the second four years. But the establishment of this system was not accomplished by consensus politics. There had been great opposition to such egalitarian and secular policies from the conservative Christian Social party. After the party established its clerical-fascist dictatorship in 1934, in fact, the school reform was completely abolished. Similar legislation under the Swedish Social Democrats came late because of the slow operation of consensus politics. Until well after World War II, Sweden had a conventional European double-track school system. Despite the egalitarian values of the Swedish Social Democrats, those values were not applied to education until the late 1940s. But when the radical reform of a nine-year, single-track school system did come about in Sweden, unlike in Vienna, it was achieved by compromise politics with a high level of consensus and little bitter opposition. After a period of two decades in which education had not been much of a political issue, all of the political parties at about the same time, though with some qualifications from the Conservatives, came to favor the introduction of the nine-year common school on an experimental basis. The central theme in the history of Swedish primary education in the twentieth century has been the bringing together of the "practical" and "theoretical" streams, the Swedish terms for nonacademic and academic education. Only in recent years have the dual systems and early streaming become political issues in other countries, such as in Great Britain where both the Labor and Liberal parties now regard these as basic domestic issues with which to oppose the Conservatives. Both the Labor and Liberal parties have taken strong stands against the eleven-plus examinations and in favor of comprehensive schools. Most other Continental European countries do not find the issue of egalitarian school structures to be as important an issue as do the northern countries and Britain, however.

The developments in education parallel the rapid development of Sweden into a highly industrialized nation as well as the coming to power and continuing dominance of the Social Democratic party in the political arena. The Social Democrats have benefited enormously by the economic success of Swedish society over the past third of this century. In addition, the Liberals, who are almost always the second-largest party, have a long tradition of radical egalitarianism, and they have supported the new directions of the school system as much as the Social Democrats. The net result has been a political party spectrum that is more to the Left in these matters than is any other Western European country.[22]

Before the late nineteenth century, Sweden had two almost wholly separate school systems, one was free and provided a basic but terminal primary education and the other was not free and provided an academic education preparing for the university. The former was called the *folkskola*, and the overwhelming majority of youths went to it and remained there for six years. It gave a "practical" education, without foreign languages, concentrating on Swedish, reading, writing, arithmetic, and religion, emphasizing Luther's catechism. Unless a youth lived in or near a town, he usually had no other choice than to attend a *folkskola*. The latter was the nine-year *läroverk* (the old academic school), which provided a predominantly classical education with a great emphasis on languages. Most students studied Latin, German, French, and English (in that order).[23] The aim of the curriculum was to pass the coveted *studentexamen* (university matriculation examination), after which one had the privilege of entering the university. The student entered the *läroverk* at about age nine, after having had some preliminary training in writing, Swedish, spelling, arithmetic, religion, and geography. A study of where *läroverk* students between 1879 and 1882 got this basic training revealed that only a minority had ever attended a *folkskola*.[24] Most had been educated at a private school or at home.

The old dual system did not necessarily prevent social mobility. In fact there are data to indicate that mobility was quite considerable. According to Sten Carlsson, who has made a statistical study of social mobility in Sweden since 1680, about 15 percent of the university students in the first half of the nineteenth century were the sons of farmers; the percentage reached up to 20 percent in the second half of the century.[25] We can probably assume that similar percentages of farmers' sons were to be found in the *läroverk*. Another historian, Gunnar Richardson, has gathered data on the social recruitment of *läroverk* students in the 1880s, and he has concluded that up to 15 percent were the sons of farm owners.[26] Carlsson shows that the Swedish educational system throughout the nineteenth century provided for a relatively large amount of upward mobility for farmers' sons as compared with Norway and Denmark. He also claims, and probably rightly, that Sweden was unique in Europe in the proportions of farmers' sons who got to the universities. On the other hand, the educational system did not facilitate social mobility for the sons of industrial workers or farm workers; they were not more than 5 or 6 percent of all university students until the mid-1940s.[27]

The debate in the 1880s about what the future structure of the primary school system should be centered around two highly discussed plans.[28] The leading proposal of the conservatives was first put forth at a national meeting of teachers by Fredrik Andersson, a gymnasium teacher of mathematics and physics and a member of the Riksdag's 1882 Education Commission. His basic assumption was the conventional one of the time, that no single primary school could satisfy the needs of all social classes. He maintained that Sweden had the *folkskola* to serve the farmers and the workers and a "learned school" in the *läroverk* to serve the needs of the professional and official classes; there was, however, no school to meet the needs of the higher artisans, the emerging business and merchant groups, and the larger farmers. He proposed the creation of a new school specifically for them to be called the *borgarskola*, which was to have two lines of specialization—business and farming—in the upper grades. This was to be a school for the lower-middle classes, with a less academic orientation than the *läroverk*, but at a less practical level than the *folkskola*, and it was to be wholly separate from both. This is in effect an outline for a tripartite school system that would allegedly have satisfied the needs of the different classes by giving each class its own school. Such a system came into existence in Germany after 1872, when regulations permitted the establishment of an "elevated and expanded common school" primarily for the urban lower-middle classes.[29] Andersson's plan was favored by the conservative press, but it was severely criticized by moderates and progressives, who believed it would increase class distinctions and make the *folkskola* even more of a proletarian school than it already was.

The leading proposals of the progressives were put forth by Fridtjuv Berg, a young *folkskola* teacher, who was later Minister of Education in two Liberal governments. His plan first appeared in an article in a teacher's journal in 1882 and was expanded into a book, which was destined to be the most discussed book in the history of Swedish education, the following year. The book was entitled *The Folkskola as the Basic School* (*Folkskolan såsom bottenskola*). In it he proposed that the *folkskola* be a six-year common school *under* and preparatory to the *läroverk*. His emphasis was on the social implications of such an arrangement, maintaining that it would lessen class distinctions, promote social equality, and prevent the *folkskola* from being a school for the poor. Such a plan was too radical for the moderates, though it was supported by most *folkskola* teachers. It was too contrary to the pedagogic assumptions of the time, which held that theoretical and practical education were fundamentally different and required separate methods of instruction.

Neither of these plans had much appeal in the Riksdag, both represented polar positions in the school debate of the 1880s, but one was attuned to the society that was passing and the other to the society that was emerging. A school system structured on the basis of class or occupational groupings, as advocated by Andersson, rapidly lost contact with political reality as the official and landowning classes lost their commanding positions in the Riksdag. But Berg's proposal remained at the center of the educational debate over how the *folkskola* and *läroverk* were to be joined, until it began to become reality in 1950, when the first school reform bill was passed. Opposition to Berg's plan soon ceased to be in terms of the Platonic ideal of separate education for the different classes. The dual system came to be defended only in terms of pedagogic theory, emphasizing its utility for academic education and the maintenance of high standards. The progressives continued to emphasize the negative social implications of the double-track system.

The first major step in the joining of the two systems was made in 1894 when direct transfer to the *läroverk* was provided for after the third year of the *folkskola*.[30] The typical student at this time was ten years old. In 1904 the Riksdag divided up the nine-year *läroverk* into a six-year junior secondary school (*realskola*) with a special examination (*realexamen*) and a four-year senior secondary school (gymnasium), which continued to be devoted to passing the *studentexamen*. The successful completion of the *realskola* at about age sixteen provided a kind of academic recognition between the completion of *folkskola* and the taking of the *studentexamen*.

In 1909 a big step toward the realization of Berg's goal was taken under his direction. In this year a four-year communal middle school (*kommunal mellanskola*) was established to follow the six-year *folkskola*. Students who completed the *kommunal mellanskola* with satisfactory grades could then enter a gymnasium. Yet the more academic and socially elite *realskola* remained, and it had the further advantage of enabling the student to reach the gymnasium one year earlier. In 1927, after several years of vigorous debate in the Riksdag and in the press, legislation was passed that made it possible to enter the *realskola* after having spent the full six years in the *folkskola*, but, to compromise with the conservatives, it was also provided that transfer to the *realskola* could be made after the fourth year. Those who made an early transfer after the fourth year went to a five-year *realskola*, whereas those who made a late transfer after the sixth year went to a four-year *realskola*. Those who went the full six years to the *folkskola* also found it necessary to take a year longer to reach the gymnasium. But at least after 1927 there was a four-year common school to age eleven.

Until 1927 girls were not admitted to the state gymnasia. However, private girls' schools received state and community grants-in-aid. In this year of so much educational legislation girls were finally admitted on a nondiscriminatory basis to the gymnasia. It was also in this year that legislation was passed establishing girls' schools (*flickskolor*), which provided a seven-year practical and academic course to which girls could transfer after the fourth year of the *folkskola*. This addition further added to the complexity of schools below the gymnasium level. There were now schools of different lengths, with different names, and with varying amounts of theoretical training and social prestige. This complexity was the net result of attempts to increase both the length of common schooling in the *folkskola* and the educational opportunities for those in the lower social groups, for those living in rural areas, and for girls, while there was at the same time a reluctance to give up select academic schooling beginning at an early age.

Progressive opinion continued to favor abolishing early transfer to the *realskola*, but there was little educational debate throughout the 1930s. In 1940, however, the government appointed a committee of experts on education to examine the question of the early transfer. In their investigation the committee approached the country's four professors of education for their considered opinions on continuing the early transfer; all four favored it in their reports. The committee itself became divided over the issue and was unable to reach agreement. In their 1944 report, they gave both the arguments in favor of early transfer and in favor of late transfer, but made no proposals for changing the system. The main reasons given in favor of early transfer were that it enabled students to finish their education a year earlier, that psychologists maintained that academic ability *could* be diagnosed at age eleven, and that the greater homogeneity that this provided in both the fifth year of the *folkskola* and the first year of the *realskola* was to the advantage of both groups. The committee also gave two arguments for late transfer. First, that the talent level, particularly for practical talent, could not be determined with enough accuracy in eleven-year-olds, and that differentiation at this age can easily be based on irrelevant social and economic factors.[31] And, second, that a common six-year school would lay the groundwork for common understanding between the different social levels and would thereby contribute to sound citizenship. One of the members of this committee, however, wrote an appendix in which he defended the view that separation should not be made before age fourteen or fifteen for girls and age fifteen or sixteen for boys, because it was not until those ages that practical talent could be sufficiently diagnosed.

It remained for the politically constituted 1946 School Commission, which was made up of members of the four major parties in the Riksdag and not education experts, to resolve the problem of the proper relation between the *folkskola* and *realskola*. Their 1948 report proposed that both be abolished and that the entire double-track system and the whole complex of schools below the gymnasium level, which had developed over the previous half century, also be abolished.[32] They recommended that there be a nine-year obligatory common school. The existing schools and organizations, with their names (and social connotations), were to be totally replaced by this new school. There were to be no more *folkskola, realskola, läroverk,* or *kommunal mellanskola.* Legislation establishing the nine-year obligatory school on an experimental basis was passed in 1950. In 1962 legislation was enacted making a revised form of this nine-year school universal throughout the nation. The revised school was given the name *grundskola* and was to a large measure based on the experience and research of the previous decade. By the 1964–1965 school year, 80 percent of the population lived in communities with a *grundskola* and a majority of students were attending them. By 1972–1973, it is anticipated that the new school will include all students in public instruction.[33]

Today there is general approval in all of the major groups of the society for the new *grundskola,* with the important exception of upper-level teachers. Even the dialogue between the progressives and conservatives around the issue of "differentiation" has abated since a 1968 decision lessening the line differentiation in the ninth year; the decision will take effect in the 1970–1971 school year.[34] In the ninth year there are a number of different courses of study, only one of which is preparatory for the gymnasium. The progressives argued that here there is a high degree of insulation of students in the different lines and that there is higher prestige and strong teacher preference for the gymnasium line. Since the differentiation that occurs in the seventh and eighth years of the *grundskola* is only for certain subjects, and since "theoretical" and "practical" students continue to come into contact with each other, with opportunities for influencing each other, the differentiation in this case is more acceptable. The progressives are now arguing for a nonselective gymnasium similar to the comprehensive American high school (though they never make the comparison).[35] This is a very real possibility for Sweden in the middle or late 1970s.

The most cogent statement of the conservative view is perhaps that of Sten Carlsson in the concluding chapter of his study of social mobility through Swedish history.[36] He begins with the basic assumption that a high degree of social mobility is to the benefit of Swedish society. In the present situation, he argues, the proper course for enhancing mobility is the maintenance of high standards in the *grundskola,* particularly in the upper stage, with an elimination of the "levelling-process" that has occurred. Mobility will be aided by preventing selection for gymnasium training of the less-talented children of the prosperous and ambitious business and professional groups, who will, he maintains, be the chief beneficiaries of lowered standards. He contends on the basis of his history of social mobility, though perhaps debatably, that ". . . raising standards, not lowering standards, has been most conducive to social mobility."[37]

Occasionally there were essays critical of the school reform in the conservative press, generally emphasizing the deterioration of standards and the failure to recognize the basic inequality of talent that exists among youth.[38] Opposition to the school reform remains strong among upper-stage *grundskola* teachers because of the heterogeneous classes they must teach and because of "discipline problems." There is also opposition among the gymnasium teachers who complain (without much publicity) of the lowered standards that have come in the wake of the enormous increases in enrollments.[39] There is probably much feeling, too, among both these groups of *akademiker* teachers, particularly the older ones, that they no longer have the prestige they did under the old system. An indication of the traditionally high prestige of academic secondary-school teachers is the observation that there are few occupational groups so strongly committed to the Conservative party.[40]

Secondary Education

There are three kinds of schools that build out from the *grundskola* to which youth at around age sixteen go. The first is the gymnasium, which gives a three-year course of "theoretical" studies.[41] More than 80 percent of those who successfully pass through the gymnasium later use their right to enroll in a university. There are three types of gymnasia—general, commercial, and technical. The large majority enroll in a general gymnasium, which offers a social science-modern language line, a scientific-mathematical line, and a classical line, but where everyone also studies Swedish, history, religion, social studies, and English. Unlike the American high school, students choose *lines* of study with little room for electives. The scientific-mathematical line is most selective and the classical line is least selective in the grade-point average required for admission. The 1960 government-appointed committee that was assigned to study the restructuring of secondary education proposed that in the future there be only one gymnasium with five different lines rather than three separate gymnasia, because the present separation tends to enhance invidious comparisons among the different programs.[42] The technical and commercial gymnasia send lower percentages of students to the universities, have students of lower social-class backgrounds, and give a more "practical" education.[43] In the 1967–1968 school year, around 30 percent of the age group enrolled in a gymnasium, one of the highest figures in Europe for academic secondary education.[44]

The second alternative is the new *fackskola*, which came into being in the 1964–1965 school year, and which offers a combined "theoretical" and "practical" education of two-years' duration.[45] This school builds directly on the nine-year *grundskola* and is open to all youths who have completed the nine-year program, and it has no selective-admissions policy. It is also open to adults who want to continue their formal education. The *fackskola* offers technical, economic, and social-studies lines, which aim at preparing for "semi-intellectual" occupations that do not require a university education, such as nursing, selling, and clerical and technical work. Yet it will be possible for the student who has completed this two-year program to take additional courses that will lead to the passing of the *studentexamen*, without educationally unnecessary detours, and to eventual entrance into a university. This is an attempt to further broaden the avenues of recruitment to the universities from outside the gymnasium. It has already been made possible for *grundskola* teachers who have not been to a gymnasium but to a teacher-training institute (and who have not passed the *studentexamen*) to enter a university if they meet certain "experience" requirements. In addition, adult education and correspondence courses have been accredited for preparation for passing the *studentexam*.

The third alternative open to youth who have completed the *grundskola* are vocational schools (*yrkesskolor*), which are well developed in Sweden.

In the 1967–1968 school year, approximately 80 percent of sixteen-year-olds continued their education beyond the *grundskola*.[46]

A fundamental aim in the present restructuring of secondary education is to introduce organizational relations and cooperation between the three orders of post-*grundskola* education and to lessen the aloof isolation that has always characterized the gymnasium. It is planned that transfer will be possible from a *fackskola* to a gymnasium or to a *yrkesskola*, and from a gymnasium or *yrkesskola* to a *fackskola*. There is not yet much experience to indicate how this new cooperative relation will work and how much transferring between schools will occur.

The *fackskola* together with the gymnasium are officially designated as providing "gymnasial education," with the obvious intention of lessening the exclusive connotations of the term. It will be interesting to observe whether the *fackskola* will become the first step in the direction of an open gymnasium without selective admissions similar to the comprehensive American high school.[47] It is quite conceivable that the *fackskola* will only be a transitional school on the path toward diversified and nonselective secondary education. While this is *not* the manifest purpose of the *fackskola*, it appears a reasonable line of development, considering the anticipated continuation of the rapid increase in gymnasium enrollment and the egalitarian value system that increasingly dominates educational planning. Even now there is a great deal of sentiment in favor of bringing all secondary education into the same building.

In the latter half of the nineteenth century, only about 1 percent of an age group entered a gymnasium. As late as 1926, the figure had increased to only about 2.5 percent, by 1946 it was up to 7.8 percent, by 1962 it had reached 23.2 percent, and by 1967 it had reached around 30 percent.[48] Among the major consequences of this extraordinary growth has certainly been some decline in *average* levels. Yet this does not necessarily mean that a given proportion of youth now learns less than a given percentage in the past, and it certainly is reasonable to assume that a larger percentage are learning more. The level and quality of work in the Swedish gymnasium has been and undoubtedly remains higher than those of the American high school, but comparisons with Denmark, the Netherlands, and Switzerland, which have not opened the gates, would be interesting. A lessening prestige of gymnasium education can be observed as it has become more common in Sweden. And there has certainly been a decline in the prestige of gymnasium teachers with the increase in their numbers and with the tremendous expansion of better-paid opportunities that have arisen with high-level industrialization. Fewer and fewer of the *lektorer* (senior teachers) in the gymnasia have the doctorate, which before 1952 was a requirement for this rank. Sven Moberg of the Department of Education and a student of the careers of Swedish university graduates has pointed out that ". . . the weakest competitor in the market for talent is likely to be the teaching function, and especially the secondary school."[49] Yet it is important to stress that the status of the gymnasium teacher remains substantially higher than that of English or American secondary-school teachers, which is partly a carryover from the high status inherited from the past, partly because they carry the prestige of *akademiker* and have attended the same universities as physicians, lawyers, professors, and civil servants, and partly because of an interchange of faculty between the gymnasium and the university.

One of the basic aims in the creation of the new *grundskola* was the elimination or at least minimization of social class and geography as factors determining the educational paths students will follow. In the 1960s, concern with these factors tended to center on secondary education. Youth in the country compared with those in the towns, those in the lower social groups compared with those in the higher social groups, and those in the north of Sweden compared with those in the center and south have traditionally been underrepresented in the gymnasia. To lessen the underrepresentation of these categories and generally to encourage education, legislation was passed in 1964 that expanded financial aid to students over sixteen, the age when compulsory education ends and the universal child allowance ceases. The principle of universal study and travel allowances has now been accepted by all of the political parties. The Conservatives parted company with the other political parties only over the issue of study allowances for university students, which they opposed, but it was also passed in 1964. To be eligible for these study and travel allowances, one need only be a full-time student. Additional allowances and loans can be obtained by youth from low or moderate-income families through a "means test." Now more than one-quarter of the newly enrolled gymnasium students have fathers who are classified as "workers."[50] While this category comprises slightly over half the male population with the right to vote, a working class representation of one out of four is very high for European secondary education. In the early 1940s the comparable ratio was more like one out of ten.[51] A comparative view of how successful Sweden has been in eliminating these class and geographical differentials will be dealt with when the recruitment of university students is discussed in the next chapter.

The first selective-admissions policy comes at the end of the *grundskola* for students who want to enter the gymnasium. For a student to be admitted, he must have studied German or French in addition to English and have achieved a certain grade-point average in the last year of the gymnasium line of the *grundskola*. This first selective admission by the school system occurs typically at age sixteen, five or six years later than in most of Continental Europe and Great Britain, but two years earlier than in the American system, where it conventionally does not occur until admission to college. As in most Continental countries, but not in Great Britain, successful completion of an academic secondary education gives the privilege of entering a university or, specifically, the free faculties of theology, law, and philosophy (in the United States, arts and sciences). Medicine, dentistry, engineering, and most technical faculties have "blocked" admissions with a specific number of entrance places determined by national legislation; there is a marked excess of applicants for the available places (generally three or two to one).

There has always been some problem in determining the level of correspondence between the gymnasium of the Germanic countries (also the *lycées* and *collèges* of France, and the English Sixth Form) and the American high school. The conventional view that has developed in Sweden and much of Europe is that completion of academic secondary education is about equivalent to the completion of the first two years of an American university. This view continues to be held by Swedes in spite of the fact that an increasing proportion of students who complete the gymnasium have spent just twelve years in school, which is the same number of years the American high school graduate has. This indicates an implicit belief that there are higher standards and more advanced levels of work in the gymnasium, an assumption which seems less and less justifiable. However, the Swedish student who finishes the gymnasium after twelve years is one year older than his American counterpart, since he began school at age seven rather than at age six, and he has spent more time in school each week (about thirty-eight hours per week). He has also worked harder; one recent study found the average gymnasium pupil spends two and a half hours a day on his homework.[52] Gymnasium students who have spent a year in American schools report that they did not work as hard here as at home.[53]

That a number of suburban and selective urban high schools and some private schools in the United States function at an equal or higher level than the average Swedish gymnasium may well be true. Yet, from some points of view, a comparison of gymnasium education with liberal arts education can be made. They have similar functions and purposes. Both come prior to specialized and professional training and both are structured around giving a general education with some degree of emphasis in languages, science, or social science. The liberal-education ideal as stressed in America (or in England) is found only at the level of academic secondary education in Sweden or in Continental Europe. The Swedish university is quite unambiguously devoted to research and training in specific disciplines. Whereas the Swedish gymnasium certainly does not now approach the level of a good American college, it may well compare favorably in quality and level with education in the first two years of lower-middle rank liberal arts colleges. Yet competence in foreign languages—for reasons of educational and occupational necessity—is far higher than that of students in the best American colleges and universities. Virtually all have a basic conversational and reading knowledge of English, somewhat less competence in German, and at least a reading knowledge of French.

A most interesting development that has come with the expansion of secondary education in the 1950s has been the formation and developing influence of the Swedish Association of Students (*SECO, Sveriges elevers centralorganisation*), a kind of trade union of secondary-school students and *grundskola* students in grades seven, eight, and nine with the purpose of bringing organized student influence to bear on school policy. The number of schools affiliated with the organization has been increasing, it has received much reporting of its activities in the press, and the government has asked its members to comment on proposals regarding the schools and has provided them with some financial support. The organization has advocated increased financial support for students, a greater role for students in the administration of the schools, the more objective teaching of Christianity, and better sex education. It is a youth organization very much dominated by the radicalism that is characteristic of Social Democratic and Liberal party youth groups, and it has been criticized as representing the views of only a small minority of students. Their functioning as an interest group is similar to, and probably modelled after, the Swedish National Union of Students (*SFS, Sveriges förenade studentkårer*) which has been so successful in acting in behalf of the interests of university students since the 1940s. It is indeed remarkable to see seventeen and eighteen-year-old "leaders" influencing government decisions. They showed their strength during the 1966 strike of teachers, when the students were able to run the schools in the absence of the teachers. *SECO* represents the beginning of student self-government among secondary (and even lower level) students in Sweden. It is developing into a more autonomous form of student organization than prevails in the United States, where the school administration generally oversees and frequently directs student government.

Organization and Control

Swedish education at all levels is a national system of education with a high degree of standardization. The general and specific aims of the educational system, course content, course sequences, grading systems, the school's role in the ability differentiation of students, and the hiring of gymnasium teachers are carried out by appropriate agencies under the Department of Education from specific legislative authority. There are a number of administrative agencies under the Department, which handle, among other areas, primary education, secondary education, and the universities. The administrative agencies function largely autonomously with a high degree of independence from and little direction by the Minister of Education.

In the years since the end of World War II, however, there has been an increase in the local administration of the schools, which remains one of the characteristics of the continuing school reform in Sweden. This is probably partly because the middle class parties are united in continually opposing the increasing centralization of Swedish government under the Social Democrats. County districts and communities now have authority to make minor adjustments in the curriculum to suit local needs and desires, to hire *grundskola* teachers, to provide book allowances for gymnasium students, to build schools, and to oversee the administration of the schools.

Teachers are hired on the basis of an objective point system. Vacancies for teaching positions are advertised. Applicants submit their credentials, and the fact of their application is duly announced in the newspapers. For positions at the lower levels, points in practice teaching are most important. *Grundskola* appointments are made by county boards by determining the applicant with the highest number of points. Senior gymnasium teachers (*lektorer*) and principals (*rektorer*) are appointed by the Board of Education (*Skolöverstyrelsen*) in Stockholm. In Sweden only gymnasium *lektorer* and *rektorer* are regarded as civil servants, whereas in France all teachers are and in Great Britain and the United States none are. Personal interviews are not part of the customary procedure, so that particularistic evaluations by the selecting officials are in this way minimized. A group of American superintendents of schools surveying the Swedish school system in 1963 commented in their final report on how much less important the superintendent's role is in Sweden in selecting staff than it is in the United States.[54]

In spite of the rather high degree of specification of course content and aims, teachers at all levels have much freedom in how they are to teach the prescribed material. At the higher levels (as in all of Europe), head teachers have the right to select textbooks. They are not required to be present in the school when they do not have classes. Teachers are allowed more autonomy than in America, where almost 10 percent of the entire school staff is engaged in "supervision," where teachers are conventionally required to submit "lesson plans," and where high school teachers rarely have any opportunity to choose textbooks, but must use the "adopted" texts.[55] Yet in Sweden there is not the unusual degree of teacher autonomy that prevails in Great Britain, where even at the elementary school level there is little supervision of teachers within the school and little direction or interference from national or local authorities, unless it is believed that a particular school is a "place afflicted with horrors."[56] In Britain there is even an absence of law prohibiting the use of corporal punishment by teachers.[57] In the words of an official publication there is ". . . freedom of teachers from official direction. Teachers are not civil servants. . . . Head teachers are free, within wide limits, to organize their schools according to their own ideas, and teachers generally are not bound by official instructions as to syllabuses, textbooks, or teaching methods."[58]

Certain consequences flow from a centralized school system such as prevails in Sweden.[59] There is little local experimentation with different "organization, methods, goals, curricula," which is carried to such great lengths in American schools. Research and experimentation are specialist tasks carried out in designated experimental schools. The local schools are also less the objects of criticism and pressure than in some decentralized systems. There are charges that there is a lack of discipline in the upper classes of the *grundskola*, that rowdyism prevails, that there has been a lowering of standards with the increased "democratization" of the schools, and there is strong criticism of the "objective" teaching of Christianity from some quarters. Yet these criticisms are almost never directed against the local schools. Rather, they are debated in the press and in the political arena, and they may become subjects of concern to the teachers' organizations. There is clear and universal awareness that authority to bring about changes in the schools rests at the national level.

Among teachers, the competition among different areas with different pay scales does not exist. All teachers are paid according to the same scale subject only to variations in the cost of living in different areas. There is less unevenness in the quality of the school systems between town and country and between rich and poor areas than is characteristic of the United States or Great Britain. The basic organization of the Swedish school system is just a variation on the Continental European form of national (or state) governance, and the differences between it and the American and British systems are fundamental. In the United States, in addition to the close supervision of the teachers within the schools, there is sensitivity to pressure from parents and all manner of organized groups (patriotic, religious, political, and so forth) in the community. In Great Britain, in spite of the high degree of local governance, the schools appear to be much less vulnerable to the pressures of parents and organized groups. The high degree of school independence and teacher autonomy that prevail is in contrast to both Sweden and the United States.

Some additional sociologically pertinent features of the organization and control of the Swedish school system are the following:

(1) The public schools contain the overwhelming majority of students. The number of private schools and schools administered under religious auspices is almost negligible. There are no legal impediments to the formation of schools outside of the state system, however.

(2) About 40 percent of the total educational budget comes from local funds,[60] which compares with about 15 percent in France[61] and an average of 60 percent in the United States in recent years.[62] The percentage of school expenses that comes from local revenues appears to be closely related to the extent of local administration that prevails. In Sweden the sources of tax support for the schools are diverse and not specifically derived from property taxes, as is the case in the United States, providing for less opportunity for opposition to school expenditures and to building from property owners.

(3) Teachers are organized in high degree into national unions that represent their interests in dealing with the government. They also exert influence on the school system by suggesting legislation and by commenting on proposed educational legislation at the request of the government. Teachers in the lower grades and without academic

degrees belong to the National Association of Teachers (*Sveriges lärarförbund*), which is a member union in the Central Organization of Salaried Employees (*TCO, Tjänstemännens Centralorganisation*). Teachers at higher levels and with academic degrees belong to the National Association of Secondary School Teachers (*Lärarnas riksförbund*), which is a member union of The Swedish Confederation of Professional Associations (*SACO, Sveriges Akademikers Centralorganisation*). In contrast, only a minority of American teachers belong to organizations that function as unions with any kind of institutionalized collective bargaining with their employers.

Manifest Aims of the Schools

The aims and values inherent in the educational reform of the postwar years represent a radical departure from the educational traditions of the prewar period. Not only was the double-track system abolished, but a new emphasis was developed that the schools must reflect the democratic values of the society and that they, in turn, should serve as an agency for spreading these values. The Board of Education has summarized the goals of the new *grundskola* as follows:

The school's goals derive from humanistic and democratic ideals. In the center of the school's activity stands the individual pupil. The school's central task is character training. However, the main responsibility for the pupil's upbringing still remains with the home. Respect for the pupil's human value, personality, and individuality ought to mark the school's activity, while at the same time the school must always take into consideration the group of which the individual is a part. The school shall consequently give all pupils equal conditions to develop their personalities and to become good members of society. In accordance with this the school will seek to foster the individual's growth and development, help the young to grow in community with others, and give them useful skills and knowledge. Within the unitary goal of character training a number of sub-goals can be distinguished which interact with each other. The grundskola's goal is partly new and different from what has hitherto been characteristic of the school. The emphasis has essentially been changed from an education aimed at the communication of limited knowledge to character training. The school shall not only correspond as closely as possible to the actual situation of society, but shall also forward society's development.[63]

The central official goal that now dominates in presecondary education in Sweden is that the school's central concern should be the general democratic development of the individual child. It is to be an education in which the influence of geography, social class, and cultural background on the educational paths a pupil will follow are to be minimized. But most significantly, it reflects a radically egalitarian philosophy of education in which academic intelligence is no longer to be considered of central importance. It is an education that has changed its major emphasis from "the communication of limited knowledge to character training." The correspondence to dominant American educational thought, particularly that stemming from John Dewey, is close here, and American thought (but not American practice) is quite certainly one of the central influences in the development of the new *grundskola*. It is important to stress that these are statements of "official" goals, and that they have not been discovered from inductive observation of the teaching in Swedish schools.

Other aims of Swedish educational reform of recent years have already been mentioned in this chapter: the effort to encourage more formal study by youth over sixteen through the establishment of study allowances, the attempt to increase the proportions of those sections of the population traditionally underrepresented in academic education, the broadening of avenues of recruitment to the universities, and the further decentralizing of the administration of the schools. Other aims of official educational policy that have relevance for the changing structure of Swedish society and that are in themselves further indicators of the new egalitarian value-orientation are:

To lessen invidious distinctions. There is an ideological concern with eliminating invidious distinctions between "theoretical" education, that which prepares for higher education and the intellectual occupations, and "practical" education. This is particularly evident in the planning of the upper stage of the *grundskola*. It is also apparent in attempts to lessen invidious comparisons among different kinds of gymnasia and between gymnasial and other types of post-*grundskola* education. The abolition by the Department of Education and Ecclesiastical Affairs of the *studentexam* in 1968 is another example of the importance of this emphasis. Admission to the universities is now based on achieving a low minimum average grade in the last terms of the gymnasium.

To minimize sexual differentiation. This has been a basic principle of all postwar Swedish school reform, and will be discussed in Chapter VI.

To change traditional teaching methods. The dominant teaching method that has prevailed in Swedish schools has been described as follows: "the teacher conducts the lesson from his desk, the children put up their hands and answer his questions, lessons are the same for the whole class and are thoroughly worked through." [64] Increasingly, new teaching methods that permit more independent work on the part of the pupils have been encouraged. The work has been adapted to differing individual capacities, and cooperative solutions to problems, which would have been "cheating" according to the traditional methods, have also been encouraged. Attempts have also been made to break down artificial boundaries between subjects. There has been much concern with helping students to develop their own ideas and to be critical of propaganda and of conventional answers to problems. (Yet Swedish students still remain reticent in class at all levels.)

To help students understand the functioning of democracy. In the *grundskola* a relatively large amount of time is devoted to social studies, civics, and history in order to give students an understanding of how modern democracy works and what the threats to it are. Emphasis is placed on modern history, with particular attention devoted to the rise of Naziism and Fascism, to the formation of the United Nations, and to giving pupils an international perspective. In the first eight years of the *grundskola* curricula, between 15 and 20 percent of school time is devoted to history and social studies (not including religion) as compared with about 10 percent in the national eight-year French elementary school curricula.[65]

Pervasive and Persistent Characteristics of Swedish Education

Following are a number of structural characteristics and trends that have persisted over a number of decades and that are not as specifically characteristic of the recent educational reforms as those items previously discussed as "manifest aims":

Uniformity of knowledge. A traditional feature of Swedish education at all levels has been and continues to be a "strict demand on a uniform level of knowledge, uniform in the sense that it must be the same for pupils all over the country, that it must contain the same items of knowledge, and that it shall be comparable in all parts of Sweden." [66] This is fundamentally similar in concept to the other Scandinavian countries and to France, although it is somewhat different from that of Great Britain, and the concept is absent in the United States. The subjects to be studied, when they are to be studied, how much time is to be devoted to each, and the level to be reached is determined by national committees of subject specialists. But in the lower grades there is less specification of what is to be taught by the individual teacher than is found in the detailed syllabuses issued by the French Ministry of Education.

Emphasis on languages. Traditionally there has been an enormous emphasis on foreign languages in academic education. This is perhaps to be expected in a small and advanced European nation that speaks a language virtually unknown outside of Scandinavia, a situation characteristic of all the Scandinavian countries, Belgium, and the Netherlands. English is a compulsory subject in the fourth (soon to be changed to the third) through the seventh grades of the new *grundskola*, but in recent years 80 to 85 percent of the students have continued with it in the eighth and ninth years,[67] which means that a substantial majority of Swedish youth have studied English for at least six years. The emphasis continues to be on British and not American English, and the learning of English is reinforced from movies, television, popular songs, books and magazines, and, for a minority, travel to Great Britain.

In practice German is the second foreign language, though officially it shares the second place with French (and Finnish in some areas) in the *grundskola* curriculum. German was, in fact, the first foreign language in the schools until 1948. In recent years when German was offered in the seventh year, about half of all students elected it, a choice highly selective of the more intelligent and more academically oriented.[68] By general agreement, French is regarded as the most difficult of the three major foreign languages for Swedish youth, since it is the most distant from Swedish and has the fewest cognates with it. There has been some discussion that Spanish, Italian, and Russian should be given equal status with French and German in the *grundskola*, but this is a long way off.

Latin has continually lost ground in Swedish education over the past century. It is not even an optional subject in the new *grundskola* curriculum, but it continues to occupy a more important place in secondary education than it does in Norway or the United States, although it is less important in Sweden than in Great Britain or Continental Europe.[69]

At the gymnasium level emphasis on language training continues with 20 to 30 percent of the student's time devoted to it.[70] By the time the student gets to the university, it is assumed that he has a mastery of English and reading competence in German and French. In some departments books are assigned in all three foreign languages. There is no basic instruction for credit in the three major European languages at the university level, such as there is in the United States.

Martin Mayer's assertion in *The Schools* that in the Scandinavian countries, "the lessons are presented *entirely* in the language to be studied"[71] is not the case in Sweden. It is true, however, as he further maintains, that there is much greater use of the "direct method" in the teaching of languages (particularly English) than is the case in the United States. Grammar is generally explained in Swedish and not in the language studied. Also, as Mayer maintains, the competence of language teachers in all of the Scandinavian countries is much higher than among their American counterparts.[72]

Language departments in Sweden's universities as compared with those of Anglo-American countries emphasize the study of a language rather than of its literature. With only two exceptions (both in English), all of the language professors in the universities in 1964 were students of language and not of literature.[73] This emphasis on the language tends to be characteristic of language training at all levels and means that the study of foreign languages is conceived of as a tool and not as a part of humanistic study. The language departments of Swedish universities are geared to the training of upper-stage *grundskola* and gymnasium teachers, and they have been shaped by this function. Anglo-American language departments, on the other hand, are attuned to the liberal-arts ideal and consequently place great emphasis on literature study, even when the students have a low competence in the use of the language, which is generally the case. The tendency of Swedish students to see the study of English as a tool, and one that is not related to any great extent to the study of literature, is disconcerting to American instructors of English in Swedish universities.[74] Yet it in good part explains the outstanding ability of Swedes to really use English and to be good teachers of it.

Emphasis on research. The findings of empirical research are important in determining school policy. Decisions that have been supported by experimental findings are that English can just as well be begun in the fourth (and now the third) rather than the fifth class, that it is probably better for an academically oriented student to study only two rather than three foreign languages in the *grundskola*, and that line differentiation into different kinds of programs is beneficial in the last year of the *grundskola* (but which was modified in 1968). But too much emphasis on the importance of research findings as a factor in determining educational policy should not be made. What research is chosen to be done is generally conditioned by ideological factors and by the structural and financial limitations of what is possible at a given time. Yet the impression remains that respect for the findings of pedagogic research is an important and somewhat independent factor in shaping educational policy and in determining curricula questions. This is a manifestation of the marked respect for expert and specialist opinion which prevails in Sweden.

Passive role for students. Swedish education traditionally has been hierarchical in form, with the teacher and the text as the sources of authority. The student was originally conceived of as "a vessel to be filled," and he was directed to answer the teachers' questions and to pass examinations. Departures from these older forms of teaching have been an important part of the educational reform of the past two decades, but established patterns change slowly. From the primary years through the university, Swedish students are reticent in class and only infrequently ask questions or make unsolicited comments,[75] as compared with their American counterparts.

In seminars, one of the principal forms of teaching in Swedish universities, there are duly appointed "opponents" who have the task of criticizing and evaluating the paper under discussion. Frequently no comments other than the opponents' are made. In any case, the proportion of those present who enter into a discussion is generally small. During the second half of the 1930s, when he was Professor of Political Science at the University of Stockholm, Herbert Tingsten made some sharp remarks on the reticence of Swedish university students to talk in class:

As a novelty I attempted for a couple of terms to get students to interrupt me at any time with questions or objections. It was an unsuccessful experiment. The few who said anything after requesting the floor asked questions which certified to their stupidity or ignorance or both together. I got the impression that the more talented and knowledgeable never said anything and that the correlation between venturesomeness and foolishness was almost total. I am convinced that at least during this time that Swedish youth were exceptionally afraid to rise and speak and spoke badly when they did; in every case my experience from English, American, and German universities has been very different.[76]

While the reserve of Swedish university students is almost certainly less now than it was in the 1930s, it remains one of their persistent characteristics. American instructors of literature at Swedish universities report (and sometimes with exasperation) that it is very difficult to establish class discussion in the manner that is conventional in the United States, and they further claim that it is not because the classes are conducted in English. (Those who study English *do* use the language well.) Swedish students who have studied in America also confirm the greater reserve of Swedish students. A study of the adjustment of forty long-term Scandinavian students at the University of Wisconsin in the late 1950s reports that their professors rated them lower in "class participation" than in any other of eight variables such as "English-language facility," "academic adjustment," and "mental ability." [77] While this reticence reflects the passive role they have learned to play in their earlier education, particularly through the gymnasium years, it is reinforced at the university level. There is an enormous difference in the normative structure of the classroom situation when compared with the United States. There is little permissiveness and certainly no encouragement given to the presentation of half-articulate, half-formed ideas (an indulgence sometimes carried to extremes in the United States). There is a marked tendency toward negative criticism, which is taken to reflect positively on the astuteness of the critic, and there is minimal approval (reward) for what are possibly positive contributions. The giving of approval is inhibited by the value placed on being regarded as "critical."[78]

Extracurricular activities directed toward the greater society. In both the gymnasium and the universities there are many fewer fraternities, honor societies, school publications, and special purpose organizations than in the United States. While physical education (with a heavy emphasis on gymnastics) is required every year from the first year of the *grundskola* through the last year of the gymnasium, there is almost no interschool competitive athletics. The consequences for "school spirit" and the prestige for school athletes that so characterize secondary education in Great Britain and the United States are nearly absent. However, organized student politics is far more developed and important at both the secondary and university levels than it is in either the United States or Britain, with respect to both internal government in the schools and student political groups that support the various political parties. There are even active temperance organizations at both the secondary and university levels. It is a fair generalization to say that extracurricular activities are directed out to the greater society in Sweden; they very much socialize for adult roles.

Much teaching of "practical" topics. In a manner similar to the United States but unlike France, there is little reluctance to teach "practical" topics, such as traffic rules, sexual behavior and ethics, the use of alcohol, and elements of domestic science including home furnishings and the care of infants, handicrafts, first aid, and fire precautions. There is substantial vocational guidance and "trial" work experience in the eighth year for all students.

Increasing secularization of the study of religion. According to a comparative study of the 1958 government commission appointed to study church-state relations, Sweden is the only country in the world that has "objective" teaching of Christianity.[79] Norway, Denmark, and Finland, which have similar state-church relationships, continue to have "confessional" teaching of Christianity in the schools, that is, instruction "in" Christianity for students who are assumed to be believers (though pupils everywhere can be excused from this instruction). Similarly, the great majority of youth in France, which is one of the few countries in Western Europe without religious teaching in the schools, and the United States get wholly confessional instruction in religion outside of the public schools. The teaching of Christianity (and other religions) is, or should be, according to legislation passed in 1950, teaching *about* religion. Bias in favor of Lutheranism or Christianity is specifically outlawed. According to Ragnar Edenman, a recent Minister of Education, the teaching of religion must "be objective in the sense that it should give factual knowledge on the meaning and contents of various creeds without trying to influence the pupils to embrace a certain creed."[80]

Strong opposition to the central place of orthodox Christianity in primary education did not develop until the latter part of the nineteenth century. Not until the teaching plan of 1919, however, was Martin Luther's Catechism abolished from the schools, after it had dominated the elementary teaching in the schools for nearly 400 years.[81] The 1919 education plan substantially reduced the amount of time devoted to religion and emphasized the ethical aspects of Christianity. As mentioned previously, legislation passed in 1950 obliged instruction to be "objective," and the religious freedom law of 1951 removed the requirement that teachers of religion belong to the Evangelical Lutheran Church. In 1958 the Church was deprived of overseeing the instruction of religion in the gymnasia, its last vestige of involvement in the schools. The secularization of the teaching of religion that has come about in the years since the end of World War I, in addition to being an aspect of the late and rapid secularization of Sweden, manifests a self-conscious and radical opposition to encouraging Christian belief in the schools. Great Britain, which also has a state church and which is also highly secularized, is quite different, according to Erik Melander, who has pointed out (perhaps in an exaggerated way) that in:

Britain there is no opinion of the kind directed in Sweden against Christian education or activities in school, such as divine service or hours of worship; on the whole it seems that authorities, school leaders, teachers and pupils look on the Christian coloring as something self evident, just as they look at the educational activities in school; the parents are also loyal to these ideas . . .[82]

The British Education Act of 1944 gave Christian training a most positive role in the ethical training of students as compared with the teaching plan for the new *grundskola*. From one point of view, the curricula adopted in Sweden in 1962 represents the culmination of the secularization of the teaching of religion in the schools. It explicitly limits Christianity to an area of study, but bases the character-training function of the schools *wholly and explicitly on democratic values*, not on values deriving from "the Christian heritage," as is the case in the British Act or in the older Swedish school tradition, exemplified in the long-lived teaching plan of 1919.[83] Beginning with the report of the 1946 School Commission, which was published in 1948, and continuing in subsequent official reports, there is a virtual absence of any tendency to attribute a positive role in character training to Christianity in particular or to religion in general. The contrast with the official British reports in this regard is marked; for example, the 1963 report of the Central Advisory Council for Education (England), whose mission was to advise the Minister of Education "on the education of pupils aged thirteen to sixteen of average and less than average ability," makes the following specific recommendations regarding "spiritual and moral development" after reaffirming the provisions for "Christian education" in the Education Act of 1944:

(a) *Religious instruction has a part to play in helping boys and girls to find a firm basis for sexual morality based on chastity before marriage and fidelity within it. (para. 164)*

(b) *The schools have a duty to give specific religious instruction, which is more than general ethical teaching. (paras. 166, 169)*

. . .

(d) *We reaffirm the value of the school act of worship as a potent force in the spiritual experience of the pupils. (para. 174)* [84]

Such propositions would be inconceivable in any contemporary Swedish government report. It should be noted, however, that there is some opposition to the policy of the objective teaching of Christianity in the schools from some believing Christians (though most support the policy). On the other hand, there is much criticism that the teaching of Christianity often fails to be objective by being biased in its favor.

Aesthetic emphasis. There is a relatively great emphasis on the aesthetic element in Swedish (and Scandinavian) education. Sweden was a pioneer in the introduction of handicraft into primary education, and it assumes a major role in the training of both boys and girls. Concerns with textiles, designing, weaving, wood and metal working are not nearly so universally developed in British and American schools. In each of the first six years of the national French elementary-school curricula, only one to one and a quarter hours per week are devoted to "handicraft or drawing." [85] In Sweden two hours per week are devoted to handicraft in the third year of the *grundskola* and four to six hours per week in the fourth through the sixth years. In the seventh through the ninth years two to four hours per week are devoted to the two categories of "handicraft" and "art." [86]

Original art work is conventionally found throughout school buildings for aesthetic and pedagogic purposes. It is common practice for schools to have budgets for the purchase of original art works. In the report of the American school superintendents previously mentioned, in fact, comment was made on the profusion of original paintings, which they observed "hanging in the corridors, cafeterias, and on classroom walls." [87]

Relatively high prestige for upper-level teachers. As we have already noted, while the prestige of gymnasium teachers has been declining, it remains substantially above that of their American and British counterparts. Some evidence of the higher status of teachers in Sweden is offered by Myron Lieberman, who calculated that the Swedish teacher's average annual salary in 1949 was 3.6 times per capita income as compared with 1.9 in the United States and 2.5 in England.[88] On the other hand, in France it was 5.1, and in West Germany 4.7. The relative income of Swedish gymnasium teachers vis-à-vis other professionals is decidedly higher than in the United States. Median annual income of senior gymnasium teachers compared with physicians stands in a ratio of around 1 to 1.5 as compared to a ratio in the United States of at least 1 to 3.[89]

If we accept the assumption of some inverse relationship between the status of a profession and the proportion of women in the field, the prestige of both primary and secondary school teachers is higher in Sweden. In 1960 men comprised 38 percent of all primary school teachers (few, however, in the first three classes) and 60 percent of all secondary school teachers.[90] In the United States in 1955 only 25 percent of all teachers were men, which was an increase from a low of 14 percent in 1920.[91]

Seven percent of those elected to the Lower House of the Riksdag in 1964 were classified as being regularly employed in "education" (17 out of 232), and 11 percent of the total number of candidates were in education.[92] Most were gymnasium teachers. In 1955, 10 percent of the combined membership of both houses of the Riksdag were in education.[93] Teachers are also well represented in the French National Assembly,[94] but they are much less common as British M.P.'s,[95] and almost negligible in the United States Congress. In Sweden three Ministers of Education in this century had been *folkskola* teachers when first elected to the Lower House of the Riksdag.

Probably in all industrial societies the prestige of grade-school teachers is not very high, and there is not much difference in this regard between Sweden and the United States. A sample of 891 Swedish and American university students ranked eight professions on the basis of prestige and intellectual ability. Both groups ranked grade-school teacher in the bottom position in both areas.[96] Unfortunately for our purposes, secondary-school teachers were not comparatively evaluated. But the prestige gap between primary and secondary-school teachers is much greater in Sweden (and in the rest of Continental Europe) than it is in the United States or England. In Sweden, distinctions are emphasized by the use of different titles for teachers at different levels, by membership in different professional organizations (*akademiker* versus non*akademiker*), and by substantially higher pay scales for teachers at the secondary level.

Heavy press coverage of education. Partly because Swedish education is nationally governed and because it is therefore an aspect of national policy, it receives a great deal more attention in the national and provincial press than is the case in the United States. In addition, in the traditional "culture page" in the daily press where a large number of topics are dealt with at some length by all manner of specialists, educational subjects are a frequent topic of discussion and debate. Reporting on and discussion of the content of the *grundskola* and gymnasium curricula, the administration of the schools, pending legislation, school problems (discipline, the teacher shortage, morale problems of teachers, and so forth), the results of pedagogical research, and the activities of the national teacher and student associations is standard fare in the press. The appointments of professors (generally with their pictures) are reported in all of the larger daily papers, and the evaluations of the committees that are appointed to judge candidates for professorships are also reported (and it is front page news when a candidate challenges the judges). In recent years the leading papers in the nation have published large numbers of long articles on such specialized subjects as the organization of the universities, the work load of professors, the place of geography, history, and other subjects in the curricula of the new gymnasium, and the question of differentiation in the *grundskola*. Outside of the *New York Times* (and perhaps a few other quality newspapers), there is little comparable attention paid to such topics in the American press.

Conclusion

In theory, the nine-year *grundskola* is as egalitarian as is presecondary education in the United States; in practice it is more egalitarian. There is substantially less residential segregation by class in Sweden than exists in the United States, and there is no ethnic or racial segregation.[97] The generally tight housing situation tends to inhibit class segregation by mixing the middle and working classes. In Sweden there is little inclination to think in terms of certain schools being "good" and others being less so, and variations in class backgrounds among pupils in the different schools of each community, except, perhaps, for the largest, are generally not great. In the United States the quality differences among schools, particularly grade schools, are often great, because the schools so closely parallel the socioeconomic status of the neighborhoods in which they are found.

In Sweden students are not homogeneously grouped by ability, as this is specifically prohibited by statute. Defenders of the *grundskola* argue that such grouping strongly reflects class background and, further, acts to the detriment of the poorer pupils who have lower morale and who learn less. Homogeneous grouping by ability is conventional in many American communities and is generally defended on pedagogic grounds with little consideration paid to the social class implications of such grouping.

Perhaps the ultimate measure of the egalitarianism of a school system is the percentage of working-class and farm youth who get to the universities. In the 1967–1968 academic year 19 percent of those who entered Swedish universities were from the working class, which meant that about 8 percent of working-class youth born in 1947 entered higher education, but this is probably as high a figure as in any country in Western Europe with the possible exception of Finland.[98]

Notes

1. Torsten Husén and Gunnar Boalt, *Educational Research and Educational Change: The Case of Sweden* (New York: Wiley, 1968), p. 9.
2. Part of the material in this chapter appeared earlier in Richard F. Tomasson, "From Elitism to Egalitarianism in Swedish Education," in *Sociology of Education*, 38 (Spring 1965), 203–223.
3. Throughout this chapter I use the term "common school" to refer to the new Swedish *grundskola* (literally: basic school), which is usually translated as "comprehensive school." I think it conveys better the idea that it is a basic school for all, without any ability differentiation. The term "university" is used in the American sense to include the five Swedish universities and the large number of institutes and special schools that the Swedes call "*högskolor.*"
4. Among discussions in English of the Swedish school reforms are the following: Stellan Arvidson, "Education for Democracy," in J. A. Lauwerys (ed.), *Scandinavian Democracy* (Copenhagen: Det Danske Selskab, 1958), pp. 294–315; Jonas Orring, *Comprehensive School and Continuation Schools in Sweden* (Stockholm: Kungliga Ecklesiastikdepartementet, 1962); Torsten Husén, "A Liberal Democracy Adopts the Comprehensive School System," *Phi Kappa Deltan* (November 1961), pp. 86–91; Herman Ruge, *Educational Systems in Scandinavia* (Oslo: Norwegian Universities Press, 1962), pp. 56–83. Summaries of most of the reports of the 1957 School Commission have been published in the *International Review of Education*, VII (1961). See also various articles in Uppsala Studentkår, *The Intellectual Face of Sweden* (Uppsala:

Uppsala Studentkår, 1964). See also Torsten Husén, "Educational Change in Sweden," *Comparative Education* I (June 1965), 181–191; Husén, "Curriculum Research in Sweden," *International Review of Education*, II (1965), 189–208; and Husén and Boalt, *op. cit.*

5. For discussions of the egalitarian Norwegian school system see Ruge, *op. cit.*, pp. 41–55, 70–83; see also the discussion in Anthony Kerr, *The Schools of Europe* (London: Bowes & Bowes, 1960), pp. 19–28. There are also some comments on the Norwegian schools in Arvidson, *op. cit.*, *passim*.

6. I eliminate here certain Eastern European countries that give special advantages to youth from working-class backgrounds and have much higher percentages in the universities than Western societies. This is true, for example, of East Germany and the Soviet Union. See Nigel Grant, *Soviet Education* (London: Penguin Books, 1964), pp. 118–119, and Anthony Kerr, *The Universities of Europe* (London: Bowes & Bowes, 1962), pp. 55, 76–77.

7. Arvidson, *op. cit.*, p. 295.

8. H. G. Good, *A History of Western Education* (New York: Macmillan, 1947), p. 356.

9. George A. Male, *Education in France* (Washington, D.C.: U.S. Government Printing Office, 1963), p. 16.

10. Good, *op. cit.*, pp. 450–452.

11. Male, *op. cit.*, pp. 7–28

12. Gunnar Richardson, *Kulturkamp och klasskamp: Ideologiska och sociala motsättningar i svensk skol- och kulturpolitik under 1880-talet* (Gothenburg: Akademiförlaget-Gumperts, 1963), pp. 80–101.

13. This does not mean that there was an absence of radical opinion opposing the church's role in overseeing education. There was some, such as S. A. Hedin and all of the early socialists, but it was not yet politically important opinion.

14. Alexis de Tocqueville, *Democracy in America* (New York: Vintage Books, 1954), Vol. 1, pp. 89–101.

15. Kerr, *The Schools of Europe*, *op. cit.*, p. 143.

16. Male, *op. cit.*, pp. 29–38.

17. Such was advocated by Süvern and Humboldt in that "great period of educational ferment" in Germany in the early part of the nineteenth century. See Abraham Flexner, *Universities: American, English, German* (New York: Oxford, 1930), p. 309.

18. The academic schools trace their origins back to medieval times, whereas the compulsory popular schools did not really become established in any country until the nineteenth century.

19. The situation has probably improved since Abraham Flexner wrote in 1930 that ". . . in the mass, it is still true that American college students are, at the close of four years, intellectually considered an unselected and untrained body of attractive boys and girls, who have for the most part not yet received even a strenuous secondary school training." Flexner, *op. cit.*, p. 67.

20. See Richardson, *op. cit.*, pp. 288–308.

21. For an excellent account of the Austrian school reform, see Ernst Papanek, *The Austrian School Reform* (New York: Frederick Fell, 1962); see also Charles A. Gulick, *Austria from Hapsburg to Hitler* (Berkeley and Los An-

geles: University of California Press, 1948), pp. 544–582, and Flexner, *op. cit.*, p. 309.

22. Norway comes close to Sweden in the Leftism of the political-party spectrum. The Social Democrats in Denmark have not had the long-term dominance they have had in Sweden or Norway.

23. Richardson, *op. cit.*, pp. 68, 71.

24. *Ibid.*, pp. 67–68.

25. Sten Carlsson, *Bonde-präst-ämbetsman* (Stockholm: Bokförlaget Prisma, 1962), pp. 81, 100.

26. Richardson, *op. cit.*, pp. 184–189.

27. Statens Offentliga Utredningar (*S.O.U.*) (Stockholm), 1963: 53, p. 56.

28. Most of the data on these two plans is from Richardson, *op. cit.*, pp. 189–205.

29. Good, *op. cit.*, p. 330.

30. The history of the coming together of these two systems has been taken mainly from the following sources: Gunnar Boalt and Torsten Husén, *Skolans sociologi* (Stockholm: Almqvist & Wiksell, 1964), pp. 52–61, and *S.O.U.*, *op. cit.*, 1963: 42, pp. 13–24. A brief history in English can be found in Arvidson, *op. cit.*, pp. 296–306.

31. While some pupils have the capacity to do academic work, they may have a greater aptitude for practical work. It is conventionally maintained by Swedish writers on education that this cannot be determined with much accuracy prior to age fourteen or fifteen.

32. *S.O.U.*, 1948: 27.

33. Orring, *op. cit.*, pp. 124, 129.

34. This information was supplied to me by Lena Johansson from Sweden in October 1969.

35. This is a demand of, for example, *TCO;* see *Dagens Nyheter*, February 4, 1968, p. 3.

36. Carlsson, *op. cit.*, pp. 146–150.

37. *Ibid.*, p. 147.

38. Two examples are Professors Erik Melander and Wilhelm Sjöstrand, both of whom have written articles strongly opposed to the school reform in the Stockholm newspaper *Svenska Dagbladet* in the mid-1960s.

39. This is based on conversations with a number of teachers and newspaper articles.

40. Joachim Israel, "Uppfostran och utbildning," in Edmund Dahlstöm (ed.), *Svensk samhällstruktur i sociologisk belysning*, third ed. (Stockholm: Norstedts, 1965), pp. 481–484.

41. The proposed future structure of the gymnasium has been published in a volume of almost a thousand pages: *S.O.U.*, 1963: 42.

42. *The Intellectual Face of Sweden*, *op. cit.*, p. 15.

43. *S.O.U.*, 1963: 42, p. 125.

44. *Dagens Nyheter*, February 20, 1968, p. 20.

45. See *S.O.U.*, 1963: 50.

46. *Dagens Nyheter*, February 20, 1968, p. 20.

47. This was in effect suggested in the conclusion to Joachim Israel's article "Social grupp och linjeval," *Stockholms Tidningen*, September 5, 1964, p. 5. Official thinking in the Department of Education is in this direction, too.

48. *S.O.U.*, 1963: 42, p. 103.

49. The words are those of A. H. Halsey, "Science and Government in Sweden," *Minerva*, 11 (Autumn 1963), p. 59.

50. *S.O.U.*, 1963: 42, p. 125.

51. Based on data in *S.O.U.*, 1963: 42, p. 127.

52. See "Stressade gymnasister," *Dagens Nyheter*, January 31, 1968, p. 2.

53. This is an observation based on discussions with several Scandinavian students who have studied for a year in an American high school.

54. Shirley Cooper (ed.), *American School Superintendents in Sweden* (Upper Marlboro, Maryland, 1963), p. 9, mimeo.

55. Martin Mayer, *The Schools* (Garden City, N.Y.: Doubleday, 1963), pp. 22–23.

56. *Ibid.*, p. 23.

57. Grant, *op. cit.*, p. 57.

58. Quoted in Erik Melander, *Etisk fostran i svensk obligatorisk skola från 1842* (Stockholm: Föreningen för svensk undervisningshistoria, 1964), p. 278.

59. The discussion in this and the following paragraph was suggested by Robin M. Williams, Jr., *American Society*, rev. ed. (New York: Knopf, 1960), pp. 301–303.

60. Orring, *op. cit.*, p. 150.

61. Male, *op. cit.*, p. 29.

62. M. Williams, Jr., *op. cit.*, p. 303.

63. Quoted in Melander, *op. cit.*, p. 258.

64. Arvidson, *op. cit.*, p. 308. The material in this paragraph is mostly from Arvidson, pp. 307–311.

65. Male, *op. cit.*, pp. 64–65.

66. Orring, *op. cit.*, p. 12.

67. Orring, *op. cit.*, p. 52.

68. Boalt and Husén, *op. cit.*, pp. 59–60.

69. Kerr, *The Schools of Europe*, *op. cit.*, p. 12.

70. Alvar Ellegård, "The University Teaching of Foreign Languages," *The Intellectual Face of Sweden*, *op. cit.*, p. 109.

71. Mayer, *op. cit.*, p. 339.

72. *Ibid.*, pp. 340–341.

73. A. Ellegård, *op. cit.*, p. 109.

74. I am indebted to Mr. Bernard Mergen, instructor in English Literature at Gothenburg University, for this observation.

75. One Swedish primary school teacher I talked with, who had been to a university in the United States and who had several years of primary school teaching experience both here and in Sweden, told me she had great difficulty in getting her Swedish pupils to ask questions, which was quite the opposite of her experience in a Denver suburb. This basic difference in the behavior of Swedish pupils has been confirmed for me in a number of talks with pupils and teachers.

76. Herbert Tingsten, *Mitt liv: Mellan trettio och femtio* (Stockholm: P. A. Norstedt, 1962), pp. 181–182.

77. William H. Sewell and Oluf M. Davidsen, *Scandinavian Students on an American Campus* (Minneapolis: University of Minnesota Press, 1961), p. 25.

78. In commenting on an early draft of this chapter, David Riesman had the following comparative observations to make on English students: "I have found English students exceedingly diffident, and unwilling to talk in lecture or seminar—perhaps they are less diffident than Swedish students but they are certainly more like your description of Swedish students than like my experience with American ones. At the same time the British students enjoy being critical and unenthusiastic in much the same way you describe for Sweden; they can be parliamentary and contentious without being really interested." Letter dated July 29, 1965.

79. *S.O.U.*, 1964: 30, pp. 94–153.

80. Quoted by Melander, *op. cit.*, p. 301.

81. See *S.O.U.*, 1964:30, pp. 9–50. For a brief discussion in English, see "Religious Instruction in Swedish Schools" (Stockholm: The Swedish Institute, no date), mimeo.

82. Melander, *op. cit.*, p. 302.

83. Melander, *op. cit.*, pp. 277–286.

84. Ministry of Education, *Half Our Future: A Report of the Central Advisory Council for Education (England)* (London: Her Majesty's Stationery Office, 1963), pp. 58–59.

85. Male, *op. cit.*, pp. 64–65.

86. Orring, *op. cit.*, pp. 70–73.

87. Cooper, *op. cit.*, pp. 6–7. In general aesthetic concern in the schools, however, I believe the contrast is greater with Britain than with the United States.

88. Cited by Richard Hofstadter, *Anti-Intellectualism in American Life* (London: Jonathan Cape, 1964), p. 311.

89. These are only my estimates. They are based on 1966 estimates of average annual income of Swedish gymnasium teachers (with some overtime) of 50,000 *kronor* and of Swedish doctors of 75,000 *kronor*. My estimates for the United States for 1966 are $9,000 and $25,000–30,000.

90. Calculated from figures in *Statistical Abstract of Sweden: 1963* (Stockholm: Statistiska Centralbyrån, 1963), p. 305.

91. Williams, Jr., *op. cit.*, p. 305.

92. Sveriges Officiella Statistik, *Riksdagsmannavalen åren 1961–1964* (Stockholm: Statistiska Centralbyrån, 1965), Vol. II, pp. 56–57.

93. Nils Andrén, *Modern Swedish Government* (Stockholm: Almqvist & Wiksell, 1961), pp. 56–58.

94. Mayer, *op. cit.*, p. 27.

95. J. Blondel, *Voters, Parties, and Leaders: The Social Fabric of British Politics* (London: Penguin Books, 1963), pp. 136–145; see also Mayer, *op. cit.*, p. 27.

96. Edward C. McDonagh, Sven Wermlund, and John F. Crowther, "Relative Professional Status as Perceived by American and Swedish University Students," *Social Forces*, 38 (October 1959), 65–69.

97. For a discussion of this question, see Leila Sussman, "Summary Review by the Rapporteur," in *Social Objectives in Educational Planning* (Paris: OECD, 1967), pp. 15–27.

98. This will be discussed, with citations, in the following chapter.

V

The Universities and
Intellectual Life

> The Swedish university is a medieval institution
> which is just now beginning to make some adjustments
> to the modern world.
> —An Uppsala University graduate student

At the outset we can classify the system of Swedish higher education
as of the Continental variety, German subtype. From the fifteenth
century, when the first Swedish university was founded, until at least
World War I, the structure, practices, methods, and philosophies of
the German universities provided the only foreign influence of any
importance on the Swedish universities.[1] In the period since World
War II, certain elements of American higher education have influenced and will probably have increasing influence upon certain directions of change in the rapidly expanding system of higher education.
The place that Germany held before 1914 as the principle foreign
country for research and study has been replaced by the United States.
The introduction of more class teaching with the lecture-discussion
method in the 1950s and the declining importance of formal *ex cathedra*
lectures are probably due in some degree to American practice. Most
of the critics of such things as the lack of research funds, the traditional
academic organization, the paucity of graduate courses, and the lack of
tenure for docents (teachers with the doctorate) and other categories
of teachers point to the situation that exists at the major American

universities for support.[2] These have become the new models for change.

The structure and functioning of the *grundskola* is clear because it is now a reality in most Swedish communities. The future structure of the whole complex of post-*grundskola* education is now taking shape, but the general directions of change are clear. The future structure of the complex of higher education, however, is not so clear. Yet it is apparent that the 1970s will see basic changes in departmental organization, the system of advanced degrees, the structure of graduate training, and the predictability and security of the academic career.

The first Swedish university, and the model for those that followed, was Uppsala, founded in 1477.[3] This university resulted from a bull issued by Pope Sixtus IV establishing a *studium generale* at Uppsala on the model of Bologna and conferring all the privileges of that university. But in spite of this declaration, Uppsala was modelled after some German university, perhaps Cologne or Rostock, with which Swedish ecclesiastics were familiar. This provided the basic structure of the division into the four faculties of theology, common law, medicine, and philosophy, the methods of study and disputation, and the governance of the university by a rector elected by the professors from their own group rather than by the students, as was done at Bologna and as is still done in the Scottish universities. The coordinating office of the Chancellor of the Universities probably has its origins as the Bishop's representative at the university. This general structure has been maintained to the present from fifteenth-century Germany, which earlier had got it from Paris and Bologna. But it was in the nineteenth century that the contemporary complex of Swedish higher education took form and established its modern role in the social order.

At the beginning of the nineteenth century, higher education in Sweden consisted of two universities in the cities of Uppsala and Lund with a few hundred students at each, and two small academies of art and music in Stockholm established by Gustavus III. In the nineteenth century, higher education became increasingly dominant in the national cultural and intellectual life of the society, though it had a place in this regard as far back as the mid-seventeenth century.[4] By the 1830s three of the four leading men of letters were professors.[5] More and more the dominant official classes were academically trained. All through the nineteenth century and up to the student explosion beginning in the second half of the 1940s, the number of students doubled every twenty to thirty years. More and more different kinds of specialists—engineers, architects, business administrators, dentists— were academically trained in special-purpose, university-level, institutions (*högskolor*).[6] At present there are five universities with a growing number of affiliated branches and around thirty *högskolor*.

The universities have manifested a marked conservatism in adding any training outside of that covered by the four traditional faculties. Only with the establishment of a dental faculty at the new university at Umeå in 1959, a commerce faculty at Lund in 1961, and an engineering faculty at Lund in 1963 has this conservative tradition been broken. All of the specialists that were demanded by increasing industrialization and higher standards of living had been trained at *högskolor* outside of the universities. Swedish universities in this respect have been as conservative as those of any European nation, many of which were not so reluctant to add faculties of dentistry, engineering, commerce, agriculture, and veterinary medicine.[7] With enormous fidelity, the Swedish universities remained true to the research and scholarship ideals of the nineteenth-century German model in the traditional fields of study. Until the 1950s, in fact, there was not even much teaching in the Swedish universities; the student just presented himself for examination in a given subject when he felt ready.

The development of the Swedish universities is indeed the polar opposite of the pattern that developed in the United States, where training in advertising, home economics, hotel and restaurant management, teacher education, engineering, journalism, commerce, agriculture, and pilot training have all been integrated into the university, in many cases through to the Ph.D. level. The isolation of the *högskolor* from the universities is declining in Sweden, and the future will see more new faculties added to the universities and the establishment of closer relations and the sharing of facilities between the universities and the *högskolor* (particularly between science faculties and technological institutes). The basic philosophy of expanding higher education, which all of the political parties accept, is to expand existing institutions rather than to create new ones.

A Comparison of Swedish, British, and American Higher Education

In 1955 the Swedish government appointed a special committee on higher education to "carry out a comprehensive and unbiased inquiry into the mission and needs of the university in modern society."[8] The appointment of this committee signifies a general awareness of the very expanded role that higher education was assuming in Swedish society. The recommendations of this committee, which published seven reports between 1957 and 1963, mark the beginning of the modernization of the whole system of Swedish higher education. These reports deal with the recruitment of academic staff, changes in the occupational distribution of academically trained people, teaching methods, research conditions and needs, the future needs of academically trained people, questions of expansion, coordination, and administration, and the overall structure of the nation's system of higher education.[9] Through most of the reports, explicit and specific proposals are made as to what actions, plans, and policies should be undertaken, much of which has since become the basis of legislation. Yet in spite of almost 3000 pages of text, these reports fail to propose sufficient solutions for lessening the stresses that are developing from the increasing size and activities of the universities, with their antiquated nineteenth-century structures that are suitable only for small numbers of students and faculty. This was partially recognized when a second committee was appointed in 1963 to make recommendations on modernizing the research role of the university.

The British counterpart to the 1955 Swedish Committee was appointed in 1961 under Lord Robbins, with a similar though somewhat broader mission, and its reports highlight the marked differences in values, aims, and structure of higher education in the two societies.[10] From some points of view, it is easier to contrast the value emphases in higher education between Sweden and Britain (particularly England) than between Sweden and the United States because the dominant values undergirding higher education are so different in the United States. The basic value system of undergraduate education in the United States represents an uneasy accommodation between the English ideal of liberal education and that of specialized vocational training, though at the graduate level the German university ideal of specialized research and training is clearly dominant. In England, on the other hand, the dominant value emphasis is clearly that of liberal education as found at Oxford, Cambridge, the new "plate glass" universities, and perhaps at some of the other universities. (Yet much of redbrick education is similar to the American situation in their conflicting educational ideals.) In Sweden, however, the situation is simpler, because liberal education is virtually irrelevant to what higher education is supposed to be about.

The mission given to the Robbins Committee was "to review the pattern of full-time higher education in Great Britain and in the light of national needs and resources to advise Her Majesty's Government on what principles its long-term development should be based."[11] This is akin to the mission given the Swedish Committee, except that the British had a more long-range view. Both countries' reports dealt with essentially the same substantive topics, although the British dealt with them in a less specific manner and with greater emphasis on finding general guiding principles rather than on making concrete proposals.

Government committee reports when they exist can be excellent sources for the study of the functioning of institutions and of national value systems. They are committee products which minimize the presentation of atypical perspectives. They are generally based on sources of data not always available to nonofficial investigators and they frequently commission expensive studies of their own. They are generally directed toward problem areas and toward institutional practices that are in need of restructuring, and they tend to emphasize the dysfunctional aspects of institutions. What the authors say (and do not say) in their consensual product together with the public discussion which ensues can be enormously useful in apprehending national values. Because these reports are written from the point of view of future national discussion and possible legislation they will tend to be moderate—even if they make radical proposals—in the sense that they will usually not diverge very greatly from the traditions and values of dominant opinion.

A systematic comparative study of the values, aims, and perceptions of higher education contained in these two national reports and the reactions to them could be a most enlightening demonstration of differences in apparently similar institutions. Some of these will be dealt with here.

In Sweden the manifest functions of higher education are research, scholarship, and the training of all manner of specialists, scholars, teachers, and professionals. Liberal education is the function of lower levels of education, of adult education, and of other agencies in society. That there should be a close relation between the output of the various university faculties and institutions and the labor market is seen as axiomatic. Estimates of the future needs of higher education are made primarily in terms of estimates of the future need for doctors, teachers, engineers, and so forth, and not in terms of the future demands of individuals to go on with higher education. How close the Swedish Committee sees the relationship between the university and the labor market is its concern with the increasing numbers of students in the liberal-arts faculties, its wish that this number decline in the future, and its proposal for a more occupation-related curriculum here.[12] Other indications of the Committee's view of higher education as the training of occupational specialists is its favoring a *decline* in the percentage of gymnasium graduates who will go on to pursue higher education and its related concern with "wastage," the problem of those who take up higher studies but do not complete them.[13] Despite this, the increase in enrollments in the liberal-arts faculties through the 1960s was enormous, and in recent years more than 80 percent of those who finish gymnasium go on to the universities.[14]

By contrast, the Robbins Report calls for a broadening of undergraduate education, and little attention is given the problem of "wastage," partly, probably, because there is so much less of it in British universities. In the United States where the English ideal of the benefits of liberal education at the university level has been incorporated into the dominant value system, though in attenuated form and with generally less concern with quality and level, for any authoritative source to advocate that fewer students be educated in liberal arts is almost inconceivable because university education is generally regarded as good per se. Much respectable opinion and perhaps most intellectual opinion (as in England) holds that nonvocationally related liberal education is the best training for business, journalism, and many other fields.[15] And, in spite of the enormous wastage in American higher education, there is not much concern with it; a little college is better than none.

At the outset of the Robbins Report, the authors state explicitly what they regard as the four equally important aims of higher education.[16] First they mention "instruction in skills" related to occupations, but they immediately go on to say, "We put this first, not because we regard it as most important, but because we think it is sometimes ignored or undervalued." A second aim is "the advancement of learning," an aim equally important to the Swedish Committee. The remaining two—"to promote the powers of the mind" and "the transmission of a common culture and common standards of citizenship"— are not held by the Swedish Committee to as great an extent as by the British Committee. These deceptively simple phrases mean the production of "not mere specialists but rather cultivated men and women," who will, in effect, be members of an educated subculture. This is the complex Anglo-American, but particularly English, ideal of the liberally educated man, one with a general education who can deal with most problems better than the specialist. It is an elitist, humanist, antispecialist, and frequently, class-conscious ideal.

An important illustration of Swedish emphasis on specialized training and English emphasis on humanist and antispecialist education is the kind of training upper-level civil servants have had. The public service has equally great prestige in both societies and both are highly selective in their entrance demands. Sten-Sture Landström found that only 17.7 percent of 840 Swedish civil servants with academic degrees in 1947 received them from liberal-arts faculties.[17] The majority had law degrees, the remainder had a wide range of specialist degrees. This contrasts with the observation that 53 percent of the university graduates who went into the British Civil Service between 1948 and 1956 read classics or history as their major field.[18]

In Britain, concern has been expressed over the increase in numbers in the universities, but this never deals with the inability of the labor force to absorb them, rather it centers on the question of quality. Indeed, one of the main themes of the Robbins Report was to demonstrate that the universities can be expanded without standards being lowered. But still "more means worse" to Kingsley Amis, F. K. Leavis, and the minority who opposed the expansionist plans of the Robbins Committee, in spite of the fact that they were among the most modest expansion plans in Western Europe. British enrollment expectations for 1970–1971 as stated in the Robbins Report were only about 55 percent as high as Swedish expectations for the same year. The former were for 344,000 students (in 1963) and the latter for almost 90,000 (in 1964), yet Britain has a population about seven times as great as Sweden.[19] However, in both countries these estimates were quickly shown to be far too low.[20] In any case, probably not more than 10 percent of British youth born around 1950 will go on to higher education as compared with close to 20 percent of Swedish youth.

Sweden and Finland are probably the only countries in Western Europe where such a high percentage of an age group now enter a university or university-level institution. Yet in Sweden there has been little concern with the quality issue insofar as higher education is concerned. Sweden in this regard is closer to the United States in the belief that "more means better." Consider the observations of the Swedish sociologists Gösta Carlsson and Bengt Geeser on the egalitarian values regarding access to the universities:

in Sweden the prevailing spirit in government and administration, among politicians, in the press and among influential spokesmen for the public is strongly egalitarian. Professional training, and to a lesser extent general education, are accepted and put in the foreground as the main tasks of university faculties and professional schools. The selective function is viewed with much more suspicion; if selection takes place through students dropping out before graduation it is regarded as a sign of inefficient teaching. The entrance restrictions now in force in many of the professional schools are officially regarded as temporary measures although it is hard to believe that they will disappear within the foreseeable future. This is a philosophy which lies behind the far-reaching reforms now underway in the Swedish educational system as a whole, starting with the elementary (comprehensive) school. Opportunity and free choice, not screening and competition, are the desired ends.[21]

The Swedish Committee's emphasis on future planning of higher education is in terms of the needs of the labor force, whereas the British Committee's emphasis is on the basis of estimates of future demands of youth for places in the universities. Despite undoubtedly technical factors that influenced the decisions, the committees' choices are consonant with the emphasis on higher education meeting the "needs and demands" of society in Sweden, and with the emphasis on making higher education available to all youth who are qualified and wish to attend in Britain. Comparing Sweden with Britain on the extent to which the universities are regarded as existing to serve the needs of society compared to serving the discrete needs of individuals is, however, not so clear as a comparison with the United States, because both Sweden and Britain have universities closely allied to the official classes and both have a more or less organic conception of the relation between the individual and society. In contrast to Sweden, however, higher education in the United States is seen to a much greater extent as existing for meeting individual needs "as a weapon or tool in individual competition."[22] This is a result of a general faith in formal education, an extraordinary heterogeneity of competing institutions free to seek their own levels and clientele, and an individualistic value system.

Standardization, Centralization, Directed Change

The Swedish Committee sees higher education as a network of educational institutions amenable to a relatively high degree of direction, planned change, and coordination. This is true in spite of the observation that change comes about slowly in Swedish universities; all Western European universities change slowly. The Committee shows little concern with institutional peculiarities because there is virtually no variation in prestige among institutions, and a high degree of organizational uniformity prevails. The Robbins Report, on the other hand, accepts prestige inequalities among institutions as "inevitable." It manifests an ambivalent respect for the unique traditions of Oxford and Cambridge, finding much value in them, yet lamenting their dominating presence in British higher education. They virtually apologize for considering higher education to be "a system" and accept strong institutional autonomy at the expense of coordination and central planning as in the best interests of academic freedom.

The situation in the United States has changed little in the four decades since Abraham Flexner wrote that there is an "absence of any possibility of centralized and intelligently directed authority and the lack of institutions which possess and may be counted on to maintain ideals, America must flounder in, and perhaps ultimately out of, chaos."[23] The planning by the state of California represents the only substantial planned coordination and is the major exception to the American tradition of academic competition. Most of the change that comes about in the United States through this competition, together with an enormous faculty mobility and a trickling down in the academic procession of methods, theories, and forms of organization, comes about in Sweden through slow, rational, planned change at the national level.

By American or English standards, higher education in Sweden is standardized, coordinated, and uniform in great degree. With one partial exception (The Stockholm School of Economics), all higher education in Sweden is public in the American sense of that term. The control of most higher education falls under the Minister of Education and Ecclesiastical Affairs. Several specialized schools fall under the control of the Ministry of Agriculture. The administrative control of the universities and *högskolor* fall under the Office of the Chancellor of the Universities, which oversees the coordination and standardization of university policy, handles personnel problems, and coordinates the budgets of the various universities to be submitted to the Riksdag. This office, intermediate between the universities and the government, is partially analogous to the English University Grants Committee, but the latter only allots money as an agent of the Chancellor of the Exchequer and does not have the coordinating and standardizing role of the Swedish office. A recent Rector of Lund University in Sweden, a man who has had much intimate contact with the United States, has written that: "The universities are being reduced to uniformity by the central bureaucracy in an unparalleled manner," and that "it is difficult for the universities to develop their own individualities or to act on their own initiative."[24] However, he very much qualifies these strong statements and sees "advantages and disadvantages" in the high degree of central governance that prevails in Swedish higher education.

There is a general absence of institutional prestige adhering to one university over another. One university may be regarded as preeminent in a given subject at a given time, as Stockholm was in economics and as Uppsala was in political science in the years between World Wars I and II, but the prestige belongs to the specific department and not to the university as such. To the Swedes, a degree is a degree, regardless of where it comes from. Most students go to the university closest to their homes, those from north and central Sweden generally go to Uppsala, Stockholm, or the new university in Umeå, those from the west coast and south to Gothenburg and Lund. The same is true of the thirty or so *högskolor*. The points, six or seven of which are needed for the first degree, are equally valid at all of the universities, and sometimes are based on precisely the same reading lists and requirements. Unlike German and Swiss students, however, there is little movement between universities even in the work for advanced degrees. The kind of prestige divisions found in England between Oxford and Cambridge and the redbrick universities or the finely graded prestige hierarchy of the American academic procession are quite absent.

And within the individual university there are no organizations that confer varying amounts of social prestige. There are no socially elite colleges, such as Christ Church, Oxford or King's College, Cambridge, and there are no fraternity prestige hierarchies as are found in most residential American universities. A functional equivalent to these intermediate organizations are the "nations" in the Swedish universities, most strongly developed at Uppsala and Lund, where membership is determined by home residence, parental membership, or some such criteria. These organizations function similarly to their American and English counterparts, but they are wholly nonselective and exist virtually without any social-prestige dimension. This in no sense implies that no informal social-status hierarchy develops within or outside the nations, but only that there are no formal organizations that institutionalize these distinctions.[25]

High Evaluation of Technology

Sweden differs fundamentally from England and to a lesser extent from the United States in the high prestige accorded to technology. There is enormous competition to enter the technical universities. A 1958 study of the Swedish Ministry of Labor Statistics found that over six times as many male students in the last year in the science line of the gymnasium gave a technological university as their first choice over a university science faculty, even though the first year enrollments run higher in the latter.[26] Many students enter the science faculties to accumulate points to increase their chances of transferring to a technical university. Admission to the liberal-arts (science and humanities) faculties, along with those of theology and law, are open to all students who successfully complete the gymnasium; all other faculties and specialized institutions have a selective admissions policy. Commenting on the tendency to regard science as "second best," Donald W. Hutchings, an Oxford education don who has studied Swedish technological education, wrote that this quite simply is "the reverse of the situation in Britain."[27] The United States is not readily comparable in this respect because most students who can graduate from high school can "get in" somewhere in the area of their first choice, but the relative evaluation of "technology" versus "science" among brighter students is probably closer in the United States to the situation that exists in Britain rather than Sweden.

A study of eight occupational statuses, previously mentioned, which used 358 Swedish students and 533 American students, found the Swedes to rank the profession of civil engineer higher in prestige, usefulness to society, and relative intellectual ability than did the

Americans.[28] In discussing the different evaluations of the two nationality groups the authors state, "The greatest discrepancy in evaluation of usefulness to society attaches to the civil engineer. In Sweden he carries a second rank (after medical doctor), but in America he is ranked a low sixth."

In Britain the prestige and professional status of the engineer is substantially below what it is in the United States.[29] The Robbins Committee states that ". . . the Colleges of Advanced Technology have not found it easy to recruit suitable teachers because the colleges lacked status."[30] The different status of technological institutions in Sweden compared with Britain has been expressed in somewhat exaggerated terms by Hutchings as follows, "It takes a little time for the British educator to grasp the fact that the two great technological institutions in Stockholm and Gothenburg enjoy a reputation and prestige in Sweden which can be likened to that of Oxford and Cambridge in Britain."[31]

"One professor, one department, one building"

University teachers with the title "professor" are much less common in Swedish than in American universities, but they are probably more common than in Britain or the Continental countries.[32] Columbia University in New York was just slightly larger than Uppsala in the mid-1960s, yet it had 540 full professors as compared with Uppsala's 143 professors. Gothenburg University, with 90 professors, had almost three times as many students as Dartmouth College, with 145 full professors. A conservative estimate is that there are three times as many full professors in an American as compared with a Swedish university of similar size, and if we include the associate and assistant professors, at least eight times as many. If the total were multiplied by a factor of three, to allow for the much larger proportion of American youth in institutions classified as "colleges and universities" and taught by persons with the title "professor," we would get an estimate of relatively twenty-four times as many "professors" in the United States. The scarcity of the title professor in Sweden, together with its prestige apart from any institutional locus of identity, make the title a precise and exalted occupational designation, whereas it is only a synonym for college teacher in the United States. This difference makes any attempt to compare the relative prestige of "professor" in Sweden (or most other European countries) with the United States most difficult.

The Swedish university department (*institution*) is a narrow pyramid with "the" professor at the top, whose prestige in most cases is about equal to that of "star" professors in American universities. In a few fields in the larger universities there are two professors in a subject, and more rarely three.

A hierarchical system of titles prevails in the universities, such as "professor," "lecturer," "docent," "licentiat," and a few others. These titles are generally known throughout the society and are used in formal intercourse. They are used in the press, follow a person's name in the telephone book, and are used in writing to an individual. Sometimes, however, there is a polite upgrading outside of the university. This emphasis on titles persists in the increasingly egalitarian Sweden. The anti-title bias that characterizes Anglo-American universities (particularly the higher status ones) must not lead to an exaggeration of the importance of this "title sickness," but the emphasis on titles in Sweden does function to make an academic's rank explicit and unambiguous outside of the university.

The Swedish professor very much determines the personality and character of his department. He has become much more of an administrator with the growth of the universities. The teaching and research staff below him have grown enormously, to say nothing of the extraordinary increase in the number of students. His latent authority remains great compared to his department-head counterpart in an American university. He can set policy, determine course content, and, above all, grant degrees. In practice many of these tasks have been delegated and democratized in large departments. The authority of the professor, as well as the absence of countervailing power in the form of other professors of equal rank, gives him a dominance rarely found in American university departments. In large departments in large American universities, there are frequently ten or fifteen or even more full professors, each with the same formal academic authority to supervise and to evaluate graduate students. In practice the Swedish and American structures do not function as differently as might be supposed, because of the common democratization of the informal departmental structure and because of the delegation of segments of professorial authority to subordinates. The dysfunctions of the two types of organization are, however, quite different. A Swedish professor who is a bad administrator, inept at handling students, or whose ideas are viewed as eccentric or worse can in a few years' time alienate students and almost stop his department from functioning, which is almost impossible in an American university department. Perhaps the major dysfunctional aspect of American departmental organization is factionalism, but this rarely incapacitates a department from effective functioning as sometimes happens in Sweden.

Swedish departmental organization is presently undergoing strains as a result of the rapid growth in the old structure; the principle of "one professor, one department, one building" continues. Between 1945 and 1963, there was more than a quadrupling in the number of students, but the number of professors less than doubled while the number of other teachers (not including assistants) increased more than fourfold.[33] In other words, the overall chances for a docent or lecturer to become a professor have declined substantially since World War II. It is contemplated, however, that this situation will be changed as a result of recommendations of the 1963 University Committee.

Only a small percentage of teachers who are not professors have tenured positions. The situation has been particularly insecure for the docents. The docent is a mid-nineteenth century German import to the Swedish academic system. One becomes a docent with a six-year contract when a sufficiently high grade on a doctoral dissertation is obtained. In the past if a professorship or tenured position was not secured within the six-year contract period, one generally had to leave the university and teach in a gymnasium. By this time the individual was frequently in his forties. Some countries, such as West Germany and Norway, have solved the problem by granting tenure to all docents. This has been suggested in Sweden, but what changes will be made remains for the future.

There are a number of dysfunctional aspects for scholarship in the present departmental organization. Most obvious is that the professors are loaded with administrative duties. At the lower levels, the relative scarcity of professorships and other tenured positions results in much competition and probably makes for much isolation among peers. At least in the social sciences, academics do little collaborative research,[34] perhaps due to pressures that inhibit the exchange of ideas and information, for a man is judged for a professorship solely on the basis of *his* scholarly contributions. Considerations of age, seniority, teaching ability, intellectuality, brilliance, or "promise" play a negligible role in the selection committees.[35] The system also has tendencies to engender scholarly conservatism because professors generally determine the areas and methods of study in their departments. The tutelary relations that frequently develop between professor and student often last well into one's thirties when the doctoral dissertation is completed. And most scholars do not have much capacity to be free in any system until they have the final degree.

On the functional side of all this is the effort and the quality of scholarship represented by the Swedish doctoral dissertation. All are published, and in the social sciences and humanities they often represent the work of many years. They tend to be long, exhaustive, empirical, and to deal with a problem of relatively narrow scope in great detail. Unlike their American counterparts, a large proportion of them are major contributions to scholarship. For many with the Swedish doctorate, their dissertation represents the pinnacle of their academic achievement. The dissertations are graded, and a sufficiently high grade ensures the awarding of a docentship, which is the first step toward a professorship, and a low grade makes it difficult. These factors act as enormous incentives to the writing of substantial, but generally methodologically conventional, dissertations.

The effort and time that go into Swedish dissertations seem to have increased directly with the extent of competition for professorships. The length of time elapsing between the first degree—which comes about three years later than in America—and the Swedish doctorate increased from a median of eight years in the 1920s to eleven years in the 1950s.[36] The median age for receiving the doctorate in the 1950s was 37.0 years in the humanities and social sciences and 34.6 years in the natural sciences.[37] This is six or seven years later than in the United States, where the median age has been declining.[38] Some years ago Professor Lars Gunnar Sillén wrote, after returning from the United States where he was favorably impressed with the comparatively rapid training of graduate students, that, "in our country one sometimes has the impression, that the students' time is reckoned almost like the air in a chemical-technical process, that is, as a natural substance which exists in unlimited quantity."[39]

With an absence of a predictable career for the majority of academics as late as their middle thirties it is understandable that an academic career does not have the broad base of interest among good undergraduate students that one finds in American colleges. In America the academic career has become secure and predictable, unlike the situation that exists in Sweden and most European countries. The Robbins Committee voices concern about the attractiveness of academic life vis-à-vis other professions and about the recruitment of university teachers in the future.[40] Stanley Hoffman comments on the relatively fewer numbers attempting to obtain the French university *agrégation* (roughly equivalent to the Swedish doctorate in level), "in higher education, the *agrégation*, necessary for obtaining the top teaching post jobs, recruits fewer and fewer people precisely because the boards refuse to lower their standards; consequently more and more teachers are not *agrégés*—a sign of change—but the *agrégation* remains the most coveted goal . . ."[41]

One of the missions of the 1963 University Committee is to work out the specific nature of a new degree comparable to the Anglo-American Ph.D., a level somewhat above that of the *licentiat*, the second Swedish degree. This may very well mean the end of the Swedish super-doctorate.

Virtually no one becomes a professor or academic in the traditional fields unless he has come up through the ranks and has the required formal credentials, generally the Swedish doctorate. Distinguished writers or statesmen do not become academics as they so frequently do in the United States. Unless they were first academics, they never have any connection with the universities.

University teachers have far more access to the mass media than in the United States. Academics are among the principle contributors of cultural articles in the daily opinion pages on current events in the major newspapers. They are sometimes on television during prime listening hours, and the fact that Sweden has only one television station undoubtedly maximizes their viewing public. Dissertations and monographs are far more likely to be reviewed in the daily press, and the results of scholarly research in all areas are more frequently reported than in the American press.

The relations between university teachers and the government and politics is more extensive and intensive than in the United States. A large proportion of university teachers, probably a majority in the social sciences, have served on governmental commissions at one time or another in this society which places such reliance on expert opinion and detailed investigation prior to enacting legislation. Also, political parties have been prone to choose professional social scientists as their chairmen, because of their knowledge and not their status. Four of the five political party chairmen a few years ago (1964) had advanced degrees in social science or law. The exception was the then prime minister, but prior to his full-time entry into politics, he was an editor of an encyclopedia, which is also a "knowledge" occupation. Academics may now be devoting less energy to politics, however, as a result of an increased workload that is resulting from the student explosion and enhanced academic competition.

The universities are free from harassing pressures from government and public opinion. A teacher's position is not threatened by the public expression of ideas of any sort or even by committing a crime. Cases of university teachers—even at the lower levels—being forced out for political radicalism, antireligious views, radical libertarianism, or "moral turpitude" are quite unknown. A tenured academic (or any civil servant) can only be removed from his position after a court trial in which gross dereliction of duty or insanity is established. Consequently, there is little concern in Sweden with academic freedom in the American sense of this term.[42]

Changing Patterns in Student Recruitment

The years since World War II have seen a rapid increase in the numbers and proportions of youth attending universities and *högskolor* in Sweden. From the mid-1920s to the early 1940s, between 2 and 3 percent of Swedish twenty-one-year-olds were enrolled in higher education, by the early 1960s this figure had passed 10 percent, and by 1970 it is anticipated that it will approach 20 percent.[43] Between 1947 and 1962 the absolute number of students enrolled in higher education more than trebled from 14,000 to 45,000,[44] between 1962 and 1967 it doubled to 90,000, and in the 1968–1969 school year it passed 100,000.[45] This represents a *sevenfold* increase in twenty-one years.

This enormous increase in enrollments has been accompanied by a lessening in the differential recruitment of students from different regions, from city and country, and from the different social strata. The proportions of students coming from the northern and western sections of Sweden have increased most rapidly. The proportion of students going on to higher education from Norrland, for example, increased from 1.4 to 7.2 percent of one-fifth of the age group 20 to 24 between 1947 and 1961.[46] In 1947 the proportion of urban youth who enrolled in universities was four times that of rural youth; by the 1960-1961 school year this factor had been reduced to less than two.[47] At a 1967 conference, Torsten Husén stated that:

From 1910 to 1943 less than 2 percent of children from rural areas graduated from gymnasium but this is now 16 to 17 percent. One factor is the location of schools preparing for the university from new areas. From 1910 to the early 1940s we had the same location of pre-university schools as we had before 1900, but they have been much more fairly distributed after 1950 than they were before.[48]

This figure of 16 to 17 percent (almost as high as the overall figure in the mid-1960s) suggests that the rural-urban differential in recruitment into higher education is approaching the vanishing point, which is a remarkable phenomenon.

While everywhere higher education is selective of the children of professionals and businessmen, of the upper and middle classes, there are marked variations among countries in the proportions of the children of the lower social classes and of farmers who get to the universities. The patterns of recruitment to the universities are strikingly different among the industrialized societies. While the children of workers, though probably not farmers, are clearly underrepresented in Swedish higher education, they are less so than in all of the Continental Western European countries.

In the Scandinavian countries in the last third of the nineteenth century there was a great increase in the proportion of the children of farmers entering the universities. This was a consequence of the diffusion of the availability of academic secondary education to the rural population. At this time 15 to 20 percent of the students at the Universities of Uppsala and Lund were the sons of farmers; such a large representation of farm youth, then as now, was probably not to be found anywhere else in Europe outside of Scandinavia.[49] From the 1920s there have been marked increases in the proportions of two new categories of students in the universities: first women and later the children of the industrial working class. Sweden and Finland, in addition to having the highest proportion of youth in higher education in Western Europe, probably also have the highest proportions of female students; in 1967-1968 42 percent of all Swedish students were females, as compared with 48.1 percent of Finnish students in 1963-1964.[50] Finland probably has the highest percentage of women in higher education in the world. The proportion of women, as with other "disadvantaged" groups, is correlated with the proportion of all youth in higher education.

One measure of the class-linkage of the educational systems of modern societies is the proportion of working-class students who get to the universities. There is greater variation in the proportion of students of working-class background in the countries of Northwestern Europe than there is in the proportion of youth in higher education. For example, the son of a Swedish or English worker is at least four times as likely to get to a university as is the son of a West German worker. Sweden, along with Norway, Finland, and Great Britain, are clearly above Denmark and the countries of Continental Europe in working-class representation in the universities. They may, indeed, be above the United States, if we limit the comparison to academically selective colleges and universities.

Among newly enrolled students in Swedish higher education in 1947, 8 percent had fathers who were workers.[51] This increased to 12 percent in 1953 and to between 14 and 15 percent in the early 1960s. Table 5.1 gives the occupations of the fathers of new students in Swedish higher education in 1961–1962. By 1967–1968, 19 percent of new students were from the working class—20 percent among males and 18 percent among females.[52] While there is frequent concern in Sweden that the working class, who make up just under half the population, are much underrepresented in higher education, their representation is relatively high when compared with other industrialized societies.

Studies published in recent years give information on the class backgrounds of students in a number of European countries. A Danish

Table 5.1 Occupations of Fathers of First-Year Students in Swedish Higher Education, 1961–1962, by Sex (Percentages).

	Male	Female	Both
Agriculture, Forestry, Fishing (excluding workers)	8.3	7.1	7.9
Primary School Teachers, etc.	4.2	4.1	4.1
Graduates (not otherwise classified)	20.7	24.0	21.9
Officers	1.5	2.0	1.7
Directors, Managers, and Wholesalers	7.3	7.8	7.5
Tradesmen, Commercial Travelers, Craftsmen	11.9	11.4	11.7
Higher Salaried Employees (not graduates), Certain Professions	16.1	17.4	16.6
Other Salaried Employees	10.7	9.6	10.3
Workers	15.0	12.5	14.1
Occupation Undetermined	0.5	0.5	0.5
No Information	3.8	3.6	3.7
	100	100	100

SOURCE: Sveriges Officiella Statistik, *Högre Studier, 1961–1962* (Stockholm: Statistiska Centralbyrån, 1964), p. 5.

study found 9 percent of university students to be from the working class in 1959–1960.[53] In the fall term of 1959, 9 percent of the male students in Dutch universities were sons of workers, which represents an increase from 6 percent in the fall term of 1936.[54] However, among the minority of female students, only 3 to 4 percent came from working-class homes in both 1936 and 1959. In Austrian universities in the fall term of 1958, 8 percent of all students had fathers who were workers, having increased from 6 percent in 1929.[55] A highly detailed statistical study of the students at the University of Bern in Switzerland in 1959–1960 reports only 4 percent to have had fathers who were workers;[56] and in French universities in 1962–1963 5.5 percent of all students were sons of workers.[57] For West Germany in the mid-1960s, the proportion was just over 6 percent.[58]

Norway, on the other hand, has a higher percentage of students from the working class than Sweden. In the fall of 1961, 25.0 percent of newly enrolled male students had fathers who were workers,[59] which is substantially above the Swedish figure of 14.1 percent for 1961–1962 for male and female students combined, or the figure for males alone, which is 15.0 percent. Yet the chance for a working-class student to go to a university is greater in Sweden than in Norway because Sweden has proportionately more than twice the number of students as did Norway.[60] However, the chance of a working-class youth going to the university is clearly higher in Finland than in Sweden or any other country in Western Europe; in 1961–1962 17.6 percent of all students were the children of workers,[61] yet Finland has a relatively smaller working-class population (and a larger agricultural population) than Sweden, but as high a proportion of students in higher education.

Great Britain is a special case. In Britain the working class representation has been very high despite the eleven-plus examination. The Robbins Report shows that in the 1961–1962 school year, 25 percent of all British university students had fathers who were workers (26 percent among the men and 23 percent among the women).[62] What is particularly interesting is that this percentage has not varied much over a number of decades; from 1928 to 1947, 23 percent of all students had fathers who were workers. Yet any overall figure like this for Britain (and even more for the United States) is in a way misleading. There is a great difference in the representation of working-class students at Oxford and Cambridge and "the rest." Only 13 percent of those at Oxford and 9 percent of those at Cambridge had fathers classified as workers, compared with 31 percent at the civic universities.[63] The most startling figure in the entire report is that 46 percent of male university students in the Welsh universities in 1961–1962 had fathers who were workers.[64] It should be emphasized, however, that Britain has had a smaller proportion of students in higher education than any other country in Western Europe except Norway.[65] So for recent years the chances of a son of a Swedish worker going on to higher education are greater than for the son of a British worker. However, this was not true earlier.

Both Canada and the United States and the countries of Eastern Europe, on the other hand, have more representative student bodies than the three northern Scandinavian countries. In Canada in 1956–1957 26.2 percent of all university students had fathers classified as workers.[66] In the United States, the overall percentage is in the 25 to 30 percent range, but the gross percentage is not very meaningful because of the inclusiveness of the American concept of higher education and the enormous variations in level.[67] The selective private universities in all likelihood have a very low representation of the children of the working class, whereas, at the other extreme, working-class youth predominate at some public junior colleges. A number of the Eastern European countries, including the Soviet Union, Poland, and East Germany, give youth from working-class and peasant backgrounds preferred treatment.[68] One estimate has it that around half of the students at East German universities have working-class backgrounds.[69]

Another way of looking at the "democratization" of higher education in Sweden is to observe in Table 5.1 that just over one-fifth of the new students in 1961–1962 had fathers who were university graduates, and fewer than half of the new students can be considered to have come from an upper or upper-middle-class milieu. Note also that one out of four male students are the children of workers and farmers combined.

It is difficult to make precise cross-national comparisons because of different conventions in classifying occupations, even within the Scandinavian countries. However, the classifications of farmer and worker are probably clear-cut enough to allow such comparison, although the comparisons should be related to the proportions of farmers and industrial workers in the labor force. But, in any case, the highly representative nature of the student population in Scandinavian higher education within the Western European context is clear. Generally in Sweden and Scandinavia, and probably elsewhere, students in the faculties of medicine and law are from higher-status backgrounds as compared, for example, with those in theology or arts and sciences.[70]

The future will quite probably see a continued decline in differential recruitment into higher education. This prediction is based on the rapid increase in the proportion of pupils of working-class background entering the gymnasium through the 1960s. Also, in 1965 *all* students engaged in full-time higher study began to receive grants of 1,750 *kronor* per year (about $350), in addition to the universal availability of generous, long term, low interest, insured loans. Sweden has come close to totally eliminating the financial factor as a deterrent to full-time study in any field for any qualified student, even if married and with a family.

Admission to the faculties of philosophy, law, and theology is open to all who have a certain minimal average in the last year of the gymnasium. Entrance to the so-called "blocked" faculties and professional schools is wholly on the basis of objective criteria: grades. This is in marked distinction from much of American and English higher education where personality, "moral capacity," well-rounded-ness, participation in extracurricular activities, and so forth are important in gaining admission to the more prestigious colleges of Oxford and Cambridge or to the aggressively elitist American universities.[71] The Swedish sociologists Carlsson and Geeser have written that, "With regard to social and other selection it should . . . be kept in mind that the Swedish university system, and educational system in general, abhors all informal and discretionary methods of selection, when selection is necessary."[72] There is no personal interviewing or reliance on letters of recommendation, not even for the medical faculty that a student enters after the gymnasium. In the words of Professor Bror Rexed of the Uppsala University Medical faculty, in referring to the admission of students to medical school, "This method of selecting medical students [using only objective academic criteria] is based on the view that medicine is a wide and varied field, in which there is scope for many different types of personality." [73]

While the Scandinavian universities continue to be elite institutions in the sense that they continue to prepare only for the professions, upper-level teaching, and the higher-status occupations in general, values regarding access to the university have become, as pointed out earlier, highly egalitarian. This is particularly true at the ideological level in Sweden, even though Finland may have gone farther in the actual proportions of working class youth who get to the universities.

How nearly universal the desire for university education has really become in Sweden in recent years is indicated in Table 5.2. In July 1955 a national sample of mothers was asked whether they would be pleased if their sons or daughters took the *studentexamen;* 65 percent answered that they would be. A similar question was asked of all parents in August 1963, and the percentage had increased to 82 percent for sons and 84 percent for daughters, and only 6 percent of the parents of sons and 4 percent of the parents of daughters answered that they did not want their children to take the *studentexamen*. It is interesting to note that there is virtually no difference in the answers for sons and daughters, or between urban and rural parents. Among working-class respondents, the percentages varied between 73 and 81, almost as high as the overall percentages. [The *studentexamen* was abolished in 1968.] Anthony Kerr, in his *Universities of Europe*, has made the flip comment that "having a son or daughter at a university carries in Sweden the same sort of prestige as running a respectable-looking car in England."[74]

Table 5.2 Desire of Swedish Parents for Their Children to Take the *Student-exam* (University Matriculation Examination, 1955 and 1963) (Percentages).

JULY 1955*

	Boys	Girls
Yes	65	65
No	16	16
Don't Know	19	19

AUGUST 1963**

	Boys	Girls
Yes	82	84
No	6	4
Don't Know	12	12

* N = "over 1000" mothers, aged 18–55.

** National sample of parents of both sexes.

SOURCE: Svenska Institutet för Opinionsundersökningar (*SIFO*) (Stockholm, July 1955, August 1963).

Student Politics

Student political organization has reached a higher level of organization, differentiation, and interest articulation in Sweden and Scandinavia than anywhere else in the world.[75] This is true both of organizations with political viewpoints and of the local and national student unions with essentially trade-union aims. Nevertheless, student politics has less importance in Sweden than in Japan or in France, or in most of the developing nations of the world. Student politics and political organization in Sweden are a microcosm of the very advanced level of political and occupational organization so characteristic of the greater society.

Compared with other societies, developed and developing, student politics in Scandinavia has been characterized by an extraordinary tranquility and little mass activism or by what Clark Kerr has called "confrontation politics."[76] Yet this does not mean that there are not strains and discontent in student life. Most important are those stresses growing out of the radical egalitarian and humanitarian values of the students and the traditional social forces represented by the university authorities and the political and economic establishment. And New Left demands for greater student power, and the restrained use of direct action to obtain it, became apparent in 1968.

Scandinavian students are about as free of university control outside of the specifically academic as it is possible to be. As Torgny Segerstedt, Rector of Uppsala University, put it, "If they [the students] are drunk or disorderly or seducing women, it is not the business of the university. They're on their own."[77] This is in contrast to the declining in loco parentis traditions of the Anglo-American universities, in which school authorities assume certain parental responsibilities. A study of the adjustment of Scandinavian students at the University of Wisconsin between 1952 and 1954 showed that, "(n)o other aspect of university life here was as frequently objected to as the regulation of social and moral behavior."[78] A similar study of the American experience of fifty Swedes who had studied at American universities reports the same kind of objections.[79] This also contrasts with German and Swiss universities, where the university rector and certain faculty committees can dismiss a student from the university or can provide disciplinary measures for political, sexual, or criminal offenses.[80]

Whether Scandinavian universities even have the authority to dismiss a student for committing a crime, for reasons of "moral turpitude," or for any such reasons—except for cheating in examinations—is not at all clear. It never seems to happen.

Among the most important student political organizations of the Left in Sweden is Verdandi at Uppsala University. The society was formed in 1882 to promote "freedom of thought and expression"; more specifically it was devoted to the rationalist criticism of the beliefs of the Swedish State Church, conventional morality, and the paternalistic and hierarchical values of the Swedish establishment.[81] Its influence has been great on many generations of Uppsala students. The strongest and purest manifestation of "cultural radicalism," the conventional term the Swedes use for the application of critical rationalism to the institutions of society, is to be found in Verdandi—unaffiliated with any political party—and in the liberal and socialist student organizations in the universities.

In recent years Verdandi has had a number of special and much-publicized symposia and has published debate books on the subjects. In 1961 they had an "Atheist Week" to which "no Christian apologists" were invited.[82] Later some of these lectures and other "atheist" writings were published in a volume entitled The Atheist's Handbook,[83] which contains articles by a number of the most distinguished Swedish intellectuals and academics. In 1964 they held a four-day symposium on sex roles, devoted to the criticism of traditional sex roles and to the inequalities still existing between the sexes. This conference also resulted in a book.[84] Other areas of particular concern at their meetings have been the developing nations, the future directions of higher education, and abortion. Since about 1965, however, Verdandi has tended to emphasize questions of foreign policy and egalitarian issues,[85] which has resulted in a lessened concern with questions of God and religion, sex and sex roles. There has been a movement from a rather positive position toward American foreign policy to an extremely negative attitude resulting from intense opposition to America's role in the war in Vietnam.

In 1891, nine years after the founding of Verdandi, a group of conservative students at Uppsala University came together to form a society to promote and defend the values of patriotism, the State Church and Christianity, the monarchy and traditional values in general.[86] Heimdal, the name of the new conservative organization, and Verdandi both were formed at a time of intense conflict between the values of the official classes and the democratic and egalitarian, rationalist and scientific ideas of the young radicals. To the present, they continue to debate many of the same topics: republicanism, the relation of the Church to the state, and traditional moral and religious values. However, even though there are basic differences on these rather intellectual and not very pressing issues, there is a high degree of consensus on the absolute acceptance of the democratic method, the essentials of the social-service state, an international point of view, and so forth. Heimdal specifically regards itself as having a "reformist conservative attitude toward politics."[87]

The de-ideologization of politics and the extent of consensus in Swedish politics has probably proceeded as far as in any of the developed societies, and this is very much reflected in student politics. The extent to which this is true is indicated in the introduction to the program adopted by the Liberal Student Association (*SLS*) in 1959 in which it is maintained that it is no longer tenable to use terms such as:

socialism, liberalism, and conservatism in regard to the democratic parties [a phrase used to exclude the Communists]. They have influenced each other so that there is more that unites them than separates them. In spite of this there is an ideological continuity in the development of the parties; the conflicts of opinion have declined, but have not disappeared. The differences which still remain SLS regards as "attitudinal differences." [88]

It is precisely because of this broad consensus on fundamentals and the extraordinarily efficient way in which the social system works that student politics can be so centered on issues of unrestricted abortion, republicanism, sex roles, sex issues, class distinctions, the developing countries, the regime in South Africa, and the role of the United States in Vietnam. These were the principal issues in all of the student political journals in the mid-1960s.[89] Probably nowhere in the world is student politics so radical in its discussion, yet so orderly in its behavior.

There are national federations of the student political organizations. The largest is the National Union of Conservative Students to which Heimdal is affiliated, followed in size by the National Union of Social Democratic Students, and then by the Liberal Student Association of Sweden. The Center Student Association is the smallest, representing students who support the Center (Agrarian) party. There is no student association in Sweden specifically for communists, but many of them, along with Left-wing Social Democrats, belong to Clarté chapters affiliated with the Swedish Clarté Association.[90] Like all of the other student political associations, except Laboremus (the Social Democratic Association at Uppsala University), Clarté is unaffiliated with any political party. It is directed to "intellectuals and others interested in socialist study and enlightenment," and "takes no position in controversies between different socialist organizations."[91] Like other radical student political associations, it is not limited to students or to academics. For example, Laboremus has always been an association of "mental and physical workers," and Verdandi has recently manifested its overall concern with egalitarian issues by dropping "student" from the organization's formal name. At Uppsala, where student politics are particularly active, not more than 15 percent of the students are members of any political association, including Verdandi. Membership in Heimdal and Laboremus has been running around 3 percent of the student population in recent years.

It is in the trade-union aspect of student organization that Sweden and Scandinavia have made such progress since the 1940s in becoming important voices vis-à-vis the government, the universities, and other segments of society in representing the interests of the students.[92] At an international student conference held in 1965, one of the principal speakers concluded that "there are still relatively few countries in Europe that allow student participation in governing bodies. The countries most advanced in this field seem to be the Scandinavian countries."[93] This can be seen as a continuation of the traditions in Scandinavian universities to leave students to themselves to handle their own affairs and to organize in order to promote their interests.

The student unions are not bound to any political party, nor are they committed to any ideology other than that of democracy and internationalism. However, a predominantly two-party political system has developed in recent years in the student-union elections in the larger Swedish and Scandinavian universities organized around more-or-less conservative-radical lines.

The general aims of the Swedish National Union of Students (*Sveriges förenade studentkårer, SFS*) include the following:

(1) to act as the unified voice of the interests of students toward the government, the university authorities, and society in general;
(2) to influence the curricula;
(3) to represent students in international organizations;

(4) to improve the general welfare and living conditions of students, particularly as regards increasing the amount of student housing;
(5) to obtain more generous loan funds and salaries for students;
(6) to gain special rates in national and international travel;
(7) to obtain discounts on books and to conduct special student stores with a wide variety of goods at discount prices;
(8) to publish periodicals for the expression of student opinion;
(9) to provide innumerable other services such as the maintenance of nursery schools for students with children and medical and psychiatric services.

The *SFS* is a confederation of thirty-five local student unions ranging in size from the Uppsala Student Union with about 19,000 members to the Dairy Farming Institute in Alnarp with only about six members. The total membership is always equivalent to the total number of students enrolled in higher education because membership is compulsory for all students. The chairman of *SFS* is employed full time and occupies a prestigious post that is in most cases indicative of future success in Swedish politics or management. Olof Palme, the Social Democratic Prime Minister, for example, was a past chairman of *SFS*.

SFS, like all professional and trade-union organizations in Sweden, places great emphasis on operating by rules and regulations, makes a great deal of representing the opinions of its membership, and is in fact very much subject to the views of the locals. The result of the highly democratic organization of *SFS* according to Lars Tobisson, who was its chairman in 1964, is that "discussion is often long-winded and slow but, on the other hand, everyone knows that the attitude adopted by the *SFS* has been preceded by thorough and expert consideration and that the views presented are representative of the country's students."[94] Perhaps there is a little exaggeration in the remarks of Tobisson, but they reflect the high order of discussion, planning, and organization that is characteristic of Swedish organizations. However, it is important to stress that only a minority of students have any active interest in the local unions or in *SFS*. One of the increasing criticisms of living in the organized society par excellence that is Sweden is that organizations do their jobs so well and the people have come to have so much faith in them that most people are apathetic and do not actively participate.

SFS, in accomplishing its purposes, never resorts to pressures other than relying on their arguments and the existence of open channels to the government and parliamentary committees. They have never called a strike or demonstration. How SFS operates has been described by Tobisson as follows:

Contacts with different government bodies play a decisive part in the daily work of the SFS . . . and if the SFS is to influence matters in favour of the students, its best plan is to present its views to the administrative authorities concerned. We therefore attempt to speak with these authorities at as early a stage as possible in the discussion of a problem. The problem is then followed throughout the whole decision-making process and all opportunities are taken to influence the form of the decision. This work is facilitated by the fact that the SFS is accorded representation on government committees appointed to investigate matters of interest to the organization. The SFS is in some cases also represented on the government bodies whose work affects the students' interests.[95]

SFS can take some or all of the credit for a number of accomplishments since the late 1940s. The organization claims major credit for the formation of the 1955 University Committee, which laid the basis for the enormous expansion of higher education. They have continued their pressures for increased expansion. Some student unions have developed detailed proposals pertaining to revisions in the university curricula, but they always canalize their opinions and proposals through the central organization, SFS. The organization also claims credit for increasing the amount and conditions of loans available to students, and for the student allowance of 1750 kronor ($350), which all students began to receive in the 1965–1966 school year. They have also succeeded in getting favorable government loans for the building of student housing. Rooms are now available in student housing for one-third of all Swedish students. The organization has also negotiated with the National Railways, providing students with round-trip tickets during the school year at one-way prices. In the 1950s, SFS entered into agreements with the Swedish Booksellers Association, obtaining a certain discount on Swedish and foreign textbooks. One present concern of SFS is to bring a credit system into the universities aimed at shortening the length of time students need to spend in the university and to bring more organization and predictability into the process of higher education.

Intellectual Style

Swedish scholarship and discussion of ideas to a very high degree reflect an empirical and positivist methodology. For example, Swedish sociology, for the most part is "hard data" sociology; it has little place for speculation, and is not comfortable with propositions that are not clearly and conventionally testable. In an overview of Scandinavian sociology Erik Allardt has written:

The positivist tradition . . . has probably been stronger in Swedish sociology than in the other three countries. There has been a cautious attitude toward speculations and loosely formulated ideas. The Swedish sociologists have in general exercised a greater care in the collection of data than their colleagues in the other [Scandinavian] countries. The tendency to use quantitative methods has been strong.[96]

Political science and history, which have been methodologically close in Sweden, place an enormous emphasis on the criticism of sources, are historically statistical, and cautious about generalization. According to Ingemar Hedenius, the well-known Professor of Philosophy at Uppsala, a basic dictum in Swedish scholarship is that after one has presented and interpreted his data and wishes to speculate on them, he should resist the impulse. Even Swedish literary criticism is characterized by a high degree of empiricism, a reluctance to use concepts without clear-cut referents, and a crisp clarity.

A word of explanation about this style: Of primary importance is the strength and pervasiveness of positivist analysis, which came to dominate Swedish philosophy in the 1920s and 1930s.[97] The potency of positivist analysis must be seen as part of the revolt against the philosophical and methodological idealism that characterized Swedish scholarship (but not at all completely) up to around World War I. The statistical heritage of Sweden, probably unequaled in the world, is perhaps another factor in the fundamental empiricism of the Swedish intellectual style. Related to this, and in contrast with Norway, is the lack of much intellectual and cultural interchange with England, to say nothing of the United States, until after World War I, and intellectual influences from the Anglo-American countries were not great until after World War II. Sweden traditionally had the kind of tutelary relation with Germany that Norway had with England prior to World War I.

The influence of analytic philosophy on the whole intellectual style of the Swedes has been stressed by Lars Gustafsson:

This, unavoidably, has left its marks on the general debate on ideas. In the first place, the influence of analytical philosophy has had an extraordinarily favorable effect on the technique of argumentation and on general conceptual clarity. The abstract, free-wheeling speaking with tongues met sometimes in literary essays is pleasantly unusual in our discussions. But most of all the philosophical influence has had another consequence—it has promoted a rational attitude, an inclination toward basing positions on facts and a definite disinclination toward accepting emotive or irrational forms of concepts in discussions about ideas and problems. Logical shortcomings and lack of clarity are not unusual, but they are not excused by saying that life is more important than logic.[98]

The Anglo-American concept of intellectual in the sense of one who plays with and talks about ideas outside of his specific area of competence has little applicability to Swedish academics and scientists. By this definition there are few intellectuals in Sweden. The whole idea of an intellectual apart from expert knowledge does not have much standing.[99] Besides academics and scientists, the other major intellectual categories are journalists and writers, and the latter's claim to expert knowledge is hard to establish. Intellectuals—in other words "experts"—are to a very great extent included in effective political and cultural life; there are few free, unattached intellectuals. This is perhaps part of the explanation of why even most radicals seem to have a respect for the fundamental soundness of Swedish institutions, even when being critical of their operation.

One of the great difficulties of communication between Swedish and Anglo-American academics and scientists is the former's reticence—and the latter's lack of it—to talk in areas where they are not expert, their literal respect for truth, and their discomfort with high-level generalization. The different styles of Anglo-American, particularly English, and Swedish "intellectuals" perhaps represent the extremes within the Northwestern European context. During my years in Sweden I observed surprisingly little interaction between visiting Anglo-American academics and their Swedish counterparts. This was more true of the English whom I believe sometimes intimidated their Swedish colleagues with their cleverness and disdain for shop talk. Typical reactions of these Englishmen to their Swedish colleagues was to see them as bores, as having "nothing to say," though certainly as competent. Much of the difficulty of interaction at this level is the specialist, as opposed to the generalist, orientation of the Swedes combined with their general rectitude, modesty, and literalness. These generalizations apply less to Swedish academics who have spent time in Britain or the United States; they seem much affected by the experience and "looser" in their intellectual style. Some corroboration of these generalizations comes from my observations of Norwegian academics whose intellectual style is closer to the Anglo-American.[100]

Notes

1. This observation was quite categorically made to me by Professor Erik Lönnroth of Uppsala University.
2. See, for example, Bror Rexed, "Universiteten i ett dynamiskt samhälle," *Tiden*, 55 (November 1963), 524–531.
3. See Hastings Rashdall, *The Universities of Europe in the Middle Ages*, 2 vols. (Oxford: Clarendon Press, 1936); Uppsala University is discussed in Vol. II, pp. 298–299. See various writings by C. Annerstedt on the history of Uppsala University. The only recent university history that I have found is Sven Tunberg, *Stockholms högskolas historia före 1950* (Stockholm: P. A. Norstedt, 1957).
4. On the place of Uppsala University in the national culture in the seventeenth century, see Alrik Gustafson, *A History of Swedish Literature* (Minneapolis: University of Minnesota Press, 1961), pp. 75–109.
5. P. D. A. Atterbom and Erik Gustaf Geijer at Uppsala and Esaias Tegnér at Lund. See Gustafson, *ibid.*, pp. 153–197.
6. For a chronological listing of the founding dates of the Swedish universities and special institutes, see Sten Carlsson and Jerker Rosén, *Svensk Historia* (Stockholm: Svenska Bokförlaget, 1961), Vol. II, pp. 446–447.
7. See *The World of Learning 1966–67* (London: Europa Publications, 1967), *passim*. For a popular survey of the Universities of Europe, see Anthony Kerr, *The Universities of Europe* (London: Bowes & Bowes, 1962).
8. Some of the material in the next four sections of this chapter appeared in Richard F. Tomasson, "Some Observations on Higher Education in Sweden," *Journal of Higher Education*, 37 (December 1966), 493–501.
9. These reports consist of the following S.O.U.'s: 1957: 24, 51; 1958: 11, 21, 32; 1959: 45; 1963: 9, 10. (S.O.U. is an abbreviation for *Statens Offentliga Utredningar*.)

10. *Higher Education: Report of the Committee Appointed by the Prime Minister under the Chairmanship of Lord Robbins,* Cmnd. 2154 (London: Her Majesty's Stationery Office, 1963).

11. *Ibid.,* p. iii.

12. *S.O.U.,* 1959: 45, pp. 118–130, 194–200, 326, 436.

13. *S.O.U.,* 1959: 24, pp. 23–77.

14. *Dagens Nyheter,* February 20, 1968, p. 20.

15. For example, William H. Whyte, Jr., Robert Hutchins, and Jacques Barzun.

16. Robbins, *op. cit.,* pp. 6–7 and passim.

17. Sten-Sture Landström, *Svenska ambetsmäns sociala ursprung* (Uppsala and Stockholm: Almqvist & Wiksell, 1954), p. 130.

18. See Anthony Sampson, *The Anatomy of Britain Today* (New York: Harper & Row Colophon, 1966), pp. 259–260. He says on p. 260, "In the 1964 examinations, out of 51 successful candidates, 15 had taken degrees in classics, 18 in history, *one* in mathematics and *none* in science and technology."

19. Robbins, *op. cit.,* p. 69. This Swedish estimate is that of the Chancellor of the Universities; see *Uppsala Nya Tidning* September 10, 1964, p. 11.

20. *Dagens Nyheter* February 20, 1968, p. 20.

21. Gösta Carlsson and Bengt Geeser, "Universities as Selecting and Socializing Agents: Some Recent Swedish Data," *Acta Sociologica,* 9 (1966), pp. 26–27.

22. Robin M. Williams, Jr., *American Society,* rev. ed. (New York: Knopf, 1960), p. 315.

23. Abraham Flexner, *Universities: American, English, German* (New York: Oxford, 1930), p. 41.

24. Philip Sandblom and Sven Kjöllerström, "The University of Lund," in Uppsala Studentkår, *The Intellectual Face of Sweden* (Uppsala: Uppsala Studentkår, 1964), p. 25.

25. A graduate student in economics who had been a student at both the Stockholm School of Economics and the Harvard Business School told me that at the former there was a well-defined informal status hierarchy among the students based on family background. He pointed out that this could be objectively observed at the school's eating facilities. However, no other Swedish institution of higher education has such a high proportion of students of upper-class backgrounds. My informant here, by the way, is a Count (*greve*) in the Swedish nobility. I doubt if such marked distinctions would be observed at other Swedish universities.

26. Cited in Donald W. Hutchings, *Technological Education in Sweden* (Stockholm: Swedish Institute, 1962), pp. 6–7.

27. *Ibid.,* p. 6.

28. Edward C. McDonagh, Sven Wermlund, and John F. Crowther, "Relative Professional Status as Perceived by American and Swedish University Students," *Social Forces,* 38 (October 1959), 65–69.

29. See the interesting article by Austen Albu, "Taboo on Expertise," *Encounter,* No. 118 (July 1963), 45–50.

30. Robbins, *op. cit.*, p. 177.

31. Hutchings, *op. cit.*, p. 2.

32. The number of professors at various universities cited in this paragraph are from *The World of Learning, 1966–67, op. cit.*, passim.

33. Calculated from figures given in *Statistical Abstract of Sweden* (Stockholm: Statistiska Centralbyrån, 1963), p. 305.

34. There appears to be little collaborative research among equals when compared with the United States. Some of the ideas in this paragraph were suggested to me by Henry Valen of the Institute for Social Research in Oslo.

35. On the selection of professors in Sweden, see Ernst Ekman, "Selecting a Professor in Sweden," *AAUP Bulletin*, 41 (Autumn 1955), 547–551.

36. *S.O.U.*, 1957: 24, p. 147.

37. *Ibid.*, p. 146.

38. Bernard Berelson, *Graduate Education in the United States* (New York: McGraw-Hill, 1960), p. 157.

39. Lars Gunnar Sillén, "Studenten, en fackla att tända eller ett kärl att fylla?" *Gaudeamus*, No. 8 (1949), pp. 14–17.

40. Robbins, *op. cit.*, pp. 174–180.

41. Stanley Hoffman, *et al.*, *In Search of France* (Cambridge: Harvard University Press, 1963), p. 73.

42. For comparisons between the United States and Sweden on this, see Herbert Tingsten, *Dagbok från Amerika* (Stockholm: P. A. Norstedt, 1968), pp. 67–69.

43. *S.O.U.*, 1959: 45, p. 19.

44. See *Statistical Abstract of Sweden, op. cit.*, for appropriate years.

45. *Dagens Nyheter*, February 20, 1968, p. 20.

46. *S.O.U.*, 1963: 53, p. 49.

47. *Ibid.*, p. 51.

48. Quoted by Leila Sussman, "Summary Review of the Rapporteur," *Social Objectives in Educational Planning* (Paris: Organization for Economic Co-operation and Development, 1967), pp. 17–18.

49. See Sten Carlsson, *Bonde-präst-ämbetsman* (Stockholm: Bokförlaget Prisma, 1962), pp. 81, 100. For data on Norway see Vilheim Aubert, *et al.*, "Akademikare i norsk samfunnsstruktur, 1800–1950," *Tidskrift for samfunnsforkning*, 1 (December 1960), pp. 185–204, esp. 196–199.

50. *Studentekonomiska undersökningen 1968* (Lund: Sociologiska institutionen, 1968), mimeo, p. 26. For the Finnish percentage, see Elina Haavio-Mannila, "Aktivitet och passivitet bland kvinnor i Finland," in *Kynne eller kön* (Stockholm: Raben & Sjogren, 1966), pp. 103–144, esp. 122. For 1963–1964 the percentage of female students was 35.1 percent.

51. *S.O.U.*, 1963: 53, p. 56.

52. *Studentekonomiska, op. cit.* pp. 121–122.

53. Torben Agersnap, *Studenterundersøgelsen, 1959* (Copenhagen: J. A. Schultz Universitets—Bogtrykkeri, 1961), pp. 22–23.

54. Frederik van Heek, "Soziale Faktoren in den Niederlanden, die einer Optimalen Nachwuchsauslese für Akademische Berufe im Wege Stehen,"

in David V. Glass and Rene König (eds.), *Soziale Schichtung und soziale Mobilitat* (Köln und Opladen: Westdeutscher Verlag, 1961), p. 245. (Vol. 5 of *Kölner Zeitschrift für Soziologie und Sozialpsychologie*.)

55. Leopold Rosenmayr, "Soziale Schichtung, Bildungsweg und Bildungsziel im Jugendalter," in *ibid.*, p. 274.

56. R. F. Behrendt, *Die schweizerischen Studierenden an der Universität Bern* (Bern/Stuttgart: Verlag Paul Haupt, 1960), p. 63. (Vol. 4 of *Berner Beiträge zur Soziologie*.)

57. *Annuaire statistique de la France, resultats de 1962* (Paris: Institut national de la statistique, 1963), p. 57.

58. Ralf Dahrendorf, "The Crisis in German Education," in Walter Laquer and George L. Mosse (eds.), *Education and Social Structure in the Twentieth Century* (New York: Harper Torchbooks, 1967), p. 43.

59. Tore Lindbekk, "Den sosiale rekruttering til de akademiske profesjoner i vår tid," *Tidsskrift for samfunnsforskning*, 3 (Oslo: Universitetsforlaget, December 1962), p. 240.

60. See *Statistical Yearbook of Norway* (Oslo: Statistisk Sentralbyrå) for appropriate years.

61. Paivi Elovainio, *Korkeakolu-uran ja opintoalan valinta*, in Research Reports from the Institute of Sociology, No. 58 (Helsinki: University of Helsinki, 1966), pp. 123, 130–132, mimeo.

62. *Students and Their Education*, in *Higher Education: Report of the Committee Appointed by the Prime Minister under the Chairmanship of Lord Robbins*, Cmnd. 2154 (London: Her Majesty's Stationery Office, 1963), Appendix Two (B), p. 5.

63. *Ibid.*, pp. 428–429. These figures are for entering students in 1955. The assumption is that they were about the same in 1961. The original source is P. K. Kelsall, *Applications for Admissions to Universities* (Association of Universities of the British Commonwealth, 1957).

64. *Ibid.*, pp. 428–429. The discussion on p. 428 gives an overall figure for Wales of 46 percent, but the table on p. 429 gives a total of 40 percent—46 percent among men and 31 percent among women.

65. Anthony Sampson, *op. cit.*, p. 218.

66. Dominican Bureau of Statistics, *University Student Expenditure and Income in Canada, 1956–1957* (Ottawa: Dominican Bureau of Statistics, 1959), Chap. 19, Table 11. Quoted in John Porter, *The Vertical Mosaic* (Toronto: University of Toronto Press, 1965), p. 184.

67. See discussion and citations in Richard F. Tomasson, "From Elitism to Egalitarianism in Swedish Education," *Sociology of Education*, 38 (Spring 1965), pp. 221–222.

68. See Kerr, *op. cit.*, pp. 55, 76–77, and Nigel Grant, *Soviet Education* (Middlesex: Penguin Books, 1964), pp. 118–119.

69. The source of this estimate is the Swedish journalist Gunnar Fredrikson.

70. See Sveriges Officiella Statistik, *Högre Studier* (Stockholm: Statistiska Centralbyrån) for recent years.

71. For example, Kingman Brewster, Jr., President of Yale, said in 1964 that "moral capacity" was a factor in the admission of freshmen; see *Time*,

October 2, 1964, p. 87. The use of any such nonacademic criteria would be looked on with abhorrence in Scandinavia.

72. Carlsson and Geeser, *op. cit.*, p. 27.

73. *The Intellectual Face of Sweden*, *op. cit.*, pp. 97–98.

74. Kerr, *op. cit.*, p. 38.

75. For a detailed account of student politics in Sweden and the other Scandinavian countries, see Richard F. Tomasson and Erik Allardt, "Scandinavian Students and the Politics of Organized Radicalism," in Seymour M. Lipset and Philip G. Altbach (eds.), *Students in Revolt* (Boston: Houghton Mifflin, 1969), pp. 96–126. See also Erik Allardt and Richard F. Tomasson, "Stability and Strains in Scandinavian Student Politics," *Daedalus*, 97 (Winter 1968), pp. 156–165. The entire issue is devoted to student politics.

76. Clark Kerr, "From Apathy to Confrontation," prepared for Conference on Students and Politics (Puerto Rico: Center for International Affairs, Harvard University and the University of Puerto Rico, March 27–April 1, 1967), mimeo.

77. *The New York Times*, March 29, 1968, p. 15.

78. William H. Sewell and Oluf M. Davidson, *Scandinavian Students on an American Campus* (Minneapolis: University of Minnesota Press, 1961), p. 19.

79. Franklin D. Scott, *The American Experience of Swedish Students* (Minneapolis: University of Minnesota Press, 1956), pp. 67–88.

80. See UNESCO, *World Survey of Education* (New York: UNESCO Publications, 1966), Vol. IV, pp. 514–515. This point has also been discussed with the German sociologist Günther Lüschen, who is now at the University of Illinois.

81. *Verdandi:'genom femtio år* (Stockholm: Hugo Gebers förlag, 1932).

82. From the introduction by Ingemar Hedenius, a well-known Professor of Philosophy at Uppsala, in C. A. Wachtmeister (ed.), *Ateistens handbok* (Verdandi: Bökforlaget Prisma, 1964), p. 12.

83. Wachtmeister, *ibid.*, passim.

84. Ingrid Fredriksson (ed.), *Könsroller* (Verdandi:. Bokförlaget Prisma, 1964).

85. The information on the activities of Verdandi since 1965 has been supplied by Sten Johansson, an Uppsala sociologist and past chairman of Verdandi.

86. For a history of the first forty years of the organization, see *Föreningen Heimdal, 1891–1931* (Uppsala: Lundequitska bokhandeln, 1931). In a very moderate way, Heimdal continues to support these same value orientations.

87. A phrase from a recent *Heimdal* pamphlet inviting membership.

88. Quoted in Jorgen Ullenhag, *Studentliberal utveckling: Liberala studentförbundet åren 1947–1962* (Stockholm: Sveriges liberala studentförbund, 1963), p. 48.

89. However, there is much in all these journals that is not narrowly political.

90. Clarté was founded in France in the 1920s by Henri Barbusse to promote international socialism.

91. Clarté constitution, revised 1966.

92. See a discussion of analogous developments elsewhere, such as, Frank A.

Pinner, "Student Trade-Unionism in France, Belgium, and Holland," *Sociology of Education*, 37 (Spring 1964), 177–199.

93. See T. Mailand Christensen, "The Participation of Students in Governing Bodies—Myth or Reality," *Social Problems of Students: Report on the Council of Europe Seminar* (Oslo: Scandinavian University Books, 1966), p. 40. The Seminar took place in Oslo, Norway, July 25–31, 1965.

94. Tobisson, "The Swedish National Union of Students (*SFS*)," in Uppsala Studentkår, *op. cit.*, p. 38.

95. *Ibid.*, p. 39.

96. Erik Allardt, "Scandinavian Sociology," *Information sur les Sciences Sociales*, VI (August 1967), 240.

97. See Lars Gustafsson, *The Public Dialogue in Sweden: Current Issues of Social, Esthetic and Moral Debate*, Claude Stephenson (tr.) (Stockholm: P. A. Norstedt, 1964), pp. 24–44.

98. *Ibid.*, p. 42.

99. Gustafsson, *op. cit.*, p. 14, writes: "With some degree of correctness, it might be said that the Swedish debate on ideas is seldom or never carried on by specialists. Those taking part in it seldom have any other possibility of influencing the society around them than that which lies in the actual expression of opinion." Here he is referring primarily to the debate on issues in the daily press. This is certainly an exception to my point, but I still regard the comparison with the Anglo-American countries as valid.

100. This is an impressionistic observation, but I believe many others would make the same observation.

VI

Men, Women, and the Family

Premarital sex, in all its
guises, is frequently associated
with Sweden, and it is candidly
admitted as well as practiced.
—BIRGITTA LINNÉR[1]

One of the areas of striking difference between Sweden (or Scandinavia) and the other Western societies is the generally advanced status of women, and the lesser degree of sex-role differentiation. Much of this chapter will deal with subjects rather closely related to this topic—various indicators of sexual differentiation, premarital sex, and the persistently low fertility that has characterized Swedish society for a number of decades.

Sex roles and the relations between the sexes are staples of the on-going Swedish culture debate, which is more vigorous in Sweden than in any of the other Scandinavian countries.[2] There are three ideal typical positions.[3] The first we might call the traditional position, the view that sees the wife-mother role as sufficient for most women and deserving of greater public prestige and respect than it receives in contemporary Sweden. This position has few articulate exponents and is viewed negatively and even contemptuously by most people who write and speak on the subject. (I would guess, however, that there is quite some support for this position throughout the society, if not among the more articulate sections of it.) A second, the moderate position, is that which holds that women have two roles, that of wife-mother and that of work, a view articulated by Alva Myrdal and Viola Klein in *Women's Two Roles* published in 1956.[4] The radical position, the third, criticizes this view for saying nothing about men's role and for assuming many of the elements of the traditional role distinctions.[5] It holds that men's role, too, must be changed, that they, for example, must share equally in parental duties and in the care of the household, and that work and career must be as important to women as to men. It is certainly the radical view that is dominant in the Liberal and Social Democratic press, among university students, and among intellectuals in general. It is the strength of this radical position and the weakness of the traditional position that is so distinctive of the public discussion of sex roles in Sweden.

A self-conscious ideological emphasis on equality between the sexes in work, education, and in all official areas characterizes Swedish society. The Labor Market Committee, the trade-union movement, the education committees that have planned the school reforms, the press, the government, all of the political parties (though least the Agrarians) are committed to the principle of absolute equality in job placement, pay, promotion, and training. Some of the press, led by *Dagens Nyheter*, now use *fru* (Mrs.) to refer to any woman over twenty, arguing that there is no distinction made in a man's title based on his marital status, so there should not be for a woman. (But it has not had much general impact.) Swedish (and Scandinavian) women are never addressed by adding *fru* to their husband's name as in the Anglo-American societies. A number of Swedish women keep their maiden names after marriage, which they can legally do, and some add their husband's name to their own. There is no sexual differentiation in room assignments in Swedish universities, and the Swedish YMCA and YWCA have been merged into one organization. Indeed it takes a certain degree of courage in contemporary Sweden to publicly defend the traditional role for women or the conventional relation between the sexes.

Yet there is a clear gap between the equality demanded by the ideological emphasis on equality and the reality of its practical application. Women are in varying degrees discriminated against in employment, their pay is lower than that of men—though mainly because they occupy lower-level jobs—they remain very much underrepresented in the highest-status occupations—though less so than in most other developed societies—and so forth. And, the norms demanding equality between the sexes are not nearly so well followed in private life as in public life.[6] Though there has been a great deal of change in recent years, the division of labor within the home could hardly be said to be egalitarian in any absolute sense. Among younger Swedes, the role of the husband in household duties and child care is probably not much different from what it is in the United States, though this will probably change in future years. The ideological pressures toward sexual equality and minimal sexual differentiation are far greater in Swedish than in American society. One indication of the general concern with the issue of sex roles is the much greater emphasis that it has as a subject of study in Scandinavian social science as compared with its American counterpart.[7]

There is interesting cross-national variation in the relation between ideology and actual behavior in this area. In none of the Scandinavian countries is the emphasis on sexual equality more intense than in Sweden. Yet in Finnish society, where the issue is much less articulated, there is less sexual differentiation in a number of areas, such as education and work, than one finds in Swedish society. Perhaps of fundamental significance is the observation that Finnish does not even distinguish between "he" and "she" in the third person singular.

In Sweden there is clearly less sex self-consciousness, less cultural emphasis on girls and women being "feminine" and men and boys being "masculine," than one finds in American society, and, of course, much less than in the Latin societies. Self-consciousness about the nude body is less among Swedes than most other Western peoples. Nude bathing among families is not uncommon. Children are not put in bathing suits until they ask to be, usually at age six or seven. Swedes, a modest people in most areas, do not disdain to remove their clothes and put on their bathing suits in public. And, a front-side view in color of the nude cast of the musical *Hair* appeared in *Dagens Nyheter*.[8] There is not much sex-role differentiation in interpersonal relations in Sweden. In spite of the ritual and formality so characteristic of social relations in Sweden, the "politeness" that middle-class etiquette prescribes for men to show toward women is less developed than in American society. The whole body of forms whereby a "gentleman" helps a "lady" on with her coat, opens the car door for her, offers her a seat on the bus, and jumps to push her chair in at the table or to light her cigarette are not commonly practiced or expected in Sweden. American movies from the 1930s and 1940s in which the good guy leaps out of his car to open the door for the good girl bring forth great laughter from young Swedish movie audiences.

Sexual Differentiation

While all societies have sexual differentiation, more or less distinct
social roles for men and women, there are sharp variations among the
industrialized societies in the extent and characteristics of this differentiation. Among Western societies, the Latin countries (least so
France) are those with the greatest sexual differentiation in most
spheres, the Scandinavian societies, Finland, and the Soviet Union
(particularly Russia) appear to have the least differentiation, and the
English-speaking societies and the other developed countries seem to
fall in between.[9]

In looking at sexual differentiation it might be useful to compare
the situation in Sweden with that in the United States. The differences are rather marked, and the trends over the past three or four
decades have often moved in quite opposite directions. In Sweden
there has been a great emphasis on lessening sexual differentiation and
enhancing female equality in all spheres, which has not been the
dominant trend in American society—at least since the early 1940s.[10]

By the early twentieth century, the United States, with its open and
fluid social structure, acquiesced rather quickly and easily to feminist
demands. With a long tradition of higher education for women behind them, American women probably had as many opportunities and
were as important in their society as were the women in any other
modern society. Into the 1920s there may have been as high a proportion of women in the free professions and in upper-managerial jobs as
anywhere. Since the early 1940s, however, there has been a decline in
the proportion of high-status positions held by women, and feminine
protest has gone out of style, though there were signs, beginning in
the late 1960s, that it may be returning. In Sweden, on the other hand,
there has been a continuing increase in the proportion of professional
and career positions occupied by women from the 1920s and earlier
to the present. Criticism of the traditional aspects of the role of women,
and radical prescriptions for change, have continued unabated in
Sweden without being regarded as eccentric. A commitment to full
sexual equality and minimal sexual differentiation is everywhere the
official ideology in Sweden.

The proportion of professional and upper-level managerial positions occupied by women is one measure of the diversity of role possibilities for women in an industrial society, and it is perhaps the most

readily available and most significant indicator of sexual differentiation in an industrial society. It is an important and perhaps paradoxical observation that the proportion of married women who work in a society is not much related to this. A few examples will make this clear. France probably has the highest proportion of married women working of any Western society, yet, outside of Paris, women make up only a small percentage of the free professions (yet higher than in the United States), and women did not get the right to vote until after World War II.[11] Switzerland, too, has a high proportion of married women in the labor force, yet only a small proportion of the professions are made up of women, and there is still no female suffrage in most of the cantons. In Sweden, on the other hand, there are many job possibilities for women, even though a lower proportion of married women work as compared with France, Great Britain, Switzerland, or the United States, but a relatively *high* proportion of dentists, doctors, lawyers, and legislators are women. Yet even in Sweden the proportion of women in traditionally male occupations is not great, in an absolute sense, and it is higher in both Finland and the Soviet Union. The majority of working women continue to be found in "female" and "neuter" types of work, in clerical and kindred occupations, light manufacturing, service occupations, school teaching, social work, and nursing.

There are a number of other diverse indicators of sexual differentiation in a society other than occupational distribution, such as education, the extent of a double-standard sexual morality, differences in political behavior and participation, legal equality, personality differences between the sexes, and mortality differences. Following is a discussion of each of these:

Education. A basic principle in all of the postwar Swedish educational reform has been the minimization of sexual differentiation and the maximization of sexual equality. All *grundskolor* are coeducational and all secondary education soon will be. By the early 1970s all of the *flickskolor* (girls' schools) will have been abolished. There is almost no differentiation in the subjects that boys and girls study in the *grundskola*. In the middle stage (fourth, fifth, and sixth classes), boys are required to have at least twenty lessons each year in textile handicraft and girls at least twenty in woodworking.[12] In grade six, boys may, by a decision of the local school board, exchange one of four weekly lessons in handicraft for domestic science, which includes teaching in the care of infants.

By the mid-1960s almost half of the *studentexamen* were awarded to girls as compared with 35.0 percent between 1941 and 1945, 18.9 percent between 1921 and 1925, and a mere 3.4 percent between 1886 and 1890.[13] Yet girls remain markedly underrepresented in the scientific-mathematical line of the general gymnasium and in the commercial and technical gymnasia.[14] Since 1873, when women were first allowed to take academic degrees in Sweden, to the present, the proportion of women in higher education has increased. For a number of years the proportion of women in higher education has been higher in Sweden than in the United States.[15] This is evident in the high proportion of women who are preparing for professional careers in Sweden. In 1967–1968 32 percent of all students in the faculties of theology were women, 20 percent in law, 24 percent in medicine, 65 percent in humanities, and 23 percent in the natural sciences.[16] In addition, 6 percent of those studying to be engineers were women, 13 percent in business administration, 38 percent in dentistry, 18 percent studying to be veterinarians, and 39 percent studying to be pharmacists. These percentages are all much higher than are found in the United States. On the other hand, the teachers' colleges—which are not considered a part of higher education in Sweden—have a larger proportion of males planning to be primary school teachers than do such programs in the United States.

Sexual Morality. There is little double-standard morality in Sweden. The whole topic of premarital sex will be dealt with in some detail in the next section.

Political behavior. Women secured the right to vote in national elections in Sweden in 1919, just a year before the United States. There has been a marked decline in the sex differential since then, which is easily measured by subtracting the female from the male voting percentage. In the 1921 Lower House election, the difference was 14.8 points, but by 1960 the difference had declined to 2.3 points, and by 1964 to 2.1 points. Rarely in national elections without compulsory voting are such small male excesses recorded.[17] In American presidential elections of the 1940s and 1950s, the differential ranged between ten and fourteen points.[18] It should be noted, however, that there is a relationship between the magnitude of the sex differential and the proportion of the electorate which votes. We might even formulate this as a proposition: the greater the proportion of an electorate that votes, the smaller will be the sex differential. Yet in spite of this, the sex differential in voting has become very small in Sweden.

In fact at all ages into the fifties there is now virtually no difference between the percentage of males and females who vote.[19]

Another manifestation of a low degree of sexual differentiation in Sweden is in *how* men and women vote. Unlike the situation in other countries, women do not appear to vote more conservatively than men.[20] In contrast to Britain, Norway, and a number of Continental countries, Swedish women are as likely to vote socialist as are men; also, women are hardly more likely to support the Conservative party than are men. How exceptional Sweden is here is indicated by Lipset's observation that "in practically every country for which we have data (except perhaps the United States), women tend to support the conservative parties more than men do."[21]

Yet while Swedish women vote almost as much as Swedish men, and do so no more conservatively, they do have appreciably less political information. A 1960 interview sample of voters included nine knowledge questions, mostly involving what party took a particular stand on certain important issues.[22] The differences between the percentage of men and women giving correct answers was over twenty points for five of the nine questions, and for the other four, the men were more knowledgeable, though to not as great an extent.

Another measure of the political participation of women that varies greatly among societies is their representation in legislative bodies. In 1963 14.7 percent of those in the Lower House and 9.3 percent of those in the Upper House of the Riksdag were women as compared with 4.2 percent of those in the United States House of Representatives and 2 percent of those in the United States Senate in the same year. The proportion of women in the Lower House of the Riksdag was the highest in any national legislature in the world, acording to a United States Department of Labor report.[23] In the 1962 Communal elections, 12.2 percent of the elected members were women; 27 percent of those elected in Stockholm were women.

Legal equality. It can probably be said of Sweden and the other Scandinavian countries that there is virtual equality of the sexes throughout the entire legal code. The legal manifestations of sexual differentiation were the first to be eliminated in the vigorous Scandinavian movement for female equality. The contrast between Scandinavia and the other developed societies is marked, particularly with a country like Italy, where, for example, adultery has been a crime for women but not for men.[24] Some of the most important dates in the movement toward full legal equality are the following:

1845   Law passed giving men and women equal rights of inheritance.

1862   Women given right to vote in municipal elections.

1863   Women given right to work in Post and Telegraph offices.

1870   Women allowed to matriculate in the universities.

1872   Certain laws repealed giving women over twenty-five complete independence from their guardians.

1873   Women allowed to take all degrees except in the faculty of theology and certain higher law degrees.

1884   Unmarried women declared of age at twenty-one.

1909   Women eligible for election to city councils.

1918   Women given equal voting rights with men in *municipal* elections.

1919   Women given equal voting rights with men in *all* elections.

1921   New marriage laws ended husband's legal tutelage. Married women now of age at twenty-one and able to take independent legal action.

1922   First women (three) elected to the Lower House of the Riksdag.

1928   Girls admitted to the public gymnasia on the same basis as boys.

1939   Law passed prohibiting women from being dismissed because of engagement and marriage; extended to include pregnancy in 1946.

1949   New parentage law provided that both parents act as guardians of children born in wedlock; Amendment to the Constitution passed holding, among other things, that appointments to the Civil Service are to be made irrespective of sex.

1958   Legislation passed giving women equal right to be ordained in the Church of Sweden; later also passed by the Church Assembly.[25]

The ordination of women was the last important legal obstacle in the battle for full female equality, although in one unimportant instance the law does not recognize female equality: the daughters of the House of Bernadotte cannot inherit the throne according to the Law of Succession adopted in 1810. There is certain differential treatment of men and women in welfare legislation in which women have certain advantages; for example, a widow above a certain age gets a pension, but a widower does not, and a housewife has sickness insurance, but a man who functions as a housewife does not.

Personality differences between the sexes. Swedish women approximate the conventional "national character" description of Swedes to a lesser extent than do the men. There is general agreement on the description of Swedes as stolid and stiff, shy or reserved, formal and conventional, inhibited—even dull, nonexpressive, more interested in things than in people, and so forth.[26] Among Western European peoples they are described—and are—virtually polar opposites of the Italians as portrayed, for example, by Luigi Barzini and certain Italian film makers.[27]

Yet what has impressed me and a number of other observers is that Swedish women approximate these labels appreciably less than do the men.[28] I might argue that the differences between Swedish and Italian women in "national character" are less than those between Swedish and Italian men. On the more outgoing personality of Swedish women, consider, for example, the observation of Kingsley Martin:

Why is it that . . . adult men are so often—the best word is perhaps 'formal,' some say 'conventional' or even 'stiff?' The women remain charming, easy to talk to, anxious at every level, it seemed to me, to make life pleasant for everyone. The men, after they have settled down and gone into business, tend only to become communicative at night when they have drunk quite a lot of alcohol. I remember on a former visit remarking that some of them have a spiritual heel-click in their voices and that their hands go automatically to the place where their swords used to hang in the days of Gustavus Adolphus, and where, as symbols from the past, the police still carry them. They are Teutons who've become good, just as Prussians are Teutons gone wrong.[29]

Herbert Hendin, who interviewed twenty-five suicidal and twenty-five nonsuicidal Swedes for his study *Suicide and Scandinavia*, points out that "the men were somewhat harder to reach emotionally than were the women."[30] He goes on to say that, after the initial barriers were overcome, "the men proved to be in much poorer contact with their own feelings than were the women. They showed evidence of emotional reactions to wives, parents, employers or friends, but seemed unaware of these reactions. Particularly difficult for them was the open expression of anger or a frank criticism of anyone in their immediate surroundings."[31] Apparently this was less true of the women.

Sweden is a society in which there is an enormous emphasis on controlling one's emotion, acting rationally, and maintaining a dignified *persona*. Hendin claims, however, that these strictures operate with less strength for girls than for boys.[32] The Swedish ideal of *tyst och lugn*, quiet and calm, is mainly for the male child and the man. Girls and women are allowed greater manifestation of emotion and uncontrolled behavior. Indeed, as elsewhere, emotional behavior is regarded as feminine.

Yet it must also be stressed that sexual differentiation in child-rearing is not great in Sweden, particularly prior to the teens. Careful comparative study would probably find it less so than in American society. One study comparing Norwegian and Italian child-rearing found the former to differentiate much less by sex.[33]

Mortality differentials. The magnitude of sex differentials in life expectancies and death rates vary substantially among the advanced societies. Everywhere the life expectancies for females are greater than they are for males, yet in no advanced society is the sex differential in life expectancy at all ages of smaller magnitude than it is in Sweden and the other Scandinavian countries (except Finland). Actually the marked variation in life expectancies among the developed societies is mainly a variation in male life expectancies. In Sweden life expectancy for females born in the period from 1961 to 1965 was 75.70 years as compared with 73.7 for American females born in 1965, a difference of 2.0 years. Among Swedish males in the same period, life expectancy was 71.60 years as compared with 66.8 years for American men, a substantial difference of 4.8 years. Table 6.1 gives excess life expectancy for females as compared with males for Sweden, the United States, and several other developed countries. Note that the female

Table 6.1   Number of Years of Extra Life of Females as Compared with Males at Specified Ages with Male and Female Life Expectancies at Birth for Sweden and Selected Countries.

COUNTRY	Age						Life expectancy at birth	
	0	1	10	20	40	60	Male	Female
Sweden (1961–1965)	4.10	3.87	3.78	3.51	3.12	2.39	71.60	75.70
U.S. (1965)	6.9	6.7	6.6	6.4	5.7	4.1	66.8	73.70
England & Wales (1963–1965)	6.1	5.8	5.8	5.7	5.4	4.3	68.3	74.40
West Germany (1964–1965)	5.86	5.58	5.48	5.23	4.58	3.42	67.59	73.45
Netherlands (1961–1965)	4.8	4.5	4.3	4.2	3.8	3.7	71.1	75.9
New Zealand (1960–1962)	5.31	5.00	4.90	4.70	4.22	3.27	68.44	73.75

SOURCE: United Nations, *Demographic Yearbook, 1966* (New York: Statistical Office of the United Nations, 1967), Table 21.

excess is less at all ages in Sweden than in any of the other advanced societies.

The high life expectancies that the Scandinavian countries show is largely the result of life expectancies for males at birth substantially above age seventy. The only non-Scandinavian country in the world that has male life expectancies at the level of the Scandinavian countries is the Netherlands, yet even here there is a greater female excess life expectancy at all ages from birth through the upper ages.

Looking at the specific causes of death in the mortality data of the advanced countries, it is clear that a large portion of the excess mortality of males is a result of greater mortality from those deaths classified as arteriosclerotic and degenerative heart disease, which are the major and most variable of the several categories of heart disease in the *International List of the Causes of Death* of the World Health Organization. At no broad age category is there more variation than at ages forty-five to sixty-four. Note from Table 6.2 that the death rate from this major category of death is lower in Sweden than in any of the other countries except the Netherlands.[34] It is substantially less than half what it is in the United States. Note further that the absolute sex differential is lower in Sweden than in any of the other countries, including the Scandinavian countries.

Table 6.2   Death Rates by Sex at Ages 45–64 for Arteriosclerotic and Degenerative Heart Disease for Sweden and Selected Countries (per 100,000 Population).

COUNTRY	Male	Female	Male-Female
Sweden (1959)	242.8	78.1	164.7
U.S. (1959)	595.8	178.6	417.2
England and Wales (1959)	374.0	105.7	268.3
West Germany (1959)	287.5	100.6	186.9
Netherlands (1960)	248.5	72.8	175.7
New Zealand (1959)	451.2	127.7	333.5

SOURCE: United Nations, *Demographic Yearbook, 1960* (New York: Statistical Office of the United Nations, 1961), Table 19.

The explanation of the difference between, for example, Sweden and the United States may ultimately be traced to differences in extent of cigarette smoking (less in Sweden), exercise (greater in Sweden), diet, overweight (less in Sweden), and other factors of which we are not aware at present. All of these factors appear to be more related to male than to female mortality. One major difference between mortality as a sex differential and the others discussed here is that the variation is largely with the males rather than the females.

Premarital Sex

In Sweden premarital sexual behavior is pretty much in the realm of the "private." In most sections of the population there is little conflict between an official sexual morality, on the one hand, and a more permissive covert morality, on the other. The permissiveness for the unmarried that prevails in Sweden appears to have its roots in the courtship practices of the rural past.[35] Premarital sexual relations, under specific conditions, such as night courtship, were more or less tolerated under surveillance of family and community, particularly the youthful peer group, which served as the dominant agency of social control. And generally when pregnancy followed, so did marriage.

Eilert Sundt (1817–1875), a great Norwegian social observer, gave a graphic description of night courtship as he observed it in rural Norway in the mid-nineteenth century. It could just as well have been Sweden:

On a dark and dreary autumn evening, a Saturday evening, Per, a young farm hand, is standing outside the kitchen window of a farm, staring in through the dull pane. The cold weather does not bother him much, for he is young, and furthermore he feels a kind of new and strange warmth in his breast every time the fire in the chimney rises so that he feels the presence of Anne, the good servant girl, who is sitting at the spinning wheel with some other women. Indefatigable, Per waits for an hour until Anne comes out into the yard on some business or other, and now he must brace himself in order to utilize his only moment in as little awkward a manner as possible. Perhaps he will ask her if she will come with him to a dance at the community meet tomorrow. Anne understands what he is after, and therefore refuses his invitation; but she is also inventive, and knows how to find a sufficiently acceptable reason for him not to be hurt by her refusal, and it may well be that he goes off with a brighter hope than he had when he came. Next Saturday he gets to talk to her again, and it is possible that he will now notice even more clearly that his visits are not disagreeable to her. So he will certainly be on the spot the third time too, and if she accepts a little cotton scarf which he has brought her, and thanks him for it by pressing his hand, he goes home oblivious of blizzard and storm. On the fourth Saturday evening he deliberately arranges matters so that he only arrives at the farm when the people of the farm have gone to bed, and he knocks at the window-pane almost as hard as his heart is beating in his chest. And he need not worry much; for naturally Anne has been lying awake with a certain expectation until now. She comes out, and in the late evening hour, when the eyes of all others are closed, she will sit for quite awhile talking to him out in the woodshed; they must be talking about the chances of getting a cottager's job in these times, or some other reasonable livelihood. On the fifth evening he has more courage. "Oh, let me come in with you, Anne!" And while two or three girls and a boy are snoring all over the room, the two sit whispering together on the bench. On the sixth evening—there must be no interruption in Per's Saturday visits, for then Anne might think that he was out hunting in other places—on the sixth evening it so happens that Anne is quite tired from some hard work during the day; so she lies down in her bed, and lets him sit on the edge of it. It is true that Anne is not in sole possession of the bed; little Mary shares it with her; but luckily, Anne has the outer place. On the seventh evening Per again sits a while on the edge of the bed— but then he unlaces his shoes and removes his sweater, and after a short and weak resistance from Anne, he is lying by her side, puts his arm round her neck, repeats all his good promises, gets her permission, and goes to sleep. Anne will be careful, however, that he is up and gone, before any of the people of the house are out. But now Per and Anne are "acquainted" (engaged), and these nightly visits are repeated every Saturday. As they are secretly engaged, it may happen that another wooer manages to slip in to Anne before Per on some occasion; but I am imagining that Anne is a good girl, and she will then know how to get him out ("No, we mustn't talk any more. I've got to get up early tomorrow morning. I am telling you, Hans, you've got to go now!") Of course, their relation cannot long remain secret; but it is a point of honor with the other servants not to reveal this kind of secret, and as soon as it is clear that they are true to each other, so that she does not receive other boys, and he does not visit other girls, no one around them has the least thing to say against them. For according to the customs of the country this is the only way, in many of our provinces, in which young people of the servant class can become "acquainted," and in many, many cases it is done honorably and faithfully. This night wooing is of course always extremely dangerous to the flesh and the blood. But it is an error of judgment to regard all the girls who receive their wooers in this manner, as lacking in modesty and honor. Even in the class where night wooing belongs, there are certain rules for it, and there is a certain strictness in the opinions of how a virtuous girl should behave; indeed, it often happens that a girl leaves her service only for the reason that she cannot reconcile herself to being in

service together with another girl who has trespassed against the prevailing
rules, and thereby acquired a bad reputation in the servant class.[36]

A transformation of the premarital sexual patterns of the rural
people came to predominate in modern Sweden (and Scandinavia),
which is one of the aspects of the continuity that modern Sweden has
with her agrarian past. This pattern of egalitarian permissiveness tri-
umphed over the more romantic Victorian morality that developed
in the nineteenth century among the urban middle classes and the
aristocracy—essentially a double-standard morality similar to that
which has traditionally prevailed in the United States and England.
As Alva Myrdal has put it, "The interesting fact is that the habit of
fairly lax authoritarian inhibitions of the sex life of youth, which
stemmed out of the agrarian society, persisted so long that it was
paralleled by more modern patterns and thus strengthened before its
ultimate decline."[37] The continuation of these permissive patterns,
but without the social controls which surrounded them in the rural
society, was enhanced by the far-reaching secularization of Sweden
that occurred along with industrialization, particularly from the 1890s
through the 1920s. During these years modern ideas of women's
emancipation, socialist and radical-liberal rationalism, modern psy-
chology, and moral individualism had gained general circulation. And
these ideas had particularly strong impact in Sweden because of the
presence of a predominantly literate, organized, and secularized working class.

Georg Karlsson, Professor of Sociology at Umeå University and
the leading family sociologist in Sweden, disagrees with Mrs.
Myrdal's interpretation.[38] He maintains that the rational sexual permissiveness of contemporary Swedish society is a result of advanced
secularization and the indifference of Swedes to the traditional
Christian position. He would probably further support this opinion
by pointing to his research, which indicates a great increase in premarital coitus over recent years.[39]

Looking at the situation cross-nationally, however, I lean toward
Mrs. Myrdal's explanation. England is certainly secular—certainly
much more than American society is—yet sexual norms there are
hardly more permissive than in American society. Also, parts of Spain,
Italy, and France are almost as statistically secular as Sweden without
the development of any permissive premarital sex ethic, particularly
as far as women go. On the other hand, self-conscious Christians in

Sweden and the other Scandinavian countries certainly do not adhere to a permissive ethic. Their attitudes would doubtless be closer to the confused and contradictory American views on the subject than to the more permissive views that predominate in Sweden.

It should also be pointed out that Sweden is not even the most sexually permissive of the Scandinavian countries; it is Iceland. And Iceland is probably no more secular than Sweden. According to Armann Snaevarr, a professor of family law and past-rector of the University of Iceland, formal marriage is of little importance in the relationship of a couple,[40] which is indicated by the observation that about 25 percent of all births and 46 percent of first births in recent years are out of wedlock.[41] This is indeed unique among the developed societies. In Sweden only about 11 percent of all births are out of wedlock as compared with 8 percent in Denmark and 4 percent in Norway and Finland.[42] Many Icelandic couples (and some Swedish couples) do not marry until after the birth of a child or two. In Iceland, there is, in fact, little stigma attached to illegitimacy (certainly less than in Sweden), and sex relations typically begin at age fourteen or fifteen (earlier than in Sweden). This extraordinary permissiveness has its roots in the same old Scandinavian patterns as in Sweden, only the traditional patterns survived with greater force in Iceland.[43] Indeed, advanced modernization did not come until after World War II. As far as I know the sexual situation in Iceland has never been studied.

Neither Myrdal's nor Karlsson's explanation is phrased in functional terms, however. A permissive sex ethic, which is essentially a premarital sex ethic that gives females the same rights and privileges that men tacitly enjoy in other more sexually restrictive societies, is only an aspect of the general status of women in a society. When women's roles are characterized by a high level of equality with males, when there is a general value orientation that minimizes sexual differentiation, when there is a situation in which females are relatively economically independent from males (as with American Negroes), or where women's status is not primarily determined by that of their husbands, there is likely to be a permissive sex ethic.

James Coleman has argued, thinking primarily of the differences in white and Negro premarital sexual codes, that "the rigidity of premarital sexual codes varies inversely with female dominance in the determination of family status. Where females are more dominant, that is, where the system is more matriarchal, the sex codes will be less rigid then where the female's ultimate status depends on the status of her husband."[44] If the last sentence is revised somewhat, we have a good proposition that explains not only Swedish permissiveness, but also cross-national and intra-national differences in premarital sex codes. I would have it read as follows: *Where females have greater equality and are subject to less occupational and social differentiation, the premarital sex codes will be more permissive than where the female's status is completely or primarily dependent on the status of her husband.* This is closely related to Ira. L. Reiss's comment on Coleman's thesis in which Reiss suggests that a permissive sex ethic is positively related to the extent of courtship autonomy the female has—of which "female power" (Coleman's concept) is only one possible factor.[45]

Swedish students who have gone to the United States to study, while generally favorably disposed to many aspects of American university life, ". . . almost unanimously dislike the American customs governing relations between the sexes, and cite them as prime examples of American immorality and hypocrisy."[46] On the other hand, the premarital relations between the sexes in Sweden have been decried and criticized by many American observers, though perhaps not so much in recent years as earlier.[47] Consider the following comments on love in Sweden, made by the generally liberal Marya Mannes, who was not at all unfriendly toward Sweden, after a trip there in 1963, ". . . love, say observers, is more of an exercise than an emotion. For with prosperity, again, has come the removal of all those self-restraints which give meaning to the acts of living."[48] Essentially what these observations manifest is genuine normative conflict and misunderstanding resulting from the differences between a permissive egalitarian system of premarital relations and a system characterized by markedly different sex-role expectation for men and women, which covertly allows the man, but to a much lesser extent the woman, varying degrees of permissiveness and initiative.

Premarital sexual intimacy follows a different pattern in Sweden (or the other Scandinavian countries) than in the United States. In Sweden there is a greater sexual reserve in boy-girl relations. Intimacy develops slowly. There is not the emphasis on kissing and petting in the early stages of a relationship. Indeed, in the early stages of courtship, Swedes are probably more inhibited or reserved than American youth. However, to a greater extent than with American youth, intimacy proceeds to sexual intercourse.[49] There is not the leveling off at necking or heavy petting or the emphasis on technical virginity that is so common in America. A couple does not reach a plateau beyond which they feel constrained not to go. Sexual relations have been traditionally sanctioned when a couple becomes engaged—engagement is a more formal occasion in Sweden than in the United States. However, in contemporary Sweden, sexual relations are generally assumed to occur between a couple at what we would call the "going steady" stage, even between couples in their mid-teens. Little attempt is made in most circles to hide the fact that a couple is living together. Indeed, it is not unusual for such a couple to live together in a university dormitory.

Dating among young Swedes illustrates their less sexually differentiated role relations. It is conventional for a boy to meet a girl at the place of their date rather than to call for her, for a girl to pay her own way, and for a girl to go to a party by herself. Dating among college and high school students in the United States generally involves rather self-conscious playing of well-defined roles, particularly for the girl; above all, it involves being "feminine," always trying to be sexually attractive and generally intellectually passive. In Sweden dating is more casual, with strikingly less emphasis on the girl playing the "feminine" role. The girl can take the initiative more openly in establishing a relationship with a boy. Among Swedish youth, it is not infrequent for a boy and a girl to have a wholly nonromantic friendship relationship. Such cross-sex friendships, by contrast, seem to be quite rare among American youth, except when they are put in exceptional situations such as the mixed dormitory at Stanford University where the students came to regard each other "more like brothers and sisters."[50] Because foreign male students have sometimes misinterpreted gestures of friendship made by Swedish university girls, such as an invitation to their rooms for coffee, some Swedish girls have had to adopt their own double standard with non-Swedish men.[51]

The concern in American society (and elsewhere) with sex in Sweden is understandable. Things *are* different in Sweden. Attitudes toward premarital sexual relations, particularly among those going steady or engaged, *are* more permissive than one finds even in liberal circles in American society. Almost half of all brides are pregnant in Sweden. Having a child out of wedlock does not doom a girl from the society of the respectable, at least not permanently. If she lives in university housing, she will generally be entitled to larger quarters. Some congruence between sexual attitudes and sexual behavior does exist in Sweden. One result is that there is less preoccupation with sex and a more matter-of-fact attitude toward it than one finds in America or England. There is much less emphasis on sex in jokes, conversation, and as a subject of general concern, which is true in spite of the fact that some recent Swedish literature and films have portrayed sexual topics with a frankness and openness perhaps surpassed by no other country.

It is clear from several recent studies that the overwhelming majority of young Swedes have premarital intercourse and that they begin at an early age. A 1968 study found 95 to 98 percent of the married population to have had premarital intercourse.[52] A 1964 study of military draftees (most were twenty year olds) in Sweden reported 83 percent to have had sexual relations, 7 percent not to have had sexual relations, and 10 percent did not answer.[53] More striking than these percentages, however, is the observation that the median age at the time of first coitus was *under* sixteen years of age. The median age at first intercourse of a *representative* sample of Swedes aged twenty-one to twenty-five in 1968 was 16.9 years.[54] The average number of sex partners of men over thirty in 1968 was seven; among those twenty-one to thirty it was eight.[55] Several studies indicate that the extensiveness of sexual relations among teen-agers has increased substantially in recent years and that the median age at first coitus has decreased. The increase appears to have been greatest among the most conservative segments of youth. For example, among a sample of female students at a folk high school with a religious affiliation, the percentage that had engaged in sexual intercourse increased from 38 to 77 percent between 1960 and 1965.[56] Among male university students, in Sweden as in the United States a sexually conservative group, 40 percent of a group born in 1922 had had intercourse by age twenty-one as compared with 75 percent of those born in 1944.[57] Related to this is the observation that there is virtually no prostitution in Sweden.

In light of this evidence it is not at all likely, as Lester A. Kirkendall has suggested, that "if the extent and amount of premarital intercourse in both countries were known, we Americans might very well find our youth as active sexually if not more so than Swedish young people."[58] Such a statement flies in the face of the sexual traditions of the two countries and what slight evidence we have for contemporary America.[59] Sweden and the other Scandinavian countries have had rural traditions of sexual permissiveness prior to marriage that were never overcome by urban bourgeois morality. The United States, on the other hand, has a puritanical heritage with little normative tolerance for permissiveness. And the effects of these traditions continue to persist in the sexual norms and behavior of both societies.

The Swedes, like the Americans, are concerned about and sometimes lament the increased sexuality of the young. But at least they deal with the subject relatively openly, rationally, and nonmoralistically in the press and the schools, and they have provided universal sex education in the schools for a number of years.[60] From primary school through gymnasium, there is instruction in the nature of birth, sexual maturation in boys and girls, the functioning of the sex organs, sexual deviation, sex relations, contraception, masturbation, venereal disease, and premarital sex. Indeed, in the fall of 1967 there was a great uproar in Stockholm over the use of a pamphlet entitled *"Samspel"* ("Harmonious Relations") in the upper stage of the *grundskola*, for pupils aged thirteen to fifteen.[61] The booklet dealt specifically and in detail with the techniques of sexual intercourse. Some of the criticism held that it was too early an age to give such instruction and that it only belonged among older pupils; some critics held that the pamphlet was wholly objective and had no "ethical component." There is little moralizing in the more recent sex education materials and little obeisance to the norms of conventional morality, yet it cannot be said that this material offers encouragement to teenage sex relations—when a position can be detected it is the contrary.

Certain points of view are to be found in the recent sex education materials.[62] These views—and they are common if not predominant among educated Swedes—are that it is essential that youth be given the sex information they are able to absorb at a given age so that they will have it before they actually need it. Implicit through the material is the view that there is no special sexual morality, but only a general morality that should be applied to sexual relations as well as to all human relations. Yet it is explicitly pointed out that Sweden is a pluralist society where people do in fact have different views on this. There is an effort to minimize the traditional cultural differences between the sexes, and there is an absolute and complete rejection of any kind of double standard. There is an attempt to deal objectively with all topics, even those rarely dealt with in such a manner. Consider the following statement from a discussion on sex education in the home for gymnasium students, "If the children have become accustomed to seeing their parents naked, they will hardly suffer any serious emotional damage from a chance encounter with an exhibitionist."[63] Earlier it is pointed out (probably accurately) that exhibitionists "are usually insecure and meek individuals, who have no desire to harm anyone."[64]

How rapid social change has been in this area is the observation that it was not until 1938 that a 1912 law prohibiting the sale of contraceptives was repealed. The law stated, "It is prohibited to sell devices which are used for immoral purposes or to prevent the consequences of sexual intercourse . . ."[65] Pharmacies were not even allowed to sell contraceptives until 1946. Contraceptive vending machines were allowed somewhat later. Now such machines are found in the most obvious and diverse places—outside of pharmacies, near bus stops, in university buildings; and contraceptives are freely advertised, even in university newspapers. Another aspect of the sexual revolution in Sweden is the full legal toleration for written and pictorial pornography that has been achieved. The late 1960s indeed saw the arrival of a boredom with pornography in both Sweden and Denmark, after the daring pornographic revolution of the mid-1960s.[66]

Marriage, the Family, and Divorce

It has already been pointed out that marriage does not have the significance in Sweden that it does in America in changing the relationship of a couple or their general status. Almost half of Swedish couples now do not marry until after pregnancy has occurred, a minority not until after the birth of a child. Swedish couples, however, know each other *much* longer than do American couples before they marry. In one national study from 1949, it was found that only 3 percent of those interviewed had known their spouses for less than six months prior to marriage.[67] The average couple at the time of their marriage in a 1950 Uppsala study done by Georg Karlsson had known each other for a period of three to four years.[68] It is no wonder that the average age at marriage is several years later among Swedish couples than among their American counterparts. However, if there were contemporary data available it would probably show a decline in the average length of acquaintanceship prior to marriage along with the average age at marriage. The median age at marriage declined between the 1920s and 1960s more than three years to between twenty-five and twenty-six for men and between twenty-two and twenty-three for women,[69] which is still around two and a half years later than in American society.

The two above-mentioned studies also show, as do American studies, a marked relationship between the length of time a couple has known each other and marital success. The 1949 national study found that among those unhappily married one out of twelve had known each other for less than half a year as compared with one out of thirty-five in the total sample. Among those who were divorced, one out of seven couples had been acquainted for less than half a year prior to marriage. Karlsson's Uppsala study shows that couples who had known each other for more than two years before marriage reported their marriage to be satisfactory to a much greater degree than those who had known each other for less than two years.

The great majority of marriages in secular Sweden are religious, only about 6 percent are civil.[70] The reason for the low proportion of civil weddings is probably that in most places sentimentally suitable places for such weddings are not available and that marriage by civil officials is not regarded as very attractive.

One more interesting observation on marriage in Sweden is that the minimum legal age is probably the highest in the world: twenty-one for men and eighteen for women. It is likely, however, that the minimum age for men will be lowered to eighteen.

The factors associated with happiness in Swedish marriages are quite similar to those associated with happiness in American marriages, according to a comparative study by Harvey J. Locke and Georg Karlsson.[71] Besides length of acquaintanceship prior to marriage, there are also similarities in the relationship between how happiness of parents' marriage is perceived and in reporting a happy childhood— both factors being positively associated with marital happiness. In terms of personality traits "the results in the Swedish study . . . were similar to the results in Indiana. . . ." [72] In both cases similarities were found in marital happiness being related to sociability, shared attitudes toward given activities, and equality in leadership in family activities.

Among the items in which differences appeared between the two societies, were religious behavior, the demonstration of affection, and frequency of premarital and extramarital intercourse. Age at which Sunday school stopped and frequency of church attendance were not related to marital happiness in the Swedish data, unlike in the Indiana data. And just the opposite from Indiana was the observation that in Sweden "usually attending religious services was unfavorable to marital adjustment." [73] The religious behavior items were used by Locke and Karlsson as indicators of conventionality. However, because formal religious activity is not conventional in Sweden, these items are not—as the authors suggest—suitable indicators of conventionality in Sweden. Conventionality would probably be shown to be associated with marital happiness in Sweden as it is in the United States.

In the Indiana study, both affectionateness and demonstration of affection were positively related to marital adjustment. In Sweden, however, only affectionateness was related to marital adjustment, demonstration of affection was associated with maladjustment. Through informal interviewing "it was found that being affectionate was expected by husbands and wives, but showing it was more or less frowned upon. Thus, being affectionate without obviously showing it appears to be a characteristic of the Swedish culture." [74]

The Indiana and Swedish studies show little meaningful difference in the extent of extramarital intercourse, except that the divorced Indiana men report having had extramarital relations to a substantially greater extent (47.1 percent) than maritally unadjusted Swedish men (26.3 percent).[75] The 1968 study of sexual behavior previously referred to indicates a very low incidence of extramarital sex relations; 95 percent of married Swedes under sixty state they have not had extramarital relations in the previous year.[76] I would guess that this is a higher degree of marital fidelity than one would find in American society. Premarital sexual intercourse was reported by seven out of ten of the Indiana men, but only by one in ten of the women. In Sweden, by contrast, premarital intercourse was practically universally reported by nine out of ten men and women.

The overall impression from this comparative study is that pretty much the same factors are associated with marital happiness in Swedish and American society. Indeed the marriage relationship in Sweden is similar to what it is in America, in that it is a basically egalitarian relationship in which personal satisfactions are paramount.

The persistently low fertility of Swedish couples will be discussed in the final section of this chapter. Two observations related to child bearing, however, might appropriately be made here.[77] First, natural childbirth has become virtually universal in Sweden. Natural childbirth came to Sweden in the late 1940s and by the late 1950s had become diffused throughout the society. Pregnant women are encouraged to exercise prior to childbirth, no anesthesia is conventionally used, childbirth is not associated with pain, and the father is encouraged to be present in the delivery room at the time of birth. What is almost a cult of an educated and sophisticated minority in America is conventional in Sweden. Also, in sharp contrast to American society, breast feeding is practically universal. Mothers generally stay in the hospital for eight or nine days—a situation conducive to successful breast feeding. In America, by contrast, the mother with her newborn child commonly returns home three or four days after birth, frequently before satisfactory breast feeding can be established. At least in regard to childbirth and breast feeding, therefore, Sweden can be regarded as more "traditional" than America.

Sweden has one of the highest divorce rates among the developed societies, though not nearly so high as in the United States, which has by far the highest of all the developed societies.[78] For a number of years there has been one divorce for every six marriages in Sweden as compared with one for every four in the United States. Between 1900 and the late 1940s, when divorce in Sweden approached a plateau, as it did in the United States, there was more than a tenfold increase in the number of divorces per 1000 marriages.

Obtaining a divorce in Sweden is easier, though it perhaps takes more time, than in most of the American states. The whole legal code pertaining to divorce and its operation is enormously more rational than in most of the American states.[79] Husband and wife are not pitted against each other; collusion and perjury are unnecessary. Some of the major provisions of the divorce law are the following:

(1) With some exceptions, before a final divorce is granted there must be a legal separation of one year.

(2) Legal separation is granted automatically when both husband and wife agree that there is incompatibility. However, this can be done only after a declaration that marital counselling has taken place. This mediation is free of charge. If both parties do not agree that there is incompatibility, a court may declare it.

(3) If fidelity continues for the year of legal separation and the couple continues to want a divorce, a final divorce is granted.

(4) There is virtual sexual equality in the divorce law and its operation. Custody of children is determined on the basis of the welfare of the child, though this is generally taken to be the mother. If both parents are equally suited to take care of the children, however, preference is given to the one who has not caused the divorce.

The reasons for the great increase in divorce in Sweden in the first half of this century and the relatively high rate that prevails in Sweden vis-à-vis other developed societies are subject only to speculation.

That Sweden should have such a high divorce rate, considering the length of time that couples know each other before marriage and the relatively mature age at which they marry, is noteworthy. Ultimately, the explanation is probably due to the relative ease of divorce in Sweden, the high degree of independence of women, and a nontraditional and rational attitude toward marriage. There is certainly no more stigma attached to being divorced in Sweden than in America.

Why Is Swedish Fertility So Low?

Swedish wives born around 1930, most of whom have now completed their childbearing, will have completed families that average around one child less than their American counterparts.[80] In fact they will have fewer children than the women of any society in the world. In most years from the early 1930s to the early 1960s, Sweden has had the lowest birth rate in the world; in recent years several Eastern European countries—Bulgaria, Hungary, and Romania—have come to occupy this position largely as a result of very liberal abortion policies.

Those Swedish wives born around 1930 will probably have an average of 2.2 or 2.3 children by the time they complete the childbearing years, as compared with an estimate of 3.3 children for their counterparts in America.[81] This low fertility of the Swedes is not the result of any unique ability to control family size; the great majority of young couples in all the developed societies control the size of their families. Nor are economic factors the heart of the matter. In fact it might be argued that the relative cost of rearing a child in the United States or most of the other developed societies is greater for its parents than in Sweden, where an expanding system of welfare legislation has provided increasing financial benefits to mothers and children; this aid was begun in the 1930s to spur the low birth rate, which for several years had run below replacement level.

All Swedish mothers, married or not, now receive a grant of $180 when a child is born, as well as free delivery and confinement, grants for postnatal health care for mother and child, and an allowance of $180 per year for each child up to the age of sixteen.[82] All of these grants are tax free, and they will probably be raised in the near future. There are no tax exemptions for children, but the married pay a lower tax rate than do the single. Comprehensive national health insurance makes the child's medical bills negligible and complete dental care is available to all children in the schools. Housing allowances to large families and paid holidays for children and mothers are given to those parents with low incomes. Apartments (in which most Swedes live), though in relatively short supply, cost substantially less than they do in the United States, though food and most manufactured goods cost somewhat more. Swedish parents do not need to be as concerned as American parents about paying for their children's education, since tuition through the university level is free and because of the universal allowances and loan programs to meet students' living costs. Employers are forbidden by law to discharge a woman employee who gets married or becomes pregnant. She is entitled to six months' maternity leave with pay, and her job must be held open for her for an additional three months. With these inducements one might expect Swedish fertility to exceed ours.

There are, however, certain differences in Swedish and American values, behavior patterns, and housing situations that at least provide some plausible explanations for the low fertility of Swedes. Of some importance is the observation that Swedes marry at older ages than, for example, Americans do. During the 1950s Swedes were three to four years older than Americans at the time of marriage. The median age at first marriage for Swedish men in the 1950s was between twenty-six and twenty-seven and for women it was between twenty-three and twenty-four.[83] Very young couples often have a longer period of fecundity, more energy to deal with the rigors of child-rearing, and a less realistic picture of the burdens of parenthood than those who marry later. It is also probably true that a girl who marries directly after leaving her parental home or directly after finishing school adjusts more easily to the confining role of motherhood than one who has had several years of bachelor freedom. Also, early marriage tends to canalize a girl's interests into the traditional roles of wife and mother before competing role possibilities have much chance to develop.

Yet the importance of age at marriage is quite difficult to assess. In Sweden there has been a decline in average age of first marriage of women between 1940 and the 1960s of 2.2 years from age 25.0 to 22.8, as compared with a decline of 1.3 years in the United States, from age 21.5 to 20.2 (which has been more or less constant since the early 1950s). Yet there has been only the slightest increase, if there has been any increase at all, in the average number of children that married Swedish women have. The increase in the Swedish birth rate that occurred after the 1930s appears to be mainly the result of a marked increase in the proportion of women who married and to having babies in the 1940s who were postponed from the 1930s. (Of the women who became thirty in 1940, 30.1 percent had never married; of those who turned thirty in 1960 only 13.5 percent had never married.) The point is that the increase in average family size that has occurred in America between women born around 1910 and women born in the decade around 1930 has little counterpart in Sweden.

In Sweden, in contrast to America, a high proportion of middle-class wives have relatively uninterrupted working lives, and there are far more women in the traditional male occupations in Sweden than in America. This is true in spite of the observation that fewer Swedish than American wives work outside the home. As I suggested earlier, the proportion of women in the professions and in the traditionally male occupations is an indicator of the general role possibilities open to women in a society. That prosperity and an increased standard of living in a highly advanced society does not necessarily result in larger families is suggested by Sweden where there has been a high level of prosperity without any marked change in average family size, despite the declining average age at marriage. What is significantly different between Sweden and the United States is the increase in acceptable role possibilities for women that has occurred in Sweden over the past generation. The neotraditional role for women has few spokesmen in the Swedish press and in the mass media as compared with the United States. The feminism that became abortive in the United States around World War II continued unabated in Sweden and has had far-reaching effects in the society. Typical views of Swedish university students on men's and women's roles, for example, are less differentiated and more egalitarian than those of American students, for the minimizing of sexual differentiation and the maximizing of sexual equality in education have been guiding principles in the radical school reforms in Sweden in the postwar years.

As to the role expectation of middle-class Swedish women, consider the following observation on Scandinavian women of the Norwegian-Danish sociologist Kaare Svalastoga:

But even if she excels in all these respects (being a good housekeeper and hostess, a loving mother and an attractive spouse), she will reap slight social esteem, because dominant middle class opinion will insist on the superior values of choosing a career outside the home and of cultivating literary and artistic interests.[84]

Contrast this role definition with that of John H. Bushnell as to the future role identities of Vassar undergraduates of the middle 1950s, an unusually intelligent academic sample of young women:

> *the validation of femininity and a full realization of the potential of woman-*
> *hood is thought to reside almost exclusively in the realm of marriage and*
> *family. . . . That the female should attempt, in their thinking, to usurp the*
> *prerogatives of the male is a distasteful notion which would seriously disrupt*
> *their own projected role of helpmate and faithful complement to the man of*
> *the house. For these young women, the "togetherness" vogue is definitely*
> *an integral theme of future family life, with any opportunities for independent*
> *action attaching to an Ivy League degree being willingly passed over in*
> *favor of the anticipated rewards of close knit companionship within the home*
> *that is to be.*[85]

There has been an expansion of role identities for young American women since the late 1960s, I believe, but conventional role possibilities are still far greater for young Swedish women than for their American counterparts. It is a conventional choice in Sweden for a bright girl to choose to enter a medical faculty or to study chemistry.

There is, however, one major factor in Swedish society that acts as a kind of brake on fertility: the generally small living quarters. Family size in the advanced societies is affected to some extent by type and size of living quarters. Apartment living and small quarters discourage families of more than two children. About three-fourths of non-farm Swedish families live in apartment houses and most families with children do not have more than two bedrooms.[86] The fact that Americans have so much living space and do not hesitate to spend a large portion of their income on housing is a basic difference between Sweden and the United States. Statistically, Americans are more urbanized than the Swedes but, unlike them, Americans are essentially anti-city. Most American parents with children prefer to live in sprawling subdivisions of one-family houses. Even if a Swede lives in a suburb, he is far more likely to live in an apartment than a single-family dwelling.

It is suggestive that more Swedish wives regard two children as "ideal" than any other number (48 percent compared with 19 percent of American wives), whereas more American wives so regard four children (41 percent).[87] Actually, the Swedish wives will average slightly more than two children and the American wives fewer than four. But the fertility conservatism of the Swedes is understandable, since most couples only have one bedroom available for children, and since there is a chronic housing shortage in a society that emphasizes maintaining a well-appointed home in which no one sleeps in the living room; having a third child therefore becomes virtually unthinkable to a large segment of the Swedish population. Having a third child in America rarely means that someone will have to sleep in the living room.

Sweden, in addition, is not a child-centered or child-oriented society; the style of life of a family is not so commonly organized around the children as in the United States, Denmark, or the Netherlands.[88] Consider, for example, the following comparative observation of Herbert Hendin:

Swedish magazines reflect the mother-child situation in a characteristic way. While in American and Danish magazines children are running all over the pages, their absence is conspicuous in the Swedish stories. If they exist, they have no character or personality, and their relations with their mothers are completely in the background. Even more important is the fact that they are not prime factors in the woman's considerations or in her deliberations about her problems.[89]

Sweden is the first (and possibly the only) industrial society in which a direct relationship between fertility and socioeconomic status has been found.[90] Karl A. Edin and Edward P. Hutchinson studied the relation of occupation, income, and education with fertility among Stockholm wives in the period around 1920. They found strong and conclusive evidence of a direct relationship between fertility and the status variables. It is important to note that Edin and Hutchinson's data refer only to women in Stockholm, yet it is indeed a remarkable relationship and one that is rarely (if ever) found even in recent fertility studies. No American study has yet found such a relationship.[91] Table 6.3 shows the average number of live births per family in the first ten years of marriage in Stockholm in 1920 by education and income.

Data obtained for the entire county in a 1935–1936 Special Census showed that while not all major occupational groups failed to manifest the usual inverse relation between status and fertility, industrial workers still did.[92] If a study were done today, perhaps a direct relationship between fertility and socioeconomic status for the entire urban population would be found. This fertility behavior indicates that an unusually high degree of rational planning has been charac-

Table 6.3   Average Number of Live Births per Family in the First Ten Years of Marriage, by Education and Income of Husband, Stockholm, 1920.

		Education		
INCOME OF HUSBAND	Total	8 years or less	Intermediate	Completion of gymnasium
Under 4,000 *kronor*	1.16	1.15	1.18	1.46
4,000–6,000	1.21	1.18	1.34	1.45
6,000–10,000	1.31	1.18	1.35	1.46
10,000 and over	1.74	1.56	1.62	1.85

SOURCE: Karl A. Edin and Edward P. Hutchinson, *Studies of Differential Fertility in Sweden* (London: P. S. King and Son, 1935), p. 78.

teristic of the industrial working class in Sweden for a number of decades.

Concluding Speculations

Why do females have more general equality in Sweden and why is there less sexual differentiation than in most of the other developed societies? Part of the explanation for the great advances of the feminist movement in Sweden in this century has been the general support it has been given by the antitraditional, secular, and rational emphasis of the dominant value system of which the feminist movement itself is a manifestation. Female equality has been a specific goal of both the socialist and radical liberal traditions, both of which have been numerically stronger in Sweden than in any other Western nation.

Yet the traditional culture of Sweden was probably less antagonistic to the movement for female equality than the traditional cultures of non-Scandinavian Western societies. In the nineteenth century and earlier, the status of women, like the status of the peasant farmers, appears to have been better in Sweden than in most other places. They even had the traditional right to half as much inheritance as male heirs. One theory to explain this is the difficulty of survival in vigorous environments like Scandinavia where the soil is rocky and the summers short. It seems reasonable that where life is hard and women have an important economic role to play they will be less oppressed and will have more equality. It is suggestive that Eskimo cultures are also characterized by a high degree of female equality.[93] On the other hand, subsistence was not nearly so demanding of energy and cooperation between the sexes in, for example, Ireland or

Southern Europe.[94] In such societies it was doubtless easier for patterns of male dominance and female subservience to emerge and to survive. High status for women appears particularly characteristic of traditional fishing cultures in difficult environments, such as those of the Eskimos and of Scandinavia, where men are away for a good portion of the time (and perhaps many are lost at sea) and where the women remain home and have crucial economic roles to play.

Notes

1. Birgitta Linnér, *Sex and Society in Sweden* (New York: Pantheon, 1967), p. 18.
2. This is also the opinion of the Norwegian sociologist Harriet Holter. See her "Women's Occupational Situation in Scandinavia," *International Labour Review*, 93 (April 1966), 383.
3. Edmund Dahlström has discussed these three positions in E. Dahlström, *Kvinnors liv och arbete* (Stockholm: *Studieförbundet näringsliv och samhälle*, 1962), pp. 17–70. An English translation of much of this discussion is to be found in Edmund Dahlström, *The Changing Roles of Men and Women* (London: Gerald Duckworth, 1967), pp. 170–205.
4. Alva Myrdal and Viola Klein, *Women's Two Roles* (London: Routledge & Kegan Paul, 1956).
5. The most well-known articulation of the radical position is probably Eva Moberg, *Kvinnor och människor* (Stockholm: Bonniers, 1962).
6. For a Finnish study on this discrepancy, see Elina Haavio-Mannila, "Sex Differentiation in Role Expectations and Performance," *Journal of Marriage and the Family*, XXIX (August 1967), 568–578.
7. See references, for example, in the items cited in notes 2–6.
8. *Dagens Nyheter, Sondagsbilagen*, September 15, 1968, p. 8.
9. For a perceptive discussion of sexual differentiation in Russia, see Wright Miller, *The Russians as People* (New York: Dutton, 1961), pp. 157–165.
10. See references and discussions in Richard F. Tomasson, "Why Has American Fertility Been so High?" in Bernard Farber (ed.), *Kinship and Family Organization* (New York: Wiley, 1966), pp. 327–338.
11. Many of the facts in this paragraph are from Myrdal and Klein, *op. cit.*, pp. 42–77.
12. See Jonas Orring, *Comprehensive and Continuation Schools in Sweden* (Stockholm: Ecklesiastikdepartementet, 1962), p. 60.
13. Calculated from data in Hans Jägerstad, *Sveriges historia i årtal* (Stockholm: Bokförlaget Prisma, 1964), p. 149.
14. See the Education section, *Statistical Abstract of Sweden* (Stockholm: Statistiska Centralbyrån) for recent years.

15. Not only is there a smaller percentage of women in America than in Swedish higher education, but the American definition includes much under higher education not so included in Sweden, most of which has a high proportion of females, such as teacher-training institutions.

16. See Sveriges Officiella Statistik, *Högre Studier, 1961/62* (Stockholm: Statistiska Centralbyrån, 1964), and *Statistical Abstract of Sweden, op. cit.*, for recent years.

17. See Herbert Tingsten, *Political Behavior: Studies in Election Statistics* (London: P. S. King, 1937), pp. 10–78; Bernard Berelson, Paul F. Lazersfeld, and William McPhee, *Voting* (Chicago: University of Chicago Press, 1954), pp. 336–337; and Robert E. Lane, *Political Life* (Glencoe, Ill.: Free Press, 1959), pp. 204–219.

18. See Angus Campbell, *et al.*, *The American Voter* (New York: Wiley, 1960), p. 484, and Lane, *op. cit.*, p. 210.

19. See Sveriges Officiella Statistik, *Riksdagsmannavalen, åren 1961–1964* (Stockholm: Statistiska Centralbyrån, 1965), Vol. II, p. 82.

20. See Ulf Himmelstrand, *Work Report on Political Conservatism among Swedish Women* (Uppsala), mimeo.

21. Seymour M. Lipset, *Political Man* (Garden City, N.Y.: Anchor Books, 1960), p. 231.

22. *Riksdagsmannavalen, åren 1959–1960, op. cit.*, p. 65.

23. U. S. Department of Labor, "Women in High-Level Elective and Appointive Positions in National Governments," in *Women in the World Today*, International Report No. 1 (February 1963).

24. Luigi Barzini, "Divorce in Italy?" *New York Times Magazine*, March 17, 1968, pp. 28ff.

25. These dates are from Jägerstad, *op. cit.*, passim, and Swedish Federation of Business and Professional Women, *History of Swedish Women* (Stockholm: Swedish Federation of Business and Professional Women, 1958).

26. Gösta Carlsson, "Swedish Character in the Twentieth Century," *The Annals*, 370 (March 1967), 93–98.

27. Luigi Barzini, *The Italians* (New York: Atheneum, 1964).

28. I believe this is true of both William Samson, the English writer, in *The Sun and the Icicle* (London: Hogarth, 1958), and Kathleen Nott, in her attack on Swedish society, *A Clean Well-Lighted Place* (London: Heineman, 1961).

29. See "Are the Swedes Happy," *New Statesman*, October 11, 1963, pp. 480ff.

30. Herbert Hendin, *Suicide and Scandinavia* (New York: Grune & Stratton, 1964), p. 43.

31. *Ibid.*, p. 44.

32. *Ibid.*, p. 67.

33. See Per Olav Tiller, "Kulturelle vanasjoner i persepjon av foreldre," *Nordisk Psykologi*, 1–2 (1960).

34. France and Switzerland have lower rates than Sweden. The rates for this cause of death are in fact so low for these countries that I am suspicious that their conventions in the classification of deaths might be sharply different from those in the other developed societies.

35. See Alva Myrdal, *Nation and Family* (London: Routledge & Kegan Paul, 1945), pp. 42–47. Mrs. Myrdal's interpretation is based largely on K. Robert

V. Wikman, *Die Einleitung der Ehe. Eine vergleichend ethnosoziologische Untersuchung über die Vorstufe der Ehe in den Sitten des schwedischen Volkstums* (Åbo, Finland: *Acta Academiae Aboensis*, 1937).

36. This quotation is from Martin S. Allwood, *Eilert Sundt: A Pioneer in Sociology and Anthropology* (Oslo: Olaf Norlis, 1957), pp. 51–54.

37. A. Myrdal, *op. cit.*, p. 45.

38. Discussion in the Higher Seminar, Department of Sociology, Uppsala University, 1964.

39. See references in footnote 56.

40. I spent two weeks in Iceland in the spring of 1964 and three weeks in the summer of 1969 on Fulbright grants. I had several conversations on this topic with Rector Armann Snaevarr. Some of my early observations on Icelandic society are contained in "Iceland Report," *New Society*, 149 (August 5, 1965), 22.

41. See *Population and Vital Statistics 1951–60* (Reykjavik: Statistical Bureau of Iceland, 1963), p. 24.

42. These statistics were provided by Rector Armann Snaevarr. See official statistical yearbooks of the respective countries.

43. Yet the proportion of all births out of wedlock increased from 13.1 percent in 1916–1920 to the present high level by the period 1941–1945. See *Population and Vital Statistics, 1951–60, op. cit.*, p. 24.

44. James S. Coleman, "Female Status and Premarital Sex Codes," *American Journal of Sociology*, 72 (September 1966), p. 217.

45. Ira L. Reiss, "Some Comments on Premarital Sexual Permissiveness," *American Journal of Sociology*, 72 (March 1967), pp. 558–559.

46. Franklin D. Scott, *The American Experience of Swedish Students* (Minneapolis: University of Minnesota Press, 1956), p. 76.

47. The article of this genre that gained the widest circulation in the United States was "Sin and Sweden," in *Time*, April 25, 1955, p. 29.

48. Marya Mannes, "Northern Places," *The Reporter*, August 15, 1963, p. 58ff.

49. For a comparative study of courtship practices among students at the University of Wisconsin and the University of Oslo, see William Simenson and Gilbert Geis, "Courtship Patterns in Norwegian and American University Students," *Marriage and Family Living*, 18 (November 1956), 334–338.

50. See "Coed Dorms Found to Shift Attitudes," *New York Times*, March 12, 1968.

51. I am indebted to Hans Berg, Department of Sociology, Uppsala University, for this observation.

52. *Dagens Nyheter*, January 21, 1969, p. 7.

53. Joachim Israel and Sten Johansson, "Ålder vid första coitus bland värnpliktiga," *Sociologisk forskning*, II (1965), 30–38.

54. See J. Robert Moskin, "The New Contraceptive Society," *Look*, 33 (February 4, 1969), 50–53.

55. *Ibid.*

56. However, the median age increased from 19.4 years in 1960 to 20.3 years in 1965. For the four folk high schools combined, the percentage who had had intercourse increased from 40 percent in 1960 to 65 percent in 1965. See Georg Karlsson, "Sexualundersökning bland folkhögskoleelever—en repli-

cation," *Sociologisk forskning*, II (1965), 169–176. See also Karlsson's earlier studies of the sexual behavior and attitudes of folk-high-school students, "Sexuella vanor och attityder bland folkhögskoleelever," *Sociologisk forskning*, I (1964), 55–63, 105–111.

57. Israel and Johansson, *op. cit.*, p. 33.
58. See Lester A. Kirkendall's Preface to Linnér, *op. cit.*, p. ix.
59. See Robert R. Bell, *Premarital Sex in a Changing Society* (Englewood Cliffs, N.J.: Prentice-Hall, 1966), pp. 89–109, and Erwin O. Smigel and Rita Seiden, "The Decline and Fall of the Double Standard," *The Annals*, 376 (March 1968), 6–17.
60. For the most recent and best account of sex education in Sweden in English see Linnér, *op. cit.*
61. See *Dagens Nyheter*, November 8, 1967, p. 2, and December 19, 1967, p. 1.
62. See the sixty-five pages of sample sex-education material in Linnér, *op. cit.*; see also *Handbook on Sex Instruction in Swedish Schools* (Stockholm: National Board of Education, 1957).
63. Linnér, *op. cit.*, p. 165.
64. Linnér, *op. cit.*, p. 156.
65. Freedom of the Press Act, para. 3:13, in *The Constitution of Sweden*, Sarah V. Thorelli (tr.) (Stockholm: Royal Ministry for Foreign Affairs, 1954). Information on the legal aspects of contraception is from Rune Persson, "Nativitet och familjestorlek," in Georg Karlsson and Jan Trost (eds.), *Familjen i samhället* (Stockholm: Norstedt, 1965), p. 122.
66. See the comments on what has happened to the sale of pornography in Denmark in Horace Judson, "The Critic Between," *Encounter*, XXX (March 1968), pp. 57ff. Linnér makes the same observation about Sweden, *op. cit.*, p. 3.
67. Sten Hultgren and Ingmar Stoltz, *Äktenskapet och lyckan* (Stockholm: Svenska Kyrkans Diakonisyrelses Bokförlag, 1956), p. 43.
68. *Adaptability and Communication in Marriage* (Uppsala: Almqvist & Wiksell, 1951).
69. Georg Karlsson, "Val av make/maka," in Karlsson and Trost, *op. cit.*, p. 63.
70. Sigrid Beckman, "Familjen i lagstiftningen," in Karlsson and Trost, *op. cit.*, p. 29.
71. "Marital Adjustment and Prediction," *American Sociological Review*, 17 (February 1952), pp. 10–17.
72. *Ibid.*, p. 14.
73. *Ibid.*, p. 16.
74. *Ibid.*, p. 16.
75. *Ibid.*, p. 16. See footnote 39.
76. Moskin, *op. cit.*, p. 53.
77. At the time of the birth of my third child in Uppsala in 1963, I became interested in the much greater acceptance of natural childbirth and breast feeding in Sweden compared with America. Still probably only a minority of young American mothers breast feed, and natural childbirth remains uncommon.
78. See William J. Goode, "Family Disorganization," in Robert K. Merton and Robert A. Nisbet (eds.), *Contemporary Social Problems*, 2nd ed. (New

York: Harcourt, Brace, & World, 1966), pp. 479–552; on divorce in Sweden see Jan Trost, "Aktenskapets upplösning," in Karlsson and Trost, *op. cit.*, pp. 154–174.

79. See Beckman in Karlsson and Trost, *op. cit.*, pp. 32–34.

80. This is only a rough estimate. The only non–United States study of expected family size that I am aware of is that of Ronald Freedman, Gerhard Baumert, and Martin Bolte, "Expected Family Size and Family Size Values in West Germany," *Population Studies*, XIII (November 1959), 136–150.

81. On birth expectations of United States wives in 1955 and 1960, see Ronald Freedman, Pascal K. Whelpton, and Arthur A. Campbell, *Family Planning, Sterility, and Population Growth* (New York: McGraw-Hill, 1959), and Pascal K. Whelpton, Arthur A. Campbell, and John E. Patterson, *Fertility and Family Planning in the United States* (Princeton: Princeton University Press, 1966).

82. See *Social Benefits in Sweden* (Stockholm: The Swedish Institute). See most current edition.

83. See *Befolkningsrörelsen* (Stockholm: Central Bureau of Statistics). See appropriate years.

84. Kaare Svalastoga, "The Family in Scandinavia," *Journal of Marriage and Family Living*, 16 (November 1954).

85. John H. Bushnell, "Student Culture at Vassar," in Nevitt Sanford (ed.), *The American College* (New York: Wiley, 1962), pp. 509–510.

86. See *Statistical Abstract of Sweden, op. cit.*

87. Swedish data from a national survey of 617 families with children reported in *Dagens Nyheter*, April 29, 1964, p. 9. The percentage of Swedish wives who regarded four children as "ideal" was not given. United States data from Freedman, Whelpton, and Campbell, *op. cit.*, p. 223.

88. On the Netherlands as a child-centered society, see Johan Goudsblom, *Dutch Society* (New York: Random House, 1967), pp. 137–138.

89. Hendin, *op. cit.*, p. 63.

90. See Karl A. Edin and Edward P. Hutchinson, *Studies of Differential Fertility in Sweden* (London: P. S. King and Son, 1935).

91. Such a relationship was found in the 1941 Indianapolis study among those couples who successfully planned the size of their families, however.

92. This information was supplied by Dennis Wrong who analyzed these data in his 1956 Columbia doctoral dissertation.

93. See, for example, the discussion of sex roles in Jeanette Mirsky, "The Eskimo of Greenland," in Margaret Mead (ed.), *Cooperation and Competition among Primitive Peoples* (New York: McGraw-Hill, 1937), pp. 65–68. P. A. Sorokin, in his autobiography *A Long Journey* (New Haven: College and University Press, 1963), p. 15, comments that among the Komi people, a Ugro-Finnish people in northeastern Russia among whom he was born, "the status of the sexes was essentially equal."

94. Cecil Woodham-Smith, in *The Great Hunger* (London: Hamish Hamilton, 1962), pp. 24–26, points out that the potato required little attention except at springtime and harvest. No one in nineteenth-century Ireland before the famine had to work very hard.

VII

Cleavages, Status, and Power

. . . we're far ahead compared to other countries.
And we're far ahead compared to what Sweden
looked like 30 to 40 years ago.
But we have *not* gone very far if you want your dream
of a classless society to come true.
In that case, most of the work remains to be done![1]
　　　—OLOF PALME, *Prime Minister of Sweden*
　　　in *I Am Curious* (*Yellow*)

When looking at stratification in Sweden one has a double image. From some angles Sweden appears to be a hierarchical and elitist society, with a royal house and a nobility, a society in which aristocratic manners permeate the whole social structure. There is a great emphasis on titles, ritual, and formality—much of which appears to be deferential (but much of which is not). It is also a society in which there is a profound respect for authority and the law.[2] Yet, on the other hand, styles of life do not differ very much between the working class and the middle class, and there is a high degree of consensus on values, including a pervasive emphasis on ideological egalitarianism. This double image—Sweden as an elitist society and Sweden as an egalitarian society—is the result of an intense commitment to modern values in continuing opposition to the values and structural remnants of the traditional society.

One of the central observations in the study of Swedish social structure and culture is that basic cleavages are and have been minimal in number, if not always in intensity. This becomes readily apparent when the cleavages in Norwegian society—analyzed so brilliantly and in such detail by Stein Rokkan—are compared with those in Swedish society.[3] This is a particularly appropriate comparison because Norway, too, is a relatively homogeneous society with a similar value system and social structure. Indeed Sweden resembles Norway more than any other Scandinavian country in spite of my earlier observation that official institutions in Finland are closest to those of Sweden.

Rokkan has put forth five basic dimensions of cleavage in Norwegian society, all of which are sharper than their counterparts in Swedish society. This is perhaps one of the reasons why Norwegian politics have a little more vitality and excitement than Swedish politics.[4] The five structural cleavages delineated by Rokkan, in terms of their historical appearance, are as follows:

The Territorial Opposition. This is the conflict between the capital and the provinces and between the center and the periphery. This cleavage has been less apparent in Sweden than in Norway because of the long-term operation of the national bureaucracy that has done so much to integrate Swedish society. Traces of this conflict dimension are most notably apparent in the south and north of Sweden and in the western province of Dalarna. There is also opposition to the increasing size of the national bureaucracy and to the increasing share of the gross national product that is being spent in the public sector. This, more than being fundamentally a part of the territorial opposition, seems to belong more to the next category, however.

The Sociocultural Cleavage. One of the distinguishing characteristics of all of the northern Scandinavian countries has been the persistent cultural differences and conflicts between town and country, which are manifested in the strong agrarian parties in all of these nations. In the three northern Scandinavian countries, urban conservatives and agrarians have never been able to unite in a national Conservative or Christian Democratic party as in other European countries.[5] The roots of this cleavage have been the opposition of the rural elements to the state bureaucracy and to the style of life and greater status consciousness in the cities. That it is reflected in political organization is a manifestation of the unique traditions of independence and of long-term political activity of the Scandinavian peasants, not to any uniqueness in the town and country conflict itself. Rural elements almost everywhere else have been very deficient in sustaining viable political organizations.[6] The cleavage in this instance is also not as great in Sweden as it is in Norway, where the cleavage is intensified by the language struggle between the *landsmål* (which is closer to Swedish) of the rural population and the *riksmål* (which is closer to Danish) of the urban population. It is still further exacerbated in Norway by the religious cleavage.

The Religious Cleavage. Until recent decades this was mainly a cleavage between the secularism and religious liberalism of the great majority of the population and the moralism and Protestant fundamentalism of those who belonged to the free churches. This cleavage has been particularly strong in several counties (*iän*) of Sweden, such as Jönsköping and Västerbotten. Again this cleavage is smaller than in Norway, where within the state church—the free-church movement has been negligible here—a fundamentalist Lutheranism has strong roots. In Sweden, however, this cleavage has changed its form in the wake of advanced secularism. It is now a division between the self-conscious Christian minority and the indifferent majority. The most dramatic manifestation of this cleavage in recent years was the vigorous debate that grew out of the report of the Gymnasium Committee in 1963, in which a decrease in the number of hours that were devoted to the study of Christianity was proposed. A result was the formation of a national committee, which gathered the signatures of over 2 million Swedes, more than one-fourth of the total population, on a petition that emphasized the need for more Christian education in the new gymnasium.[7]

The Commodity Market Conflict. This is the conflict of the agricultural and other primary producers with the consumers; it is also to a great extent a conflict between the rural and urbanized segments of the population. The rural point of view is manifested in the Center party (the old Agrarian party) and in the organized groups representing the interests of primary producers. Here again the language issue and religiosity overlap and intensify the cleavage in Norway but not in Sweden.

The Class Cleavage. This is the classic conflict between employers and wage earners, a cleavage which has increasingly, though certainly not completely, become one between employers and salaried employees. This is apparent in the strategic change since the 1950s in the appeal of the Social Democrats to all salaried employees rather than just to workers. In this case, the conflict is also less sharp in Sweden than it is in Norway.[8] The attitude of Swedish businessmen toward the Social Democrats is more tolerant and less harsh than it is in Norway. Norwegian businessmen, particularly on the west coast, frequently sound like conservative American Republicans.[9]

The basic cleavages in Swedish society are the divisions between rural and urban interests and between class interests; there are no structurally important religious, linguistic, ethnic, or regional cleavages in contemporary Sweden.[10] What is notable is that in Sweden cleavages are so few and so lacking in intensity, even when compared with tranquil Norway, so similar in culture and social structure to Sweden.

The "Old Class Society"

Before class differences in modern Sweden are discussed, some of the characteristics of the "old class society" will be outlined to show the enormous diminution of class differences that has accompanied the modernization of Sweden. It is opposition to many of the hierarchical characteristics inherited from the past that has shaped the nature of Swedish egalitarianism as distinct from its American form. This great transformation in the status system, combined with the phenomenally rapid rise in standards of living, is central to the way Swedes view their history. This theme runs through Åke Elmér's book *From Poor Sweden to the Welfare State*, in which he summarizes the class situation at the beginning of this century as follows:

Poverty, overcrowding, starvation, and sickness were common in Sweden around the turn of the century. And in contrast to this there was an upper class (överklass), *which in magnificence and wealth stood far above the great mass of people. An intermediate level was made up of the propertied farmer class, the lower middle class craftsmen and merchants, and the beginnings of a white-collar class, each group of which looked down upon the others, but all of whom were objects of contempt to the upper class and envy to the working class.*[11]

Most of the urban proletariat and much of the rural proletariat lived near the subsistence level, though the Swedish accounts of living conditions during early industrialization do not approach reports of the misery of the comparable but earlier period in England. Particularly in the rural areas the proletariat was highly deferential to members of the *överklass*. They were referred to by the personal *du* form, whereas they addressed their betters in the third person and tipped their caps in respect. And they were assigned to pews in the back of the church.[12] It was from this rural proletariat, in fact, that most of the Swedish emigrants to America were drawn.

Conditions were in general the worst for the workers in the north of Sweden (Norrland), where there was a rapid development of the lumber industry in the latter decades of the nineteenth century. Many small but independent landowners sold their land at low prices to large lumbering interests and were turned into a proletariat class that was paid pitifully low wages. Many were injured by the dangerous working conditions that prevailed in the sawmills. The misery of this area has had no counterpart in Sweden, though conditions have greatly improved in recent years in what is still the poorest region in the country. To the present time, no area has had such a high proportion of Communists and religious fundamentalists, both within the State Church and in the free churches.[13]

Living standards varied enormously in Sweden.[14] Differences in income were great as in all traditional societies. Pay scales of civil servants illustrate this. Around 1880, members of the cabinet had annual incomes of around 17,000 *kronor*, county governors 13,000 *kronor*, and department chiefs between 7000 and 10,000 *kronor*. Other civil servants had incomes as low as 600 to 1000 *kronor* (though often with free housing). Professors made around 6000 *kronor*, gymnasium teachers between 1500 to 4500 *kronor*, but rural *folkskola* teachers had incomes of only 500 to 600 *kronor* (in addition to house and firewood). However, teachers' salaries in certain larger cities were twice this. A member of the cabinet might then have had a salary thirty to thirty-five times higher than that of a rural *folkskola* teacher. There was an income tax at this time in Sweden but it was proportional so that it did nothing to equalize incomes. The diffences in living standards and the generally hierarchical nature of the society are further suggested by the extraordinarily great difference in travel allowances for state employees.[15] Between 1865 and 1881 there was a schedule of nine categories. The highest category of employees received a daily allowance of 15 *riksdalers* (the old currency measure) and the lowest category received only 2 *riksdalers*. After 1881 this was lessened to six categories, but the differential between the lowest and highest class was almost as great; the range was from 15 to 2.5 *kronor* per day. At this time there were three different classes on the railroad and four different classes on boats; now there are two on both, and few people use first class.

There were also enormous differences in standards of dress and in housing accommodations.[16] The lower classes frequently could not go to church or to lectures at the workers' institutes because they did not have the proper clothing. Often they could not send their children to school. Variations in housing were enormous. One study of Stockholm workers in 1895 showed that 16.5 percent lived in one room with no kitchen, 42.2 percent had one room and a kitchen, and 25.7 percent had two rooms and a kitchen.[17] There were also vast differences in the amount of leisure time. The average working time of 1292 workers in Stockholm in 1891 was 12.4 hours per day.[18] People commonly worked from 6 A.M. to 8 P.M., although on Saturdays they frequently stopped two hours earlier. It is no wonder that at this time both the Liberals and Social Democrats had the eight hour day as one of their central goals. By contrast, office workers worked much less. The daily working time for office workers around 1901 was generally between four and five hours per day.[19] And, because servants were paid very small wages, even people with very modest incomes could hire one or two general servants. The term for female servant has undergone very revealing changes; around the turn of the century she was commonly called *piga* (a term with a very subordinate connotation), which was later replaced by *jungfru* (literally, virgin or young girl), but in modern Sweden she is a *hembiträde* (literally, home assistant).

Then—and to some extent even now—the highest class in Sweden was the upper civil servants, and nothing was higher than being a minister in the government except being king. To be an official in the goverment—even at a very modest level—conveyed special distinction. A Swedish diplomat, Einar Modig (born 1883), whose father was an auditor in a state office, has pointed out how he saw the social-class system during his youth in the 1890s:

> Even if our living standards were not so splendid my father was in any case a state official, and there was nothing more important at this time. When I in distaste ladled out the unbearable Tuesday soup or when I had dry French bread without butter at evening tea, I could just think that pappa one time a year was invited to the castle, to the royal ball. . . . Indeed a civil servant was a civil servant and fully entitled to look down on merchants, manufacturers, and builders—executives were still rare in the 1890s. . . . With these circles we had nothing in common. Those who were not civil servants should be officers, doctors, maybe engineers. Possibly gymnasium teachers (läroverkslärare), in spite of the touch of the comic which for some reason was associated with the work. Foundry proprietors, estate owners, and university professors were certainly respected, as were bank directors. Lawyers, on the other hand, were a suspect relation, and because of an awareness of this camouflaged their work with titles like deputy district judge,

which for the most part embellished even the younges[lawyers. Priests who played cards (vira) were approved of, but Methodist or free church ministers absolutely not. . . . Really one ought to be a bureau chief, a judge in a court of appeals or have a judicial district. Of the living conditions of the workers, I had no conception. I was only certain that an ill-clad person was a worker; the concepts worker and ruffian were not sharply distinct . . . their main occupation after working hours seemed to me to be buying and drinking whisky (brännvin).[20]

Herbert Tingsten (born 1896) comments in his memoirs on the extreme class distinctions in the years after the turn of the century.[21] His father, too, was a modest official, the director of Stockholm's Sanitation Department. Not even as a child did he use the personal *du* form with the children of the foreman and workers who lived on his parents' property, however. Workers and workers' children in his world were seen as hostile and dangerous. There was some objective basis for this because of hostility and fighting between the children who went to the *läroverk* (the academic school) and those who went to the *folkskola;* the former wore little caps that flagged their *överklass* status. He also points out how the farm workers tipped their caps to his father in deference, and whom his father would recognize only by their last names.

The great status gulf and social distance between the working class and the higher-status groups pointed out by these typical examples should help us understand the early radicalism of the Social Democrats and the great hostility shown to them by the respectable classes.

Correlates of Stratification in Contemporary Sweden

In this section we will look at a number of diverse areas of behavior in terms of how they are related to social status. In a number of these areas, class differences are as minimal as are to be found in any modern society.

Speech. In Sweden there are a few variations of speech that are great enough to be regarded as dialects (most notably in Dalarna), but these are now rapidly disappearing, and, as everywhere, the educated have a more extensive vocabulary, use better diction, and use more correct grammar than the less educated. Yet patterns of speech and accent are not much related to social status. The situation is probably little different in this regard from "general American," the American English spoken in the west and midwest of the United States. This is in contrast to England and Germany and even to some extent the northeastern United States, where there is some relationship between high status and the patterns of speech and accent cultivated in certain private schools.

Names. In Sweden and in all the Scandinavian countries, surnames are indicators of social origins or at least of some of one's paternal ancestors. There is a clear distinction between country names, on the one hand, and town and noble names, on the other. These distinctions are less and less meaningful as the great social circulation of Swedish society continues to mix the population and as more and more Swedes with common names change them, as they are encouraged to do by the government. Yet some correlation between family names and social status continues to exist.

Country names are all the names ending in "son"—the Johanssons, Carlssons, Svenssons, Erikssons, and so forth. This is from the traditional Scandinavian pattern of naming sons after their fathers—a tradition now practiced only in Iceland. Thus Erik, son of Johan, was called Erik Johansson, Erik's son Sven would be known as Sven Eriksson, and so on. An alternative pattern of obtaining permanent family names in the nineteenth century was the practice of adopting some geographical place name. For example, Ekström means literally "oak stream," Lindström means "linden" or "basswood stream," Lindahl means "linden" or "basswood valley," Berg simply means "mountain," and Myrdal means "swamp" or "bog valley."

Long-term upper-class and noble names are very different. For example, Hammarskjöld, Rudenschöld, Silverskjöld, or Leijonhufvud are immediately recognized by any Swede as noble names. A common pattern was to add the suffix "skjöld" (literally, shield) to one's family name when one was ennobled. Many Swedish noble names, however, came from Scotland, Belgium, and Germany, such as Hamilton, de Geer, and von Sydow; many noble families came originally at the invitation of Gustavus Adolphus in the seventeenth century. Having a latinized Swedish name, such as Linnaeus, Tiselius, or Celsius, is also generally an indicator that one had high status forebears in the eighteenth century when it was high style, particularly among priests and members of the learned professions, to latinize one's surname.

Gunnar Boalt some years ago studied the relation between family name and social class.[22] Using a register of Stockholm citizens, he found that 9 percent had upper-class names. However, among those with the thirteen most common names (mostly names ending in "son" and comprising 1073 columns in the register), only 3 percent were classified as upper class. Among the next fifty-four names in frequency (539 columns), 7 percent were classified as upper class. In contrast 63 percent of those with noble names were classified as upper class. Yet it should be noted that a study by Hans L. Zetterberg found 3 percent of those listed in the *Nobility Register* (*Adels Kalender*) to have working-class occupations.[23]

Voting. In the earlier discussion of political parties it was pointed out that the relationship between class and occupation with political party preference is as close in Sweden as in any country in the world. However, the class differential in voting is quite small in Sweden; it is certainly much smaller than in the United States. Table 7.1 shows the percentages of people voting in national elections in 1964 in Sweden and in the United States, by occupation and income. Note that the breakdown of the Swedish data both in terms of occupation and income is more refined than the American data. Yet the voting differentials are substantially less in Sweden than in the United States. For example in 1964 91 percent of the highest occupational-status category voted, as compared with 87 percent of non-farm workers, a differential of only four points. In the United States, for the more general categories white-collar and manual workers, the percentages are 82.7 and 66.3, a differential of 16.4 points. Using income, the difference between the lowest income category and the highest of the six Swedish categories—less than 5000 *kronor* as compared with 30,000 *kronor* and over—is only 17 points. In the United States, however, the differential between the lowest income category of under $2000 as compared with the highest category of $10,000 and over is 35.3 points.

Part of the explanation for these differences is the much greater organization of the Swedish workers and the virtual absence of any culturally deprived and alienated minorities. It should also be pointed out that a great deal has been done in Sweden to make voting easy. For example, everyone is permanently registered, one spouse can vote for the other, and voting is done on Sundays rather than on Tuesdays, so it is not necessary to take time off from work. Also, migration does not temporarily disfranchise a sizeable minority in Sweden as it does in the United States. In any case, it is noteworthy that the percentage of non-farm workers who voted in Sweden in 1964 was 4.3 points

Table 7.1   Percent of Voters Among Population of Voting Age in 1964 National Elections in Sweden and the U.S., by Occupation and Income.

OCCUPATION			
Sweden		U.S.	
Owners of Large Businesses, Executives, Higher Civil Servants, etc. (6% of population)	91		
Farmers (10%)	91		
Owners of Smaller Enterprises, Not Farmers (9%)	82		
Lower White Collar, Clerks, etc. (26%)	89	White-Collar Workers	82.7
		Manual Workers	66.3
Farm Workers with Subsidiary Activities (6%)	82	Service Workers	66.9
		Farm Workers	65.2
Remaining Workers (43%)	87		
INCOME			
Sweden		U.S.	
30,000 and over	94	10,000 and over	84.9
20,000–29,999	93	7,500–9,999	78.3
15,000–19,999	88	5,000–7,499	72.4
10,000–14,999	86	3,000–4,999	62.7
5,000–9,999	87	2,000–2,999	57.6
0–4,999 kronor	77	Under $2,000	49.6

SOURCE: Central Bureau of Statistics, *Riksdagsmannavalen åren, 1961–1964* (Stockholm, 1965), pp. 93, 97; U.S. Department of Commerce, *Current Population Reports* (Washington, D.C.: Bureau of the Census, October 25, 1965), Series P–20, No. 143, pp. 24, 40.

greater than the percentage of white-collar workers who voted in the United States in the same year.

Religion. There is much less relation between social status and religion in Sweden than in American society and perhaps most other societies. The great majority of Swedes are quite indifferent to organized religion even if nearly all of them are baptized, confirmed, married, and buried by the Church. However, there are some slight differences. Membership in the free churches is certainly skewed toward the lower social classes. It is also true that the lower-middle classes evidence more measurable religiosity than either the higher social groups or the working class.[24]

Demography. Life expectancy for both men and women in Sweden is as high as in any country in the world, and from this observation we can probably assume that class differentials in mortality are minimal.

In any case, I have found no data on the subject. The same guess might be made about infant and maternal mortality rates, which are both at the lowest levels. As was previously mentioned, class differences in fertility are clearly minimal; aside from the rural population, there is probably no inverse relationship in Sweden between social status and fertility; and, indeed, the situation now may well be the opposite, a direct relationship between status and fertility.[25]

Education. It has been made clear that the structure of the Swedish educational system is highly egalitarian by Western European standards.[26] It is also clear that students of working-class backgrounds are less likely to choose a second foreign language in the seventh year and that they are less likely to enter the gymnasium and to go on to the universities than higher-status youth. However, the proportion of working-class youth who go on to academic secondary education and to the universities is higher in Sweden (along with Norway, Finland, and Britain) than elsewhere in Western Europe, though it is not as high as in the United States, Canada, or the Eastern European countries. As in the United States, however, the desire of Swedish parents to have their children complete academic secondary school and go on to higher education has become virtually universal. This is still far from the case in England or in the Continental European countries. That English working-class parents are commonly opposed or ambivalent even over sending their children to grammar schools has been made clear by Brian Jackson and Dennis Marsden in their study *Education and the Working Class*.[27] In a seminar of university students in Germany which I taught in the summer of 1965, I asked the students to estimate what percentage of German parents would like to send their children to the universities. Most guessed in the 20 to 30 percent range.

Dress. The Swedes are probably the best-dressed people in the world. They are more formal in their dress than are the other Scandinavians. In any town of any size, as in Stockholm, one would have difficulty telling working-class people from middle-class people by their dress or their appearance, though there is less high style and more homogeneity in Sweden than one might observe on Fifth Avenue or North Michigan Avenue in America. Few working-class women would go downtown without wearing a "dress" coat and a hat. Cleaning women, when they come to the house, are generally formally dressed and change to work. This is part of the enormous emphasis on appearance that one finds throughout Swedish society.

The cult of informality in dress that has become so predominant in America has little counterpart in urban Sweden, except now among the young. There are also few peasant types left in rural Sweden, people who have grown stout with age and dress in the dark traditional garb of the old, a type still common in rural Germany and France.

Newspaper reading. The press of some modern societies is sharply divided between a quality press and a popular press, whereas in some other societies—most notably the Scandinavian countries—there is little distinction. In England there is a small number of quality dailies, above all *The Times* and *The Manchester Guardian* that have a combined circulation of a little more than half a million.[28] At the other extreme are a number of low-level popular newspapers, such as *The Mirror* and *The Daily Mail*, that have circulations of many millions each. The situation is very much the same in West Germany, where there are a small number of quality papers, such as Hamburg's *Die Welt* and the *Frankfurter Allgemeine*, and probably the lowest-level popular press to be found in any of the developed societies. The largest and most well known (even notorious) is Axel Springer's *Bild Zeitung*, a four or six page daily full of sex, scandal, homely wisdom, and conservative politics, which has a daily circulation of well over 4 million. Even in the United States in some cities, such as New York, Washington, D.C., and St. Louis, there is a clear distinction between a quality press and a more popular press, though in no sense is this as marked as in Britain, West Germany, or France. In Sweden, by contrast, there is virtually no distinction between a popular press and a quality press. In Stockholm, until April 1966, there were three morning papers—one Conservative, one Liberal, and one Social Democratic —and all of them had a wide, across-the-board appeal, with a culture page, discussion of books, and articles by academics, combined with all sorts of popular features. Since 1966 there have only been two morning papers, one Liberal and one Conservative.[29] It would be impossible to say that *Dagens Nyheter* (Liberal) is more of a quality newspaper than *Svenska Dagbladet* (Conservative), or the other way around. In the evening there are two tabloids, *Expressen* (Liberal) and *Aftonbladet* (Social Democratic); one could not easily say that one was more of a quality paper than the other, and neither deals much with scandal— though there is much more here than in the morning papers—and both are of higher quality than their British or German counterparts.

Only in Gothenburg does one find something of a distinction, but not a large one, between a quality paper and a more popular paper. *Göteborgs-Handels- och Sjöfarts-Tidning* (Liberal) has one of the most respected "culture pages" in Sweden and is clearly a quality paper as compared with *Göteborgs-Posten* (also Liberal), a more popular paper with a circulation almost five times as great.

Sweden has the largest circulation (and presumably readership) of newspapers in the world—54 copies per 100 people per day.[30] The figure for Denmark is only 34 per 100 and in Norway it is 38; Britain is almost as high with 51 per 100 persons, but the quality of most of the press is low.[31] For the United States the comparable figure is only 32 copies per 100 people per day with a lower average intellectual level than in Sweden. *Dagens Nyheter*, the largest morning paper in Sweden, claims that 62 percent of the households in greater Stockholm subscribe to it,[32] and there are four major dailies in the city. According to a 1954 study (see Table 7.2), the reading of at least one daily newspaper is virtually universal in Sweden, even in the working class. Note also that the average working-class household reads 1.53 newspapers daily, a figure somewhat higher than the rural middle class (1.41) and not far behind the urban middle class (1.87). Even allowing for some exaggeration, these are indeed impressive figures. In France, by contrast, a 1955 Worker Survey found that 60 percent of the unskilled workers read a daily newspaper, 69 percent of the skilled workers, 73 percent of the white-collar workers, and 78 percent of the supervisors.[33] Richard F. Hamilton, in commenting on the attention French workers pay to the mass media, states that "again we find the workers isolated" from events outside of their immediate

Table 7.2   Number of Newspapers Read, by Social Class, 1954 (Percentages).

| | *Number of Newspapers* | | | | | | Number of | |
	0	1	2	3	4	5–8	Households	Average
Better situated	2.0	23.4	36.9	21.4	11.6	4.7	190	2.38
Middle class, urban	1.0	38.9	40.0	13.9	5.2	1.0	1385	1.87
Middle class, rural	2.1	60.6	32.5	4.3	0.5	—	933	1.41
Working class	2.8	52.9	34.5	7.7	2.0	0.1	2186	1.53
Total	2.1	49.6	35.7	9.2	2.9	0.5	4698	1.63

SOURCE: From a study by Jörgen Westerståhl and Carl-Gunnar Janson, cited in Gunnar Boalt, *Masskommunikation* (Stockholm: Bokförlaget Aldus/Bonniers, 1965), p. 52.

Table 7.3 Percentage of Total Income Before Taxes Received by Top 5 percent in Sweden, the United States, and Selected Other Countries.

Sweden	(1948)	20%
United States	(1950)	20
Denmark	(1952)	20
Great Britain	(1951–1952)	21
Barbados	(1951–1952)	22
Puerto Rico	(1953)	23
India	(1955–1956)	24
West Germany	(1950)	24
Italy	(1948)	24
Netherlands	(1950)	25
Ceylon	(1952–1953)	31
Guatemala	(1947–1948)	35
El Salvador	(1946)	36
Mexico	(1957)	37
Colombia	(1953)	42
Northern Rhodesia	(1946)	45
Kenya	(1949)	51
Southern Rhodesia	(1946)	65

SOURCE: Simon Kuznets, "Quantitative Aspects of the Economic Growth of Nations," in *Economic Development and Cultural Change*, XI (January 1963), Table 3.

personal sphere.[34] It would be difficult to make such an observation of the Swedish working class, at least as far as newspaper reading is concerned.

Income Distribution. Income distribution in Sweden before taxes is probably about the same as in the United States. Both countries have among the most egalitarian income distribution in the world. In Table 7.3 note that in both countries the top 5 percent of income recipients have 20 percent of the total income. However, after taxes, Swedish income distribution is more egalitarian than the American. The progressiveness of taxation in Sweden is appreciably greater at the middle levels than in the United States, and there are not so many devices, such as a ceiling on tax rates for capital gains and various depletion allowances, to aid the rich. There is also an additional wealth tax, which makes it difficult to amass a sizable fortune. Another factor that tends to make for more equitable income distribution is the system of welfare allowances, which disproportionately aids the lower-income groups. For example, they gain from the child allowances, from the national health insurance, from the basic pension, and from other welfare benefits.[35] Related to this is the observation that variations in the wages of the skilled and unskilled are less in Swedish society than in American society.[36]

The progressiveness and magnitude of income taxes in Sweden are among the highest in the world, though they do not reach Norwegian levels, which are probably the highest in Western Europe. Table 7.4 gives the 1967 Swedish income-tax schedule. A highly successful professor, for example, who has a total income of $20,000 a year— $14,000 from his salary and $6,000 from outside income—pays just about $10,000 income tax, or about half of his total income.[37] An American professor with a similar income and perhaps two children would probably not pay more than $4000 income tax, about 20 percent. A Swedish skilled worker who makes $5000 per year would pay $1400 per year in income taxes, or about 28 percent. His counterpart in America would probably not pay much more than $500 a year, or a mere 10 percent.

However, in Sweden one gets more for the taxes he pays compared with the United States. He gets full medical insurance, a genuinely adequate retirement pension, tax-free child allowances, educational

Table 7.4   1967 Swedish Income Tax Rates for a Married Man Living with His Wife.

Annual Income in *kronor*	Tax Rate, Percentage
5,000	2.4
10,000	13.6
15,000	22.4
20,000	25.5
25,000	28.1
30,000	31.0
35,000	33.2
40,000	35.4
45,000	37.3
50,000	38.9
60,000	41.7
70,000	44.0
80,000	45.8
90,000	47.7
100,000	49.2
120,000	51.3
150,000	54.2
200,000	57.7

NOTE: 5.17 *kronor* = $1.
SOURCE: *Dagens Nyheter*, October 29, 1967, p. 2.

Exhibit 7.1   Attitudes Toward Happiness of People in Sweden and in Different Countries, 1958 (Percentages).

Question: "In which country do you believe people are happiest?"

Sweden	47
Other countries	17
There is no such country	36
	100

Percentage who mention Sweden:

Workers	49
Middle class	47
Better situated	29

Reasons for naming Sweden as the country where "people are happiest."
Some persons gave two reasons.

Our neutrality, spared from war	26
High standard of living	25
Social welfare	13
Security	8
It is a free country	8
Good care for the aged	1
No class distinctions, good possibilities for education for all	1
We have it good here, am personally satisfied to live here	15
Cannot explain why	14

NOTE: N = 750.

SOURCE: Svenska Institutet för Opinionsundersökningar (SIFO) (Stockholm, August 22, 1958).

allowances for the children, and so forth. Undeniably the upper-middle and higher income groups get less than they pay for and the lower income groups get more.

Views toward their society. Swedes are very much aware that they are living in an affluent, secure, and successful society. When Swedes are asked, "in which country do you believe people are happiest," most of those who choose a country pick Sweden (see Exhibit 7.1). Almost half the Swedes asked believe people are happiest in Sweden. Seventeen percent mentioned other countries—3 percent mentioned the United States and 2.5 percent mentioned Switzerland. More than one-third gave the sensible answer that there is no such country where people are happiest. It is also interesting to note that there is an inverse relationship between those who believe that people are happiest in Sweden and social class. Among the working class, 49 percent believe people are happiest in Sweden, as compared with 47 percent of middle-class respondents; only 29 percent among the "better situated"

—the Swedish euphemism for upper class—responded that people are happiest in Sweden. The lower percentage in the highest-class group may simply reflect a greater sophistication on the part of the better-educated, yet it is notable that there is virtually no difference between the working and middle class here. Note that the reasons most often given for people being happiest in Sweden are neutrality and being spared from war. Another study has shown that more working-class people believe that their class has the most power in society than members of the other classes.[38] This is undoubtedly a direct consequence of the long-term dominance of the Social Democrats.

Another pertinent observation about how Swedes view their society is that middle-class people and working-class people do not differ much in their conceptions of the status system. In a national study of occupational prestige done in the late 1950s, Gösta Carlsson concluded that "the two sub-samples [working and middle class] did not to any considerable extent differ in the way they judged the prestige of occupations."[39]

Interpersonal relations. One vestige from the traditional society that frequently causes difficulties and embarrassment in interpersonal relations is how one should address another. In 1958, *SIFO* asked a cross section of the population how they would address a person who was obviously working class and how they would address someone who was obviously "better situated." Some of the findings of this survey are found in Table 7.5. In Sweden there are a number of subtle class differences in how people address each other. For example, there are two forms in the second person singular—*du*, which is the intimate you, and *ni*, which is the impersonal you but which sometimes has a connotation of a social superior talking to an inferior or of a customer talking to a service person. On the other hand, *du* is sometimes used nonreciprocally by a person of high status talking to someone of lower status. To avoid these problems, the third person singular is often used, a man is addressed as *herrn* (the gentleman) and a woman as *damen* (the lady). This, however, is a very formal way of addressing people and is most common among older people, particularly those of high status. Somewhat less formal is the use of a title, for example, when asking whether "the professor is enjoying the party." These problems are certainly an impediment to interpersonal relations, and they are perhaps partly a reflection of the general difficulties the Swedes seem to have in communicating with each other in an intimate way. Frequently social equals will address each other in the

third person, because *ni* (formal you) sometimes has a superior connotation and *du* is regarded as too intimate. It is a revealing observation that the third person is rarely used in Norwegian and Danish and
that the second person singular does not have the problematic connotations that it does in Swedish. Strong class distinctions in forms of
address are indicated in Table 7.5, which shows responses to the question "How do you usually address an unknown male who seems to be
about the same age as yourself and who belongs to the working class
(the better-situated class)?" The data show that men are far more likely
to address someone of about the same age who is obviously working
class with the intimate *du* form rather than with the impersonal *ni* or
with the third person. Similarly men who are obviously "better situated" are more likely to be addressed with the impersonal *ni* or with
the third person.

**Table 7.5   Terms of Address to Unknown Males and Females of Different Social
Classes, by Sex, 1957 (Percentages).**

MEN

	To male worker	To "better situated" male
Du (you, personal)	56	21
Ni (you, impersonal)	30	44
Herrn (the gentleman)	12	29
Other	1	4
It Varies	1	2
	100	100

WOMEN*

	To female worker	To "better situated" female
Du (you, personal)	13	7
Ni (you, impersonal)	40	34
Frun (the Mrs.)	4	5
Fröken (Miss)	8	3
Damen (the lady)	33	43
Other	2	2
It Varies	2	2
	102	96

* The question for women included the condition "when you cannot tell whether she
is married or unmarried."

NOTE: N = 1,000; 900 answered these questions.

SOURCE: Svenska Institutet för Opinionsundersökningar (*SIFO*), Stockholm, June 21,
1957.

Note also from Table 7.5 that the situation is more complicated for women, that there are more possible terms of address. It is also clear that class variation in who is addressed is substantially less among women than it is among men.

There is concern with this problem of address among the Swedes. In political parties, for example, everyone is supposed to call each other *du*, and a number of private offices have, by edict, put forth the policy that everyone is to use the *du* form with everyone else, which is difficult for some people, particularly older people. However, there seems to be little question that more and more people, particularly the young, are using *du*. Some self-consciously egalitarian Swedes make it a practice to use only *du*. It is interesting to note that in the 1930s Herbert Tingsten, in writing about this problem in his memoirs, made the prediction that *ni* would become the more universal form.[40] But it is now clear that it is *du*.

It is important not to confound reserve and formality in interpersonal relations with deferential behavior, and this can easily be done by the casual observer of Swedish interaction. Yet interpersonal relations are not as egalitarian as they are in the United States, even after we make due allowance for the ritual and reserve (or inhibition) that characterize interpersonal relations. One of the strongest criticisms of New-Left radicals in Sweden is the persistence of a class consciousness that permeates the society, which is evidenced by the class bias in terms of address.[41] In terms of egalitarianism in interpersonal relations, the Scandinavian countries would seem to rank as follows: Iceland, Norway, Sweden, Finland, and Denmark. This is largely an impressionistic rating, but I think it would be accepted by most close observers of variations among the Scandinavian countries.

Iceland is a radically egalitarian society, probably more than any other modern society. Everyone in Iceland is addressed by his first name, except for the President and the Bishop. Indeed, people are listed in the telephone book by their *first* names followed by their second name, which is based on the father's name, and then by their occupation. Social rank, education, and age appear to have minimal influence in interpersonal relations.[42]

In all of the other Scandinavian countries except Iceland, there is a great emphasis on titles, particularly those of occupation. A person's occupation or other title precedes his name in the telephone book, in the newspaper, and on the gravestone. It is an integral part of one's identity. The status implications of this, however, must not be exaggerated. A functional explanation for this pattern is that since so many people share so few names, it is necessary to have another means by which to identify people. For example, there are about forty-three pages of Johanssons in the Stockholm telephone directory. To find a Johansson's number, it is often not enough to know his first name. Indeed there may be scores of Johanssons with the same first name. So it is advantageous, if not absolutely necessary, to list all the Johanssons first by occupation and then by first name. The number of common occupations is much greater than the number of common first names. This observation, I think, makes Lipset's "evidence" about the continuing elitist character of Swedish society quite irrelevant. He has written that "Swedish telephone books still list individuals alphabetically *within* occupational groups. So to look up a Swede in the phone book, you must know his occupation. He is still a doctor, printer, or carpenter before he is a person."[43]

A pertinent observation about the use of titles in Sweden as compared with Finland has been made by Erik Allardt.[44] In Sweden the emphasis is generally on occupational titles, whereas in Finland there is greater use of educational degrees as titles. There is probably also greater use of nobility titles in Finland than in Sweden, where occupation almost always takes precedence over nobility. Yet there are occasional exceptions to this in Sweden; if a man is an ambassador and a count (*greve*), the latter usually takes precedence.[45] A baron who is also an ambassador, on the other hand, would probably be called ambassador. The greater emphasis in Sweden on occupational titles rather than on educational degrees or titles of nobility indicates a stronger value emphasis on both egalitarianism and achievement.

Yet it is clear that there are specific patterns of deference operating in Swedish society, but the nature of this deference is clearly different from that in England, where it is directed to gentlemen and to the upper classes, to "them" as opposed to "us." In Sweden deference is made to those who have high *achieved* position and to those who have expert knowledge, such as for professors, engineers, and specialists of all kinds. Only in certain specific ways, therefore, can we call Sweden an elitist society, and not at all in the same way that we generally regard England an elitist society. A Professor Karlsson, of whom there are many in Sweden, who is the son of a farmer, will receive more deference and respect than one who is a gentleman farmer and a member of the nobility. Nobility in Sweden, as compared with England and perhaps even Denmark, means quite little. Middle-class parents whose daughter married someone with a title might view it as a small garnish, but generally not much more. In most cases they would prefer their daughter marry an aspiring academic or engineer rather than one who is only a count or a baron.

Material level of living. Differences in material level of living among the social classes is probably less in Sweden than in any non-Scandinavian European society. With respect to living quarters, Kurt Mayer says about Australian housing what might be said about Swedish living quarters: "The overall impression is that of relatively small difference in the quality of housing for the great majority of the population." [46] About three-fourths of non-farm Swedish families live in apartments, and while there is certainly variation in size and appointments, particularly in the largest cities, there is not much variation in quality. Outside of Stockholm, Gothenburg, and Malmö, however, it is interesting to note how very similar and homogeneous the apartment houses and neighborhoods look, and it is very difficult to tell which are working class and which are middle class; most in fact are neither. Because of the acute housing shortage that has plagued Sweden for several decades, there is a great deal of mixing. This is characteristic, for example, of Vällingby and Farsta, which are the largest and most well known of the planned suburbs outside of Stockholm.

Class differences inside the home are not so striking as one would observe in England or America. Most furniture that has been produced in recent decades has contemporary lines. There is little class difference in taste in furniture style. The cheapest and the most expensive furniture is, for the most part, Scandinavian contemporary. The living rooms of working-class homes typically have oil paintings on the wall, a bookcase with a number of books, and a set of encyclopedia, all of which are considered necessities for a respectable home throughout Scandinavia. Indeed the living rooms of professors and workers are not as different as they are in America. In fact one of the first observations that Scandinavians make about American homes is the absence of paintings on the walls and books in the bookcases.[47] It should be mentioned, too, that there is relatively little variation in rents by urban American or Parisian standards. In 1968 the "extremely high rents" of some of the new and large apartments in Stockholm was a subject of much concern in the press. These rents were in the area of $120 to $200 per month for large two-bedroom apartments with balconies, which are virtually universal in Scandinavia now. In the largest city of a country with a per capita income as high as

Sweden has, this does not seem high at all, but still many remain vacant because the market for expensive apartments is quite small. Typically, the rent for a modern two-bedroom apartment is $60 to $80 a month.

Sweden does not quite approach American levels in the number of automobiles, appliances, and telephones, but they are close. The distribution of these items is more equitable, however, than in the United States. There is one personal automobile in Sweden for every four persons, as compared with every three persons in the United States; many fewer families have two or more cars, as compared with the United States.[48] Refrigerators and modern stoves are virtually universal in the cities and throughout most of the country, but individual automatic washing machines and dryers are not yet. The proportion of households with telephones is greater than in the United States, but relatively fewer homes have more than one.[49] Sweden is surpassed only by the United States in the ubiquitousness of the television set.

Related to the level of living is the great decline in the proportion of families with domestic help. In a 1963–1964 study, only 6 percent of Swedish families had any domestic help, full- or part-time; just over 1 percent of Swedish households had full-time help.[50] Domestic help is more common in Denmark, where 11 percent of the population reports having such help, but it is less common in Norway, where only 4 percent do.

Book reading. Book reading is high in Sweden as compared with the United States, which has repeatedly been shown by comparative polls to have the lowest of all the advanced societies.[51] Sweden is at the other end of the continuum in book reading. A 1957 *SIFO* study asked a national sample of Swedes whether they had read at least one book in the past four weeks. The percentages answering in the affirmative, by class, are as follows: 70 percent among the better situated, 42 percent among the middle class, and 37 percent among the working class.[52] Again we can observe that there is only a small difference between the middle and working class. A Malmö study of reading habits, which was done in the mid-1960s by Harald Swedner, found differences between the middle and working class to be somewhat greater than the 1957 figures suggest, but he came forth with some remarkable observations about book reading in the working class.[53] The two most popular Swedish writers for a number of years have been Selma Lagerlöf (1858–1940) and Vilhelm Moberg (born

1898). Swedner found 72.1 percent of the male workers interviewed to have read at least one book by Lagerlöf and 70.3 percent to have read at least one book by Moberg. Among foreign writers, the following percentages of working-class males claimed to have read at least one book of the following authors: Ernest Hemingway, 38.7 percent; Charles Dickens, 26.1 percent; Agatha Christie, 25.2 percent; John Steinbeck, 24.3 percent; Erich Maria Remarque, 21.6 percent. Very few, however, had ever read books by Franz Kafka or Alberto Moravia, who were read widely in the highest social class. The middle and upper classes had read more of all of the many writers asked about in the interview, but the striking observation is the proportion of the working class who read novels. A study of the Swedish as compared with the English or American working classes would doubtless show the Swedes to be far more active readers of serious books.[54]

The Universities and Stratification

One of the most well-known Swedish novels from the 1920s, *Lacemaker Lekholm Has an Idea* by Gustav Hellström, deals with the idea of a lower-middle class lacemaker as to how his descendants might rise in Swedish society.[55] The answer would have been obvious to a Swede even forty or fifty years ago: by taking the *studentexam* and going to the university. In the novel a third generation Lekholm who did go to the university said of his grandfather who was born in 1829:

It is not likely that grandfather had even the faintest notion of how genuinely Swedish he was when he got it into his head that his sons should be learned men. One can surely safely maintain that this idea, which apparently was the only idea the Old Man had in his head, has been responsible for eight-tenths of Sweden's cultural values and Sweden's cultural history.[56]

This quotation illustrates the traditional importance of the university in Sweden as a means of rising in the social order. Perhaps since as early as the mid-eighteenth century, the universities have been the major vehicle of upward mobility into the upper-middle and upper classes, because they have functioned to train the dominant official elites since then. That the universities functioned to train the members of the national bureaucracies, the professors and gymnasium teachers, the clergy, and the doctors is not unusual. But the lateness of industrialization gave the universities a near monopoly in training the elites;

indeed, virtually all the elites (except the military) and only the elites were trained in universities until the beginning of this century. These groups may be called the "old" elites of Swedish society. It was really not until after the beginning of the twentieth century that the new industrial, financial, and mercantile elites began to have numerical importance.

A similar relation between the universities and the old elites existed in pre-World War I England, except that in England there were large nonuniversity-trained commercial and industrial elites that did not have a counterpart in nonindustrialized and rural Sweden. Because of this, the English universities did not have the near monopoly on the means of social mobility into the upper reaches of society that the Swedish universities have had. And, as bestowers of social prestige, the public schools in England were more important than the universities. In 1880 in Sweden 93 percent of the 126 members of the upper chamber of the Riksdag had a higher education, which was an extraordinarily high figure for the time.[57] In addition, and quite unlike England, virtually all scholarship was carried out within the universities.[58] This central and commanding role of the universities in preindustrial Sweden was perhaps similar to the role of universities in much of nineteenth-century Germany, but it continued a generation longer in Sweden because of the later industrialization.

The relationship between higher education and the public service has been close in all the Scandinavian countries, but particularly so in Sweden and Finland. At the end of the 1880s, there were sixty-six students in higher education per 100,000 population in Sweden as compared with seventy-six to seventy-eight in Denmark and eighty in Norway, yet the number of higher civil servants around 1880 was 350 per 100,000 population in Sweden as compared with 280 to 300 in Denmark and Norway.[59] An indication of the extent to which Swedish higher education has continued to train "the official classes" is the estimate that as recently as the late 1950s 70 percent of all Swedes aged twenty-five through sixty-four with academic degrees were employed by national or local government.[60]

It is at the middle levels of social and occupational status that higher education in Sweden (and all of Europe) has played a small role as compared with the United States. Yet, with the tremendous increase in enrollments, there has been an abatement of the elite focus of higher education in Sweden.

Even the Swedish labor movement has placed a great stress on formal education, both in terms of explicitly formulated policy goals and in terms of latent effects. One can argue that in spite of the fact that the entrance of the lower classes into politics has opened new channels for social mobility, higher education is still regarded as the ideal channel for upward mobility. Regarding the place of higher education in the Scandinavian value system compared with other countries, one can present an argument analogous to that used by Lipset and Bendix to deal with social mobility in the United States.[61] While overall mobility is not higher in the United States than in a number of Western European countries, the belief in individual social mobility plays a greater role in the American value system than in that of other societies. In the same vein, one might say that, in spite of the opening of new channels for social mobility in Sweden and Scandinavia, higher education carries with it the distinction of being the most legitimate channel. This is reflected in the studies of the prestige of different occupations. In all of the Scandinavian countries, occupations requiring higher education are systematically and highly evaluated. Harry Eckstein, in his analysis of authority patterns in Norway, makes the following remarks about the importance of schooling and education:

Norwegians tend to define in highly specialized terms a remarkable variety of social roles and to recruit men to such roles on the basis of formally acquired qualifications, particularly special schooling. Special functional training is, of course, typical of modern societies, for functionally specific relations play a large role in all of them. But the Norwegians go much farther in this distinction than others: they even insist on considerably special schooling for such people as postal or cafeteria workers. . . .[62]

This emphasis on schooling pointed out by Eckstein is even stronger in Sweden and Finland than it is in Norway. Schooling and education are evaluated highly as such. Against this background it can be understood why higher education has a particular legitimacy as an avenue for social mobility. It is sometimes assumed that European workers are not interested in individual social mobility since their main access to a better life has been through political organization. In Sweden and the other Scandinavian countries, however, special value has been attached to academic studies in all social classes. As pointed out earlier, virtually all Swedes want their children to complete gymnasium and go to the university.[63] Such a statement could probably not be made of any non-Scandinavian European society.

Is There a Power Elite in Sweden?

Looking at the elites in Swedish society, it becomes rather clear that there is a high degree of concentration of power, particularly as regards the ownership and control of Swedish industry. Indeed, economic concentration is relatively greater in Sweden than it is in either the United States or West Germany.[64] A great increase in the concentration of ownership of Swedish industry has occurred since World War II. Yet Swedish corporations tend to be small. There are no Swedish corporations as large as several Dutch and Swiss corporations.[65] Fifteen families together with two corporations have majority control in 200 large Swedish industrial concerns that employ over 450,000 people, almost half of all those employed in private industry.[66] This represents a very high degree of economic concentration.

This came to be regarded as a central problem of Swedish society by the Left in the late 1960s. While this concentration of power is accepted as economically efficient, it is questioned from a democratic point-of-view. Indeed there has been increasing cooperation between the government and the industrial giants. In several instances the government has entered into joint ventures with large Swedish corporations, particularly in the atomic energy field. The formation of ASEA-ATOM on a 50-50 state-private (Wallenberg) ownership basis for the manufacture of atomic reactors is the most well-known example.

Yet the owners of Swedish industry are very much in the background. Few are known to the general public. Neither they nor members of their families are in any public way involved in politics, nor is there any evidence that they are involved in much "behind the scenes" activity. What Frederick Eggleston has written about Australia applies as well to Sweden except that the Swedes might show a little more respect for wealth. He maintains that "in Australia, there is little respect for wealth as such . . . . It is harder for an industrial magnate to enter politics than for a camel to pass through the eye of a needle. . . . The wealthy classes have never provided leaders or shown the community any guidance in political matters."[67]

The most economically powerful family in Sweden is the Wallenberg family. They own a major interest in seventy corporations with over 180,000 employees,[68] which represents almost 20 percent of those employed in private industry. They have majority interest in

AB Svenska Maskinverken (heavy industrial equipment) and Järnvägs AB Stockholms—Saltsjön (a small railroad). They also hold dominating minority interest in Allmänna Svenska Elektriska AB (the Swedish General Electric Company), Atlas Copco AB (shipbuilding), AB Electrolux (vacuum cleaners, appliances), AB Garphytte Bruk (steel mills), AB Investor (mutual funds), Kohlsva Jernverks AB (iron works), AB Nordströms Linbanor (tramways), Nymölla AB, Oppboga AB, AB Papyrus (quality papers), AB Scania-Vabis (trucks, buses), Stockholms Superfosfat Fabriks AB (fertilizers), Stora Kopparbergs Bergslags AB (iron mines), Svenska Aeroplan AB, Saab (jet planes, automobiles), AB Svenska Fläktfabriken (light industrial equipment), AB Svenska Järnvägsverkstäderna (locomotives, trains), Svenska Tändsticks AB (matches), Wifstavarfs AB (shipbuilding), Wikmanshytte Bruks AB (steel mills), and AB Incentive (mutual funds). They hold strong majority interest in AB Alfa-Laval (centrifuges, farm equipment) and Barnängens Tekn. Fabriker AB (paper diapers, surgical products). And, together with other owners, the Wallenbergs also have majority interest in AB Söderhamns Verkstäder (light industrial equipment), AB Nordiska Syrgasverken (gas works), and Unifors Kemiska AB (chemicals), as well as dominating minority interest in Telefon AB L.M. Ericsson (telephone equipment), AB Svenska Kullagerfabriken (*SKF*, ballbearings, many factories in the United States), AB Kopparfors (mining), AB Astra (drugs), and AB Nordiska Kompaniet (Sweden's most elegant department store).

The Wallenbergs also control one of the largest private banks in Sweden, Enskilda Banken. Yet their personal fortune is not much above $25 million (125 million Swedish *kronor*). However they have established family foundations over which they have control with assets in recent years of between $70 and $90 million. The total holdings of the Wallenbergs rank them only with the lowest levels of the richest Americans according to a recent *Fortune* survey,[69] which is an indication of the difficulties of becoming super-rich in Sweden.

The second greatest family fortune in Sweden is probably that of the Broström family (Swedish American Line, other shipping interests), whose total wealth is just a little over $30 million (165 Swedish *kronor*). Another of the richest and most economically powerful families, the Bonniers, owns a number of newspapers and magazines, publishing houses, and printing establishments. It is interesting to note that in Finland, which is just over half the size of and less economically developed than Sweden, there is a Left-Wing concern with "the twenty-five families," which suggests that there is less economic concentration there than in Sweden.

Occupational Prestige

There is now substantial literature that shows that in both modern and developing societies there is gross cross-national similarity in occupational prestige.[70] Everywhere, for example, doctors rank higher than salesmen, and salesmen rank higher than unskilled workers. What is interesting, however, are the smaller, more subtle variations in occupational prestige that basically reflect differences in national values. Even today, for example, it is clear that occupations in the civil service, particularly those requiring a university education, bestow greater prestige in Swedish as compared with American society. The enormous competition of university graduates to enter government service in Sweden is one indicator of this. And, another difference is the greater prestige of teachers in Sweden, particularly academic secondary-school teachers, though it has been declining in recent years.[71] The extraordinary prestige of primary-school teachers as indicated in Exhibit 7.2, however, is inexplicably high. If one is to accept this kind of survey-research evaluation of occupational prestige as valid,[72] a Swedish primary-school teacher is at the same prestige level as a shipowner and is ahead of a captain in the merchant marine. As we noted earlier, the prestige of professors in Sweden is especially high. Those in the military, both officers and enlisted men, probably have more prestige than they do in the United States in spite of the fact that Sweden has not been involved in a war for nearly 160 years. They, too, are employed by the government. This is probably true also of policemen, even though they are employed by lower levels of government.

Journalists and editors have particularly great prestige in Sweden. To be an editor of a major newspaper in Sweden places one very much at the top of the national status hierarchy. The editors of major papers are frequently scholars in their own right. And, because of the tendency of the Swedish press to quote the editorials of other papers, editors of provincial papers frequently develop national reputations. Relatively high prestige as compared with America also adheres to journalists, who are certainly one of the major groups of intellectuals (experts) outside of the universities, and they are so regarded.

Exhibit 7.2   Prestige Ratings of Twenty-six Occupations.

Professor	1.5
Company Director	1.6
Teacher, Elementary, Secondary*	1.9
Ship Owner	1.9
Pharmacist	1.9
Head Cashier	1.9
Colonel in the Armed Forces	2.0
Grocer, Shop Owner	2.1
Captain in Merchant Marine	2.2
Barber, Independent or Employer	2.3
Goldsmith, Employee	2.3
Carpenter, Independent or Employer	2.3
Accountant	2.4
Typographer	2.8
Taxicab Owner	2.8
Policeman	2.8
Shop Salesman	2.9
Noncommissioned Officer in Armed Forces	2.9
Building Laborer	2.9
Travelling Salesman	3.0
Actor	3.0
Waiter	3.1
Postman	3.2
Tailor, Employee	3.2
Shoe-Shiner	4.2

* Primary and secondary school teachers were given the same rating.
NOTE: N = 1700.

SOURCE: Gösta Carlsson, *Social Mobility and Class Structure* (Lund: CWK Gleerup, 1958), p. 148. Study originally done by *SIFO*.

In Sweden, there is not the prestige differential between theoretical and generalist work as compared with technical and applied work that one finds in England and to a lesser degree in the United States. Highly skilled technical workers have more prestige than in the Anglo-American countries. This is true of engineers at the expense of scientists.[73] And the status differential between doctors and dentists is probably less in Sweden than in the United States. On the other hand, work that generally does not require specialized or professional training, such as the occupations of businessman, clerk, and salesman, probably has less prestige in Sweden than in the United States.

What we see in Sweden is a great emphasis on occupation and specialized education as conveyors of prestige rather than wealth.

The income and wealth of a family is less visible in Sweden than in the United States, partly because the actual variations are less.[74] This is not to imply that Swedes are less immediately concerned than Americans with material goods, but only that material goods are less important in determining social status. Related to this is the observation that in Sweden there is little conception of a man who does not have a specific occupation, or of a gentlemanly style of life, such as one finds in England. A Harold Nicholson, the quintessence of the general unattached intellectual, writer, and man of affairs, is a type that is even rarer in Sweden than in the United States.[75]

Social Mobility

One of the striking observations about social mobility in Sweden is that even before the modern period there appears to have been a great deal of "status circulation" (which is the literal translation of the Swedish term for social mobility) relative to other Western countries. In an enormously informative book on social mobility in Sweden from 1680 to the present, the Swedish historian Sten Carlsson has shown the most typical pattern of upward generational mobility through Swedish history to have been that of farmer, clergyman, government official.[76] Indeed this is the translation of the title of his book: *Bonde-präst-ämbetsman*. An ideal typical example of this mobility pattern can be seen in Figure 7.1, which shows the rise and decline of the male descendants of Thorsten Rudenschöld, a seventeenth-century Swedish farmer. A later typical pattern of upward generational mobility that developed along with the establishment of compulsory education in the mid-nineteenth century was from farmer, to primary-school teacher, to government official.

As early as the latter part of the seventeenth century 30 percent of all clergymen were the sons of farmers, the only larger category (40 percent) were the sons of clergymen.[77] This is a high percentage for the time considering that the State Church clergy in Sweden has always had an upper-class status—all were products of Uppsala and Lund Universities—unlike the clergy of many other countries. In the eighteenth century the membership in the Swedish Academy of Science was heavily represented by clergymen and about one-quarter of all the members were the sons of clergymen.[78] Yet only between 3 and 4 percent of all the members in the year 1739 were the sons of farmers.

Figure 7.1   The Rise and Fall of Thorsten Rudenschöld's Descendants.

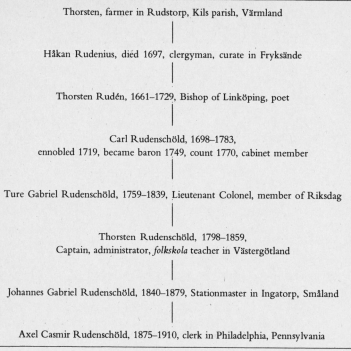

Thorsten, farmer in Rudstorp, Kils parish, Värmland

|

Håkan Rudenius, died 1697, clergyman, curate in Fryksände

|

Thorsten Rudén, 1661–1729, Bishop of Linköping, poet

|

Carl Rudenschöld, 1698–1783,
ennobled 1719, became baron 1749, count 1770, cabinet member

|

Ture Gabriel Rudenschöld, 1759–1839, Lieutenant Colonel, member of Riksdag

|

Thorsten Rudenschöld, 1798–1859,
Captain, administrator, *folkskola* teacher in Västergötland

|

Johannes Gabriel Rudenschöld, 1840–1879, Stationmaster in Ingatorp, Småland

|

Axel Casmir Rudenschöld, 1875–1910, clerk in Philadelphia, Pennsylvania

SOURCE: Adapted from Sten Carlsson, *Bonde-präst-ämbetsman* (Stockholm: Bökförlaget Prisma, 1962), p. 77.

In a classic statistical study of the Swedish nobility by Pontus Fahl-beck, the frequency of the disappearance of noble families and the entry into the nobility of new families is striking.[79] From the thir-teenth through the nineteenth centuries, one-third of all the noble lineages survived only one generation and few lasted more than four. Many, perhaps most, of those ennobled through Swedish history were the grandsons or, more frequently, the great grandsons of farmers. The last Swede to be ennobled was the famous Asian explorer Sven Hedin in 1902.

It must be pointed out, however, that the sons of farmers who went to the universities (most of whom became clergymen until this century) were only a small minority. Throughout the nineteenth century, when the overwhelming majority of the population were farmers, only 15 or 20 percent of the students in the universities were the sons of farmers.[80] Yet this was probably a higher figure than anywhere else in Europe at the time.

The proportion of outstanding Swedes who have been sons of the clergy is striking.[81] They include the biologist Linnaeus, the religionist Swedenborg, the astronomer Melanderhjelm, the chemist Wallerius, the mechanical genius Polhem, the astronomer Celsius, and perhaps *most* academics and authors prior to this century. In addition, many of the early liberal politicians were the sons of the free-church clergy. And it should be noted that many of these clergymen fathers were the sons of farmers.

Mobility to the upper levels of the Church of Sweden, however, generally took two generations in the clergy. The sons of farmers were most frequently lower-level clergy. Their sons, however, had a much greater chance of becoming bishops or cathedral priests. Yet the direct mobility from son of farmer to bishop seems to have increased after the mid-nineteenth century.[82] In the period from 1700 to 1865, only nine out of 117 clergymen who became bishops were the sons of farmers. Of the twenty-five clergymen who became bishops from 1865 to 1914, five were the sons of farmers.

Increasingly through the nineteenth century, however, becoming a primary-school (*folkskola*) teacher presented an alternative path of upward mobility for the sons of farmers. By the first decade of this century not fewer than 40 percent of the students in teacher-training institutions were the children of farmers; an additional 3 percent came from the homes of the rural proletariat.[83] Primary-school teachers have always disproportionately sent their children on to the universities. During this century, around 5 percent of the students in higher education have had fathers who were primary-school teachers, a percentage far in excess of their representation in the general population.[84]

Another path of upward mobility in Swedish society that began in the last decade or two of the nineteenth century has been through the great popular movements that have so shaped modern Sweden: the labor movement in both its trade-union and its political aspects, the cooperative movement, the free-church movement, and the temperance movement. All of these great movements appealed disproportionately to the lower-status groups in Sweden and achieved their successes as a result of a great emphasis on organization and popular education.[85] All provided a means of upward mobility from the lower orders of society. The leadership of the trade-union movement has always come from the industrial working classes. The Social Democratic party (disproportionately the party of the industrial working class) provided a means of sending many sons of workers and workers themselves to the Riksdag. Table 7.6, based on a 1945 study during which time the Social Democrats held more than half the seats in the two houses of the Riksdag, shows that 55 percent of the party's representatives were the sons of workers and 23 percent were the sons of farmers. Many were themselves workers. Even today a sizable minority of the Social Democratic delegation in the Riksdag are workers.[86] Also notable as an avenue of upward mobility has been the temperance movement with its emphasis on training youth in organizational work. At present around one-third of all the members of the Riksdag are members of temperance organizations, which is a far greater representation than they have in the general population. They are represented in all of the parties, but particularly among the Liberals. The cooperative movement and the free-church movement, the great proportion of whose preachers have been the sons of farmers and workers, have also provided avenues of upward mobility outside of the universities for ambitious lower-status youths. The role of the universities is increasing in Sweden, but they have not yet become the almost sole means of mobility into the middle and upper-middle classes that they now are in America.

There is evidence that in terms of the crudest measure of generational mobility—the movement from manual to nonmanual occupations and vice versa—that there is not much difference among modern societies. However, these data are crude and open to much question and conflict with other data.[87] In any case, these studies show that the

Table 7.6 Occupations of Fathers of the 193 Social Democratic Riksdag Representatives, 1945.

	Number	Percent
Big Businessmen	0	0
University Graduates	9	5
White-Collar Workers	16	8
Small Businessmen	18	9
Farmers	44	23
Rural Proletariat	33	17
Industrial Workers	73	38
Total	193	100

SOURCE: S. Carlsson, *op. cit.*, p. 128.

amount of manual-nonmanual generational mobility is very similar in Sweden to what it is in the United States. In both countries, for example, about one-third of those with nonmanual occupations are the sons of fathers with manual occupations.[88] It is interesting, however, to look into some of the components of this mobility and to compare mobility in specific occupations in Swedish society with American society. No longer do we see such similarity.

In our earlier discussion of higher education we discussed the recruitment of working-class and farm youth into academic secondary education and into the universities. We concluded that it is high in Sweden relative to the rest of Western Europe. Considering the more select nature of academic secondary and higher education in Sweden and the fact that it prepares for a narrower range of occupations than does higher education in America, meaningful comparison as to which system provides for more upward mobility is difficult. It is somewhat easier to compare mobility into the ranks of specific occupations. Tables 7.7, 7.8, 7.9, and 7.10 provide some generational mobility

Table 7.7   Fathers and Fathers' Fathers Occupation of 245 Swedish Big Businessmen, 1957; Occupation of Fathers of American Businessmen, 1952 (Percentages).

SWEDEN	Fathers	Fathers' Fathers
Owner and Leader of Enterprise with over 200 Employees	30	9.5
Owner and Leader of Enterprise with 10–200 Employees	10	10.5
Owner of Enterprise with Fewer than 10 Employees	7	8
Upper White Collar (for most part university graduates)	27.5	22.5
Lower White Collar	12	6
Farmer	10	29.5
Worker	3.5	9
No Data	—	5
	100	100

U.S.	
Business owner or executive	52
Professional man	14
Clerk or salesman	8
Farmer	9
Worker	15
Other	2
	100

SOURCE: For Sweden, from Carlsson, *op. cit.*, p. 115; for U.S., from W. Lloyd Warner and James C. Abegglen, *Occupational Mobility in American Business and Industry* (Minneapolis: University of Minnesota Press, 1955), p. 46.

Table 7.8 Occupational Origins of Higher Civil Servants, Sweden and the U.S. for Selected Years (Percentages).

SWEDEN

	1900	*1949*	*1961*
	(N=86)	(N=170)	(N=180)
Owners and executives in big businesses	20.9	12.4	17.4
University graduates	69.8	49.4	44.6
White collar	5.8	12.9	15.8
Small businessman	1.2	8.8	7.6
Farmer	1.2	5.8	4.9
Worker	1.2	10.0	9.2
No data	—	.6	.6
	100.1	99.9	100.1

U.S.

	1940	*1959*
	(N=180)	(N=10,851)
Professional	28.3	18.5
Business owner or executive	26.1	35.9
Government service and military	3.3	.9
White collar	3.3	9.1
Farmer	29.0	14.7
Worker	10.0	20.5
Other	—	.4
	100.0	100.0

SOURCE: Data for Sweden calculated from Carlsson, *op. cit.*, p. 139; U.S. data for 1940 from Reinhard Bendix, *Higher Civil Servants in American Society* (Boulder: University of Colorado Press, 1949), p. 26; U.S. data for 1959 from W. Lloyd Warner, *et al.*, *The American Federal Executive* (New Haven: Yale University Press, 1963), p. 29.

data on business executives, civil servants, military officers, and writers.

It appears from Table 7.7 that there may be less mobility of the sons of workers into the upper ranks of Swedish big business than into the upper ranks of American big business. A difference between 3.5 and 15 percent is large enough that even if the American sample is more inclusive it represents a significant difference. It should be pointed out, however, that at the time the Swedish business leaders were born, most typically between 1900 and 1910, the proportion of workers in the Swedish labor force was much smaller than in America. And the proportion of farmers was much larger, so we can also assume that relatively fewer sons of farmers became big businessmen in Sweden (10 percent) than in the United States (9 percent). However, the sons of lower white-collar fathers appear to have greater representation among Swedish business leaders (12 percent) than among their American counterparts (8 percent). The lower white-collar category, too, was appreciably smaller in Sweden in the early years of this century as compared with America.

Mobility into the ranks of upper-level civil servants does not appear to be very much less in Sweden as compared with the United States in recent years, in spite of the fact that the upper civil service has so much greater prestige in Sweden than in the United States (see Table 7.8). Note the great "democratization" that has occurred in recruitment between 1900 and 1949 in Sweden. However, it should be pointed out that there are great differences in patterns of recruitment within the Swedish civil service. The foreign service continues to recruit disproportionately among those of high-status background; the top levels of the postal service, on the other hand, contain large proportions from modest backgrounds.[89]

An enormous change in the composition of the entering students at the Swedish War College occurred between the 1920s and the 1950s.

Table 7.9   Class Background of Entering Students of the Swedish War College 1925-1927 and 1956-1958, and Father's Occupation of West Point Graduates, Class of 1960 (Percentages).

SWEDISH WAR COLLEGE

	1925–1927	1956–1958
Social Group I (upper class)	72	26
Social Group II (middle class)	25	52
Social Group III (working class)	3	22

WEST POINT, CLASS OF 1960

Business	15
Professional and Managerial	50
White Collar	13
Farmer	—
Worker	19
Other	3
	100

NOTE: N = 765.

SOURCE: Swedish data from Carlsson, op. cit., p. 140; West Point data from Morris Janowitz, The Professional Soldier (New York: Free Press of Glencoe, 1960), p. 91.

Between 1925 and 1927, a mere 3 percent of the entering students in the War College were from the working class, whereas 72 percent were from upper-class backgrounds. Three decades later, the career of army officer could no longer be regarded as an upper-class preserve. Between 1956 and 1958, only 26 percent of the entering students were from upper-class backgrounds and the proportion of students from the middle and upper working classes had increased to 52 percent and 22 percent respectively. According to data in Table 7.9 the occupational background of West Point students in the class of 1960 seems to be somewhat higher than that of the entering students at the Swed-

Table 7.10 Social Class Background of Swedish Authors by Decade of First Novel (Percentages).

	1880s	1890s	1900s	1910s	1920s	1930s	1940s
	(N = 83)	(N = 86)	(N = 112)	(N = 140)	(N = 115)	(N = 136)	(N = 142)
Upper Civil Servants, Free Professions Requiring Academic Degree	34	31	25	31	21	18	19
Upper White Collar (father with student-examen, but no higher education)	19	13	15	17	16	18	22
Estate Owners	10	10	6	5	5	4	3
Upper Middle and Middle Class (businessmen, executives, etc.)	20	21	23	16	10	17	14
Farm Owners	5	7	11	8	9	6	5
Lower Middle Class (craftsmen, small businessmen, lower white collar)	7	12	9	12	14	15	15
Working Class	1	2	6	4	14	11	16
Rural Lower Class	0	0	4	3	8	7	3
No Data	4	5	1	4	4	2	3
	100	101	100	100	101	98	100

SOURCE:: Adapted from Lennart Thorsell, "Den svenska parnassens 'democratisering' och de folkliga bildningsvägarna," in *Samlaren*, 1957, p. 86.

ish War College. However, top-level officers in the Swedish army are still disproportionately from high-status backgrounds.[90] This will probably change in the future. Perhaps no occupation other than that of the clergy has so declined in prestige along with modernization as that of military officer.

Table 7.10 gives some interesting data on the class background of novelists by the decade in which their first novel appeared; data are from the 1880s through the 1940s. From the 1920s, about one out of every five new novelists came from the working class or the lower rural class. Even as late as the 1940s a majority of Swedish authors making their debuts had never been to a university.[91] Note also in this table the decline in the proportion of writers whose fathers were upper civil servants or in the professions. Alrik Gustafson has written of the "proletarian authors" that:

during the 1920s they had established for themselves a position not far below the ranking authors of the day, and in the 1930s they threatened to take over command of Swedish literary developments. The majority of the more important novelists and several of the leading poets of the 1930s were of lower-class origins, and they have also contributed significantly to the drama. The rise of a literature of what may loosely be called proletarian origins is, indeed, the most important fact about Swedish literature in the twentieth century. It has poured into the bloodstream of a literary culture which had long been the special if not exclusive holding of the academically trained middle classes certain new, vital, distinctly forward-looking elements. [92]

Even without comparative data, the proportion of Swedish writers from low status backgrounds is probably higher than elsewhere and this is doubtless a reflection of the comparatively high cultural level that prevails among the Swedish working class.

Conclusion

This chapter has dealt with a broad range of stratification phenomena. Some of the important points I have attempted to demonstrate are that:

(1) An enormous diminution of class differences has occurred along with the modernization of Sweden in this century.

(2) Class differentials, for the most part, are less in Swedish than in American society, and they are probably as minimal as in any modern society. (Iceland may be an exception to this statement.)

(3) There is a high degree of economic concentration in modern Swedish society, but those who control economic power have in the past been quite uninvolved with the political elites, but this may be changing.

(4) While there is general similarity in the evaluation of occupations in Sweden and the United States, there are a number of small prestige variations. Occupations involving expert knowledge and involvement in the national bureaucracy are more highly valued in Sweden compared with similar occupations in American society. On the other hand, occupations lacking these attributes, but with high incomes, are generally not so highly valued in Sweden as in the United States.

(5) There is a relatively high degree of social mobility in modern Sweden, certainly as much as in American society. However, there are many differences in the specific patterns of mobility.

Notes

1. Vilgot Sjöman, *I Am Curious (Yellow)*, Martin Minow and Jenny Bohman (trs.) (New York: Grove Press, 1968), p. 33.
2. The view of egalitarianism implicit here is essentially the same as that of Seymour M. Lipset in *The First New Nation* (New York: Basic Books, 1963), *passim*.
3. See "Geography, Religion, and Social Class: Crosscutting Cleavages in Norwegian Politics," in Seymour M. Lipset and Stein Rokkan (eds.), *Party Systems and Voter Alignments* (New York: The Free Press, 1967), pp. 367–444.
4. Herbert Tingsten, too, has commented on the greater vitality of Norwegian politics compared with those of Sweden. See *Fran idéer till idyll* (Stockholm: Pan/Norstedts, 1967), p. 10.
5. See discussion by Stein Rokkan on this in "Electoral Mobilization, Party Competition, and National Integration," in Joseph La Palombara and Myron Weiner (eds.), *Political Parties and Political Development* (Princeton: Princeton University Press, 1966), pp. 241–265, esp. 256–265.
6. See Maurice Duverger, *Political Parties*, Barbara and Robert North (trs.) (London: University Paperbacks, 1964), pp. 6–7, 203–205, 233–239.

7. Jörgen Westerståhl, "Samkristna skolnamndens namninsamlingsaktion," *Statsvetenskaplig tidskrift*, 67 (1964), 277–290.

8. I have talked about this with Erik Allardt (Sociology) at the University of Helsinki, Nils Elvander (Political Science) at Uppsala University, and Henry Valen (Political Science) at the Institute for Social Research in Oslo, all of whom agree that there is less conflict and greater consensus between the Conservatives and Social Democrats in Sweden as compared with Norway.

9. The whole value system of the west coast of Norway with its egalitarianism, moralism, and individualism more resembles the dominant American value system than any other area of Scandinavia.

10. Perhaps the temperance issue might be regarded as a source of cleavage in Sweden on some issues.

11. Åke Elmér, *Från fattigsverige till välfärdsstaten* (Stockholm: Bokförlaget Aldus/Bonniers, 1963), p. 13.

12. See Berndt Gustafsson, *Kyrkoliv och samhällklass i Sverige omkring 1880* (Stockholm: Svenska Kyrkans Diakonistyrelses Bokförlag, 1950) for an account of the relation between social class and religion in the Church of Sweden around 1880.

13. See Sven Rydenfelt, *Kommunismen i Sverige* (Lund: Gleerupska Universitetsbokhandeln, 1954).

14. See the excellent discussion on variations in living standards in Gunnar Richardson, *Kulturkamp och klasskamp: Ideologiska och sociala motsättningar i svensk skol— och kulturpolitik under 1800-talet* (Gothenburg: Akademiförlaget-Gumperts, 1963), pp. 4–19.

15. *Ibid.*, p. 12.

16. *Ibid.*, p. 13.

17. *Ibid.*, p. 13.

18. *Ibid.*, p. 13.

19. *Ibid.*, p. 14.

20. *Ibid.*, p. 15. Quoted from E. Modig, *Diplomattjanst med mellanspel*, (Stockholm, 1954), p. 8.

21. Herbert Tingsten, *Mitt Liv: Ungdomsåren* (Stockholm: Wahlström & Widstrand, 1961), pp. 46–48.

22. Study cited in Kaare Svalastoga and Gunnar Boalt, "Social Stratification and Social Mobility in Scandinavia," *Sociological Inquiry*, XXXI (Winter 1961), 23–46, esp. 29–30.

23. Told to me in a conversation with Hans L. Zetterberg.

24. See the discussion in Chapter 3.

25. See the discussion in Chapter 6.

26. See the discussion in Chapter 5.

27. Brian Jackson and Dennis Marsden, *Education and the Working Class* (New York: Monthly Review Press, 1962).

28. See the interesting discussion on the British press in Anthony Sampson, *The Anatomy of Britain Today* (New York: Harper Colophon, 1965), pp. 138–161.

29. The Social Democratic paper *Stockholms Tidningen* had been losing money for years and ceased publication in April of 1966.

30. See Anders Y. Pers, *The Swedish Press* (Stockholm: The Swedish Institute, 1963), p. 1.

31. *Ibid.*, p. 1; see also The Nordic Council, *Yearbook of Nordic Statistics, 1968* (Stockholm: P. A. Norstedt, 1969), p. 158.

32. *Dagens Nyheter*, November 2, 1967, p. 1 of Sect. 2.

33. Richard F. Hamilton, *Affluence and the French Worker in the Fourth Republic* (Princeton: Princeton University Press, 1967), p. 95.

34. *Ibid.*, pp. 94–96.

35. See the annual *Social Benefits in Sweden* (Stockholm: The Swedish Institute).

36. Charles A. Myers, *Industrial Relations in Sweden* (Cambridge: M.I.T. Press, 1951), p. 41; see also discussion on this point in Lipset, *op. cit.*, pp. 182–187.

37. In addition to this must be added various excise taxes and also, a sales tax on all purchases of 10 percent.

38. Torgny Segerstedt, "An Investigation of Class-Consciousness among Office Employees and Workers in Swedish Factories," *Transactions of the Second World Congress of Sociology* (London: International Sociological Association, 1954), II, 300–301, 305.

39. Gösta Carlsson, *Social Mobility and Class Structure* (Lund: Gleerup, 1958), p. 150.

40. Herbert Tingsten, *Mitt Liv: Mellan trettio och femtio* (Stockholm: P. A. Norstedt, 1962).

41. See Andreas Murray (ed.), *Det svenska klassämhallet* (Stockholm: Bokförlaget Prisma, 1967).

42. Richard F. Tomasson, "Iceland Report," *New Society*, 149 (August 5, 1965), 22.

43. Lipset, *op. cit.*, p. 236.

44. In a personal conversation.

45. This observation was made by Tingsten in *Mitt liv: Ungdomåren, op. cit.*, p. 231.

46. Kurt B. Mayer, "Social Stratification in Two Equalitarian Societies: Australia and the United States," in Reinhard Bendix and Seymour M. Lipset (eds.), *Class, Status, and Power*, 2nd ed. (New York: The Free Press, 1966), p. 156.

47. Franklin D. Scott, *The American Experience of Swedish Students* (Minneapolis: University of Minnesota Press, 1956), p. 114, and William H. Sewall and Oluf M. Davidson, *Scandinavian Students on an American Campus* (Minneapolis: University of Minnesota Press, 1961), pp. 40–41.

48. See *Statistical Abstract of Sweden* (Stockholm: Statistiska Centralbyrån), for a recent year; see *Svenska Institutet för Opinionsundersökningar SIFO* (Stockholm, May 20, 1965).

49. SIFO, *ibid.*

50. *Scan Gallup Statistics 1963–64* (Copenhagen: Scan Gallup AS, 1964).

51. See George Gallup, *The Miracle Ahead* (New York: Harper & Row, 1964), pp. 34–39, 41–43. Gallup has written on p. 42: "In the most recent study

(1963) nearly two-thirds of all adults in a representative sample of citizens of the United States reported that they had not read a book all the way through during the previous year (excluding the Bible and textbooks)."

52. *SIFO*, May 15, 1957. N=about 800 persons over sixteen.

53. Harald Swedner, "Läsvanor-några reflexioner och empiriska resultat," *Sociologisk forskning*, II (1965), 197–215.

54. Several Swedes have asserted to me that some American best sellers sell more copies in Sweden than they do in the United States.

55. This novel has been translated into English by F. H. Lyon (New York: Dial, 1931).

56. This quotation is from Alrik Gustafson, *A History of Swedish Literature* (Minneapolis: University of Minnesota Press, 1961), p. 383.

57. Richardson, *op. cit.*, p. 23. Of this total 36 percent were graduates of the military academies. Only two of the 126 had no education above *folkskola*.

58. There were no Swedish counterparts to scholars like David Ricardo, Charles Darwin, John Stuart Mill, Herbert Spencer, or Hastings Rashdall, none of whom had any university position.

59. See Herbert Tingsten, *Den svenska socialdemokratiens idéutveckling* (Stockholm: Tidens Förlag, 1941), Vol. I, p. 21.

60. *Statens Offentliga Utredningar* (*SOU*), 1959:45, p. 168.

61. See Chapter III of Seymour M. Lipset and Reinhard Bendix, *Social Mobility in Industrial Society* (Berkeley and Los Angeles: University of California Press, 1960).

62. Harry Eckstein, *Division and Cohesion in Democracy: A Study of Norway* (Princeton University Press, 1966), p. 166.

63. See Chapter 5.

64. *Dagens Nyheter*, February 15, 1968, p. 24.

65. "The 200 Largest Industrials Outside the U.S.," *Fortune*, LXXVIII (September 15, 1968), 130–136.

66. *Dagens Nyheter*, February 15, 1968, pp. 1, 24.

67. Quoted by Lipset *op. cit.*, p. 254; see also Frederick W. Eggleston, "The Australian Nation," in George Caiger (ed.), *The Australian Way of Life* (London: Heinemann, 1953), p. 11.

68. *Dagens Nyheter*, February 15, 1968, p. 24.

69. See Arthur M. Lewis, "The Richest of the Rich," *Fortune*, LXXVII (May 1968), p. 156.

70. For a comparative look at these studies, see Robert W. Hodge, Donald J. Tremain, and Peter H. Rossi, "A Comparative Study of Occupational Prestige," in Lipset and Bendix, *op. cit.*, pp. 309–321.

71. Though it remains substantially higher than in the United States.

72. I do not regard these kind of surveys as valid because they appear to tap other dimensions of evaluation besides prestige, such as value to society and moral worth.

73. On the high status of engineers in Sweden, see Chapter 5.

74. Yet income is not as private a matter in Sweden as in America. In fact everyone with an income above 7000 *kronor* has his name and income listed in a readily available government publication.

75. See Harold Nicholson's memoirs, *Diaries and Letters*, 3 vols. (New York: Atheneum, 1966–1968).

76. Sten Carlsson, *Bonde-präst-ämbetsman* (Stockholm: Bokförlaget Prisma, 1962).

77. *Ibid.*, p. 23.

78. *Ibid.*, pp. 56–58.

79. Pontus E. Fahlbeck, *Der Adel Schwedens (und Finlands): Eine Demographische Studie* (Jena: Gustav Fischer, 1903). An overview of this study can be found in Suzanne Keller, *Beyond the Ruling Class* (New York: Random House, 1963), pp. 228–231.

80. S. Carlsson, *op. cit.*, pp. 81–82.

81. S. Carlsson, *op. cit.*, pp. 57–58.

82. S. Carlsson, *op. cit.*, pp. 83, 100–101.

83. S. Carlsson, *op. cit.*, pp. 101–102.

84. In 1961–1962, the children of primary-school teachers were 4.1 percent of all first year students in Swedish higher education; see Sveriges Officiella Statistik, *Högre Studier 1961–62* (Stockholm: Statistiska Centralbyrån, 1964), p. 5.

85. This is discussed in some detail in Chapter 8.

86. See Sveriges Officiella Statistik, *Riksdagsmannavalen åren, 1961–1964* (Stockholm: Statistiska Centralbyrån, 1965).

87. For example, Finland has the highest proportion of working-class youth in higher education in Scandinavia, yet Finland has the lowest rate of manual-nonmanual generational mobility. See Chapter 5, and Svalastoga and G. Carlsson, "Social Stratification and Social Mobility in Scandinavia," *op. cit.*, esp. pp. 35–36.

88. See Seymour M. Lipset and Hans L. Zetterberg, "A Theory of Social Mobility," in Lipset and Bendix, *op. cit.*, pp. 568–569.

89. S. Carlsson, *op. cit.*, p. 138–139.

90. S. Carlsson, *op. cit.*, pp. 139–142.

91. Lennart Thorsell, "Den svenska parnassens 'democratisering' och de folkliga bildningsvägarna," *Samlaren*, 1957, p. 86.

92. A. Gustafson, *op. cit.*, p. 348.

VIII

Organizations

> The propensity [of Swedes] to organize for all
> sorts of purposes is nothing short of incredible.
> It may be that it is the Americans who have publicized
> the Organization Man, but almost certainly
> his forefathers were Swedish emigrants.
> . . . —T. L. JOHNSTON, *a Scottish economist*[1]

Even if Johnston misinterprets William H. Whyte's concept of the Organization Man in the above quotation, his meaning is clear. And he is not alone in his observation on the extraordinary development of all manner of voluntary associations; indeed, virtually every serious observer of Swedish society makes the same observation.[2] Among modern societies, only the other Scandinavian countries approach Sweden in the development of organizational life, but here again Sweden is the most advanced and frequently the model for Norway and Finland and to a lesser extent for Denmark. As the Swedes say, their society is *genomorganiserad*, which means saturated with organizations. In this chapter we will give an overview of the different types of national organizations, their structures, and how they work; first, however, we will glance at the historical background of the Swedish capacity to organize.

We might speculate that the long-term national integration of the Swedes and the "fundamental strain of liberty" that they boast of in their constitutional development are crucial background factors.[3] For generations the Swedes have had the right to organize to protect and to enhance their economic interests and to form special-purpose organizations without repression and often with success. The ruthless suppression of peasant revolts in Continental Europe in the sixteenth century has no analog in Swedish history. As a result of the high degree of national integration and consciousness together with the basic homogeneity of the Swedes, local groups have tended to form into national federations.

A sort of local democracy has been functioning in Swedish villages for a thousand years.[4] The Catholic Church was unable to diminish the power of the common man, and the medieval church was consequently more "democratic" than in Continental Europe. The peasants developed a corporate consciousness early, and they have been represented in the Swedish Riksdag since the first half of the fifteenth century. Imagine the overall organization that made it possible for Sweden to be a major European power in the seventeenth century with a population of under 1 million! The dignity of the common man and his capacity to take the initiative to organize to further his special interests has a longer and stronger tradition in Sweden (and Norway) than anywhere else in Europe.

But it was not until the 1880s and 1890s with the beginnings of urbanization and industrialization that the organizations that have come to dominate modern Sweden were formed. In 1881 there was the first socialist meeting in Sweden, which began the activities leading to the foundation of the Social Democratic Party in 1889.[5] If we go back far enough to the 1840s and 1850s, we find the beginnings of what look like modern trade unions; the typographers and bricklayers appear to have been the first to adopt modern organization.[6] But the trade-union movement did not begin to develop numerically until the 1880s, leading to the formation of the Swedish Federation of Trade Unions, or *LO*, in 1898. For self-protection against the organized workers, the employers reacted by forming the Swedish Confederation of Employers, or *SAF*, in 1902.

The temperance movement, with its great emphasis on popular education, can be traced back to the 1830s.[7] At this time it was an upper-class, noblesse-oblige movement directed to the poor, and it soon failed. But it was reborn as a popular movement in the 1880s and began to attract sizable numbers of people. The free-church movement developed rapidly at the same time, even if the roots of the movement can be traced back to English and American influences of the early 1830s. The feminist movement, so much more serious and vigorous in Scandinavia than elsewhere, can be traced back to Fredrika

Bremmer and her invidious comparison of the status of women in Sweden as compared with America.[8] The situation now is quite the opposite, but the national association for women's rights in Sweden is today called the Fredrika Bremmer Society. Of significance is her novel *Hertha* published in 1856.[9] Yet the feminist movement was a relatively unimportant upper-class movement until the end of the century. The cooperative movement also traces its origins to the 1880s; particularly significant was the formation of the national Cooperative Association, or *KF*, in 1899.[10]

What is notable about these "popular movements," as the Swedes call them, is that *all* of them really "took off" in the last two decades of the nineteenth century and had become important national organizations by the first decade of this century. Again we must make the observation that Sweden was superbly prepared for modernization; the population was literate, nationally integrated, and homogeneous, and there were strong traditions of civil liberty including the right to freely form associations. Two kinds of motivation were responsible for this profusion of organization in the period from 1880 to 1914. First, there was the rapid growth of urbanization and industrialization and the reconstruction of the rural society that had previously changed little from medieval times.[11] Traditional social organization and social ties were broken. The new organizations replaced the old social ties. The uprooted common people joined the temperance societies, free churches, political parties, and trade unions in great numbers; all of these movements provided a substitute for the close relations of the village communities. The second kind of motivation had its roots in class conflict. The industrial workers and the lower-middle classes made up for their lack of resources through organization. They wanted the right to vote, better working conditions, shorter hours, job security, and equality in the newly industrializing society.

The extraordinarily rapid spread of the popular movements must be seen both as the result of modernization and as a factor that further enhanced its tempo. Modernization proceeds most rapidly in an organized society where communication with the people is easy and where interest articulation is well developed. The advanced degree of organization that has brought the high degree of modern integration to Swedish society and that is both a result and a cause of its smooth operation will be spelled out in this chapter. As Gerard De Gré and others have pointed out, it is precisely in those modern societies characterized by a multiplicity of great organizations where freedom is most secure.[12] These are also the societies with the greatest internal stability, and, further, this multiplicity of organizations and internal stability are mutually reinforcing. Sweden is indeed the prototype of this modern multi-group society.

There seem to be five types of national organization that have major importance in the development and present functioning of Swedish society: (1) the labor market organizations, those of employees and employers, (2) other economic interest organizations, those that represent the interests of specific segments of the economy—big business and small business, property owners and renters, (3) the cooperatives, both of consumers and producers, (4) "the idealistic organizations," the name the Swedes give to those interest groups that do not primarily serve economic purposes, and (5) the organizations of the political parties, the most important subcategory of the idealistic organizations. Table 8.1 lists the major economic interest groups with their membership figures for 1945 and 1967.

The Labor Market Organizations

Any discussion of labor-market organizations would begin with the Swedish Federation of Trade Unions, or *LO*.[13] It is without question the largest and most influential economic interest group in Sweden. When Nils Elvander, in his recent study of interest groups in Sweden, questioned twenty-nine political and interest-group leaders as to which three organizations had the best contacts with the government, all twenty-nine mentioned *LO*.[14] The second most mentioned organization was *LO*'s opposite number, the Confederation of Swedish Employers, or *SAF*, with sixteen votes. In other words, thirteen of these leaders did not even regard *SAF* as among the top three most influential interest groups vis-à-vis the government.

The great political influence of *LO* can be attributed to two factors. First, it represents a very large group of voters. Perhaps three-fourths of all Social Democratic voters are members of or are married to members of *LO*. Second, there has always been a strong ideological communion between *LO* and the Social Democratic party, though there are no organizational links between them at the national level.

LO was formed as a federation of a number of craft unions just before the turn of the century. A decade later, after the disastrous general strike of 1909, *LO* saw the advantage to its growth of organizing whole industries rather than just crafts. *LO*'s growth has been very

Table 8.1 **Membership in Major Swedish Economic Interest Groups, 1945 and 1967.**

	1945	1967
LABOR MARKET ORGANIZATIONS		
Swedish Federation of Trade Unions	1,106,900	1,607,077
(*Landsorganisationen, LO*)		
Central Organization of Salaried Employees	204,650	504,861
(*Tjänstemännens centralorganisation, TCO*)		
Swedish Confederation of Professional Associations	Ca:15,000**	98,720
(*Sveriges akademikers centralorganisation, SACO*)		
National Federation of Civil Servants	18,100*	18,325
(*Statstjänstemännens riksforbund, SR*)		
Swedish Employers' Confederation		
(*Svenska Arbetsgivareforeningen, SAF*)		
Part-owners	7,890	24,523§
Employees	513,170	1,244,417
ECONOMIC INTEREST ORGANIZATIONS		
General Export Association of Sweden	1,050	1,270†
(*Sveriges Allmänna Exportförening*)		
Association of Swedish Industries		
(*Sveriges Industriförbund*)		
Organizations	2,440	4,300†
Employees	373,400	Ca:720,000
Swedish Organization of Trade and Industry		
(*Sveriges hantverks- och industriorganisation, SHIO*)	Ca:45,000	Ca:45,000†
National Association of Rural People		
(*Riksförbundet Landsbygdens Folk, RLF*)	154,340	176,170
Swedish Property Owners Association		
(*Sveriges fastighetsägareförbund*)	24,500	32.730†
National Association of Renters		
(*Hyregästernas riksförbund*)	102,500	362,780†
COOPERATIVES		
Cooperative Association		
(*Kooperative Förbundet, KF*)	828,790	1,355,834††
All Consumer Cooperatives	—	1,726,616††

* 1946.
** 1947.
† 1964.
†† 1966.
§ 1968.
SOURCES: *Statistisk årsbok för Sverige 1968* (Stockholm: Statistiska Centralbyrån, 1968), passim.; and Nils Elvander, *Intresse organisationerna i dagens Sverige* (Lund: CWK Gleerup, 1968), 21–49, esp. p. 49.

rapid, from 43,500 in 1900 to substantially more than one-quarter of a million by 1920.[15] The million mark was passed in the early 1940s, and today membership is in excess of 1,600,000. *LO* comprises thirty-seven separate unions, most organized on the basis of the industrial principle. These are listed in Exhibit 8.1. The number of unions has been declining in recent years as a result of mergers. Something on the order of 95 percent of all wage workers belong to *LO*-affiliated unions. Among men in industry, membership is virtually 100 percent. In America, by contrast, only between 50 and 60 percent of all wage workers belong to unions.[16] If the AFL-CIO were as relatively large as *LO*, it would have between 40 and 41 million members rather than the 14.9 million it in fact has.[17] (To get an idea of the relative size of Swedish organizations, multiply their membership by a factor of 25.)

The only competition *LO* has among manual workers is from the syndicalists who formed the Central Organization of Swedish Workers, or *SAC*, in 1910 after the great strike of 1909, which was a major defeat for *LO*. It reached a peak membership of 37,400 in 1924, declined in the 1940s and 1950s, but has been picking up membership in the 1960s. The 1967 membership was almost 23,000.[18]

The extraordinary degree of union organization in Sweden is surprising considering the relatively small size of most Swedish industrial establishments and their vast dispersion in a rather large country. The average size in the late 1950s was forty-one employees per establishment, and 47 percent had fewer than ten employees.[19] However, 173 establishments (.1 percent of the total number) employed over 500 workers each, which accounted for 29 percent of all manual workers.

In the early years of its history, *LO* had a weak central organization with few functions other than collecting statistical data and supporting affiliated unions in defensive actions. What radically changed the functions of *LO* was the formation of the Confederation of Swedish Employers, or SAF. A number of successful strikes in the 1890s drove a group of employers to organize a national confederation in 1902. From the start, *SAF* had a strong central organization and immediately became the dominant association of employers.[20] Its principal weapon against the unions was the lockout. This, in turn, led to strong centralization in the trade-union movement. The principle of national collective agreements between *SAF* and *LO* was accepted by the former as early as 1905, which greatly strengthened the position of *LO*. In effect, this meant the recognition of the legitimate role of the union move-

Exhibit 8.1 Membership in *LO* Unions, December 31, 1967.

Union of Metal Workers	355,041
Union of Municipal Workers	185,212
Union of Building Workers	177,894
Union of Commercial Employees	109,515
Union of General Factory Workers	82,758
Union of Wood Industry Workers	69,726
Union of Railwaymen	57,325
Union of Food Workers	50,974
Union of Pulp and Paper Workers	46,171
Union of Transport Workers	46,065
Union of Garment Workers	32,085
Union of Hotel and Restaurant Workers	30,800
Union of Forest Workers and Craftsmen	30,497
Union of Postmen	27,874
Union of Building Maintenance Workers	27,869
Union of Textile Workers	26,776
Union of Telecommunication Workers	26,139
Union of Electricians	26,100
Union of Painters	24,257
Union of Road Construction Workers	19,866
Union of Civilian Personnel in Defence Establishments	18,752
Union of Typographers	17,572
Union of Agricultural Workers	17,064
Union of Insurance Employees	15,822
Union of Musicians	15,381
Union of Seamen	14,916
Union of Bookbinders	12,806
Union of Shoe and Leather Workers	12,450
Union of Miners	12,298
Union of Civil Servants	8,667
Union of Hairdressers	7,188
Union of Lithographers	6,521
Union of Sheetmetal Workers	4,505
Union of Stoneworkers	3,580
Union of Custodial Workers	3,508
Union of Power Station Workers	1,699
Union of Chimneysweeps	1,304
Total	1,607,077

SOURCE: *Statistisk årsbok för Sverige 1968, op. cit.*, p. 241.

ment. Thus began a short-lived period of relative power balance between *SAF* and *LO* that was similar to that which has characterized labor relations in Sweden since 1936. But this was broken by the general strike of 1909, caused by the large-scale use of the lockout by *SAF*. This was a disastrous defeat for *LO* and showed that *LO* was not nearly as strong as its large membership indicated. Half its membership was lost. It also marked the end of collective agreements between *LO* and *SAF*, which were not resumed until 1936. The power balance was disrupted, *LO* was not strong enough. The centralization of collective bargaining that had begun ceased. Calls for governmental control of labor relations, however, were unsuccessful.

Industrial relations were indeed stormy until the mid-1930s, but all along *LO* was growing rapidly in size, strength, and central organization. During the 1920s and early 1930s, labor relations were frequently hostile. The number of strikes each year was in the hundreds, and the number of worker days lost annually was in the several millions. Relations improved briefly in the late 1920s, but the power balance was upset in favor of *SAF* as a result of the Great Depression and the mass unemployment that occurred in the late 1920s and early 1930s. The nadir in industrial relations and class conflict is signified by the Ådal massacre of 1931 in which five striking workers were killed by the army.[21] Such an incident had not occurred in Sweden since the Sundsvall strike of 1879. It continues to be the only civil disorder in Sweden that has involved any loss of life in almost a century. There were calls for governmental regulation of industrial relations from the bourgeois parties, but again without success. The growing power of *LO* was regarded as a threat to individual freedom and the authority of the state; there was particular concern with the rights of neutral parties, the innocent "third man."

The Social Democratic victory of 1932 forced the party and *LO* to see that they had a special responsibility for maintaining social and industrial peace. Thus began a new thrust toward accommodation, first from *LO*, then from *SAF*. In 1936 there were the first central deliberations since 1909 betwen *LO* and *SAF*, beginning the new and present era in Swedish labor relations. Two years later, in 1938, came the Basic Agreement between *LO* and *SAF*, frequently called the Saltjöbadan Agreement after the name of the resort just outside of Stockholm where the officials met. The fundamental factor leading to this enormously significant agreement was the passionate desire of both *LO* and *SAF* to preserve their autonomy from government regulation, a real and persistent threat of the time.

The Basic Agreement of 1938, which in revised form continues, in effect contains five chapters.[22] Chapter 1 deals with the organization of a Labor Market Council for handling disputes with neutral third parties. It consists of six members, three from *LO* and three from *SAF*. Chapter 2 spells out the negotiation procedures to be used. Chapter 3 considers how dismissals, layoffs, and related questions are to be handled. Chapter 4 deals with the limits of economic sanctions and the protection of third parties. Chapter 5 deals with how disputes that are a threat to basic public services are to be handled. With their "typical empiricism," the committee that was convened by *LO* and *SAF* to draw up this Basic Agreement has continued to the present as the vehicle for the discussion of wider problems between the two organizations.[23] In the more than three decades since the Basic Agreement, *SAF* and *LO* have established a number of additional permanent bodies for cooperation and information.

The Basic Agreement has had a strong centralizing effect. It has resulted in agreements between centralized organs of labor and management that directly determine the pay scales of the majority of Swedish manual workers and indirectly determine those of nearly all employees in the country. But this centralized tendency was wholly in accord with the revised view of *LO*'s task, which became accepted in the mid-1930s, that *LO* must present a unified front for the entire trade-union movement so that a policy of wage solidarity could be maintained for the benefit of the low-paid groups and also in order that the union movement could maintain a solid front vis-à-vis *SAF* and the government. This new view is expressed in the thorough revision of the *LO* constitution undertaken in 1941. Since that time, the power of *LO* over its member unions has increased substantially.

LO is still organized on the basis of the tripartite structure developed in 1898; there is a congress, a representative assembly, and an executive committee (or secretariat). The congress is the fundamental decision-making body of *LO*. It meets every five years and is made up of 300 delegates representing the member unions in proportion to their size with at least one delegate from each union; it also includes the members of the representative assembly (about 125) and the executive committee (13). The representative assembly is the supreme authority between congresses and is made up of the members of the executive committee and representatives of the member unions, again in proportion to size. The assembly generally meets twice a year. The executive committee provides day-to-day continuity. The thirteen members are all from member unions elected by the congress. The positions of chairman, vice chairman, and secretary are full-time paid positions; they are *permanent* officials. They hold their offices until they retire or are perhaps voted out in a special election of the congress. The executive committee meets once a week.[24] (The *SAF* congress, unlike that of *LO*, meets annually.) This is very much *representative* democracy, but it does function without corruption and in close accordance with *LO*'s statutes. A persistent criticism of *LO* is the apathy of most of the membership in the new affluent society. The New-Left criticism centers around the pragmatic materialism of *LO* and their loss of socialist goals—the same criticism leveled at the Social Democrats. Yet *LO* has probably shown more concern with international problems, the developing nations, achieving sexual equality in work, and other issues than the labor movement of any other Western country.

As has already been mentioned, employers' organizations were formed in response to trade unionism. Since the founding of *SAF* in 1902, it has been the preëminent organization of employers in Sweden. It is a central organization of forty-four affiliated employers' organizations in various sectors of the economy. However, *SAF* does not have the inclusiveness of employers that *LO* has of manual workers. In fact, *SAF* employers in 1968 employed only half the total number of employees belonging to *LO*. Other employers' organizations that are not affiliated with *SAF* exist for retail and wholesale trade, agriculture, forestry, banking, shipping, insurance, newspapers, and cooperatives. There are also a number of employers' organizations in the public sector. Most of the largest companies in Sweden are members of employer associations affiliated with *SAF*. Still, almost three-fourths of the almost 25,000 firms in the Confederation employ fewer than twenty-five workers.

The system of collective bargaining between *LO* and *SAF* has achieved admiration throughout the world. The Swedish system was eulogized at the 1961 Conference of the International Labor Organization. No aspect of Swedish society—not even the political system—has been studied so much by foreign observers.[25] The Norwegian and Danish systems are similar in having counterparts to *LO* and *SAF*, but they do not work with such well-oiled smoothness, and there is not such astounding cooperation between the organs of labor and management.[26] Since the early 1950s, the relative number of strikes and working days lost have been greater in both these countries than in Sweden.

The accommodative and cooperative relations between LO and SAF since the adoption of the Basic Agreement in 1938 have had a major effect on the shape of Swedish democracy and how it functions.[27] These good relations have been a great factor in the stability and attenuation of class conflict. The assumption for the successful agreement reached in Saltjöbadan in 1938 was that both parties were equally strong. They had learned to respect each other as equals, that to cooperate and to compromise would be to the benefit of both, and that to fail to do so would be to the detriment of both. And with their great strength came a genuine social responsibility on both sides. To avoid any government regulation of collective bargaining is a continuing incentive for the manifestation of their social responsibility, such as not making inflationary wage agreements.[28] There have been three important consequences of the Saltjöbadan agreement and its operations. First, a precedent has been created whereby any interference by the government ought to be avoided except in a crisis situation. Second, there has been a general recognition in all quarters of the great importance of large-scale organization; the strong hostility toward organizations among nonsocialists in the discussions of rights of neutral parties has disappeared. Finally, and, most important, the Basic Agreement has become both "a symbol of and an enhancer of the consensus which is a vital necessity for democracy."[29] The Saltjöbadan Agreement has become a fundamental aspect of Swedish democracy. Indeed, the centralized negotiations of LO and SAF have become the model for all of the remaining segments of the labor market.

The most influential and the largest labor-market organization after the two giants is the Central Organization of Salaried Employees, or TCO.[30] The relative growth of the white-collar national confederations that began to organize in the 1930s has also proceeded further in Swedish society than in any other modern society.[31] Between 1945 and 1967, membership in TCO has increased two and a half times to include over a half million members. However, membership in TCO is not nearly as close to saturation as with manual workers. According to Elvander's estimate, about 60 percent of all white-collar workers are organized.[32] This definition of white-collar workers excludes professionals and all those with academic degrees (who we will see are even more organized). He further estimates that 50 percent of those in private employment and 75 to 80 percent of those in government employment are organized. About 40 percent of all white-collar workers are organized in the twenty-six *TCO*-affiliated unions; a substantial number of lower-grade white-collar workers are organized in *LO* affiliates. In the United States, by contrast, only about 11 percent of all white-collar workers belong to unions.[33]

White-collar workers in Sweden as everywhere else have been slower and more reluctant to organize than blue-collar workers. The history of white-collar unionism has been little investigated in Sweden, but it appears that with few exceptions, such as the Association of *Folkskola* Teachers, founded in 1880, that they engaged in little trade-union activity prior to the 1930s. Some local white-collar organizations, however, were in existence prior to World War I. The inflation and the failure of employers to raise salaries during World War I gave a boost to the trade-union organization of white-collar workers.

A number of white-collar organizations in the private sector formed a central organization in 1931 (*DACO*). White-collar workers in the public sector, municipal and governmental employees, had formed the *TCO* in 1937, and in 1944 both confederations of white-collar workers, the private (*DACO*) and the public (*TCO*), united under the latter name, *TCO*. The affiliated *TCO* unions with their 1967 memberships are listed in Exhibit 8.2.

The development of *TCO* has followed the same progression as that of *LO*. At first it organized horizontally, that is, by specific categories of workers. After the 1930s, however, it has increasingly turned to vertical organization, that is, organization by industry. Still, there are more differences between *LO* and *TCO* than there are similarities. *TCO* still has great room for expansion, which *LO* does not. *TCO* has relatively little control over member organizations as compared with *LO*; salary policy is more decentralized and the scope for local bargaining is greater. Most of the *TCO*-affiliated unions could stand alone in a way that *LO*-affiliated unions could not. Interests within *TCO* are more diverse than they are with *LO*. *TCO* (and the other unions of salaried employees) follow a policy of strict political-party neutrality unlike *LO*, which at all levels officially supports the Social Democratic Party. This is understandable considering that membership of *TCO* is centered in the lower-middle class, which is more politically diverse than either the working class or the upper-

Exhibit 8.2   Membership in *TCO* Unions, December 31, 1967.

Swedish Union of Clerical and Technical Employees in Industry	176,342
Swedish Union of Municipal Employees	47,568
Union of Commercial Employees	42,562
Federation of Civil Servants	41,865
Union of Swedish Teachers	38,144
Union of Health and Sick Care Personnel	25,986
Union of Bank Employees	19,640
Swedish Union of Subject Matter Teachers	17,242
Union of Civilian Employees in Defense Forces	14,753
Swedish Union of Policemen	13,119
Union of Insurance Employees	11,910
Union of Non-Commissioned Officers (lower ranks)	9,127
Union of Telephone Employees	6,801
Union of Pharmacists' Assistants	6,251
Union of Post Office Employees	5,825
Swedish Union of Non-Commissioned Officers (higher ranks)	5,816
Swedish Union of Journalists	5,038
Swedish Marine Engineer Officers Union	3,744
Union of Customs Officers	3,161
Swedish Union of Navigation Officers	3,061
Union of State Waterpower Department Employees	2,404
Swedish Union of Theatrical Employees	1,542
Union of Forest and Agricultural Supervisors	1,078
Swedish Union of Ship Stewards	843
Union of Folk High School Teachers	735
Union of Controllers' Assistants	304
Total	504,861

SOURCE: *Statistisk årsbok för Sverige 1968, op. cit.*, p. 241.

middle and upper classes. *SACO* and *SR* (which we will discuss shortly), while also neutral regarding political parties, are more homogeneous in their membership and frequently parallel the Conservative party in their general policies.

A number of attempts have been made to increase collaboration between *TCO* and *LO*, mostly from *LO*'s side. But there is little collaboration between them. Most of their discussions involve jurisdictional disputes, which are solved on an empirical basis. The lines between them are by no means clear; for example, musicians are in *LO*, whereas actors are in *TCO*.

The largest group of salaried employees outside of *TCO* are organized in The Swedish Confederation of Professional Associations, or *SACO*.[34] While the great majority of all organized salaried employees belong to *TCO*, a sizable number of lower-grade salaried employees belong to *LO*, and most upper-level civil servants belong to *SR*, *SACO* is principally the central organization of professionals with academic degrees. It includes the associations of secondary-school teachers, engineers, physicians, dentists, lawyers, architects, academics, clergymen, physiotherapists, curators of museums, veterinarians, and so forth. *SACO* comprises some thirty-four organizations, and in 1967 it had 98,720 members. Two-thirds of the membership is accounted for by the teachers, engineers, doctors, dentists, and lawyers. Elvander estimates that around 75 percent of all those in the labor force with university degrees belong to organizations affiliated with *SACO*.[35]

A number of national professional associations were formed in Sweden by the early part of this century—for example, the doctors, dentists, and gymnasium teachers all had their own organizations. But these organizations were for the most part only professional associations without trade-union characteristics. In the early 1940s, a group of young university graduates formed an organization to reverse the worsening economic conditions during their early years of work and the absolute decline in the living standards of professionals that was occurring as a result of inflation. The apprentice lawyers led the way by extending their membership to include all lawyers. Other young professionals took over several of the older professional organizations. Many new organizations were formed and in 1947 they consolidated as *SACO*. This is the first of such organizations in the world, and even now organizations like *SACO* seem limited to the Scandinavian countries. A number of Continental European countries have central organizations of professional associations but they do not have a definite trade-union character.

Several groups of higher civil servants and military officers formed a central organization in 1917, an organization which through reorganization and expansion in 1946 became the National Federation of Civil Servants, or *SR*, the most homogeneous and the smallest of all the labor-market federations. It includes some forty-four organizations of civil servants in the middle and higher-income ranges. Its total membership in 1967 was 18,325, which was just slightly greater than it was in 1945. It serves mainly to maintain the salary positions of higher-level government employees. *SR* has the confidence of the government to speak for this group in central negotiations along with the *TCO*, *SACO*, and the *LO* cartel of civil servants.

There are a number of stresses and strains among the three confederations of salaried employees, but there are also attempts to cooperate and even consolidate. The three confederations are based on different criteria of membership. TCO attempts to organize salaried employees at all levels on the vertical industrial principle, while SACO is organized wholly on the horizontal craft principle and includes only those with academic degrees or those who have passed certain exams. However, there is some overlapping between membership in SACO and in TCO. SR, which is confined to senior civil servants, is organized like SACO on a horizontal basis, but the criterion here is salary grade. SR sometimes views SACO as a threat to its existence, and with reason; several SR groups went over to SACO in the early 1950s. In recent years TCO has approached SACO about merging into one organization, but there is little interest in SACO in such a merger. This is understandable in the light of the fact that SACO is committed to a policy of taxation that is similar to that of the Conservatives, and SACO is also committed to greater salary differentials between professionals and other white-collar workers. Indeed their attempt to improve their relative salary position in relation to lower-status workers has been successful; as a result, to join a much larger organization with just the opposite view does not seem reasonable.

We might also note that the Swedish Federation of Students, or SFS, has a strong trade-union orientation, a development which has proceeded farther in Scandinavia than anywhere else and which we have already discussed in Chapter 5. The same can be said for the rapidly developing Swedish Central Organization of Secondary School Students, or SECO, which is a secondary and junior high school version of SFS and which we have also already discussed in Chapter 4.

This brief review of Swedish labor-market organizations should give some idea of how far centralized organization for the furtherance of individual economic interests has progressed. The trade-union principle of organization over the past quarter of a century has spread to the entire labor force and beyond to university and lower-level students. Indeed there are now national organizations based on trade-union principles for virtually all Swedes over age thirteen, not excepting housewives and the retired. The experience of Sweden shows not only that organization breeds organization, but that successful organization does so even more rapidly. The Swedish employers organized as a reaction to the organization of labor. The salaried groups organized as a result of the successes of organized labor. The professions organized after that, followed by the university students, who took their example from those in the professions they would soon enter. And finally the secondary-school and *grundskola* students followed them.

Economic Interest Organizations

The two most influential groups representing business and industrial interests, in addition to *SAF*, are the Federation of Swedish Industries and the General Export Association of Sweden.[36] The Federation of Swedish Industries was founded in 1910 to consolidate business interests against the growing tendency of the state to intervene in business activities. This organization entered into close activities with the conservative and antiparliamentary Hammerskjöld government (1914–1917) during the crisis caused by World War I, carrying out many administrative and regulatory functions for the government, with which it had much in common ideologically. This established a new cooperative pattern in the Swedish development of interest organizations. Just before and during World War II, a broad array of interest groups entered into similar cooperative relations with the Social Democratic government, including those representing business interests. As Elvander has put it, "Saltjöbadan had found a counterpart in the political sphere."[37]

The three groups that represent business interests cooperate among themselves in a number of areas; all are concerned with creating larger foreign markets and insuring that the government maintains minimal interference in the activities of business. While all follow a line of political-party neutrality and cooperate with the government, their views on most issues of taxation, defense, and welfare frequently parallel those of the Conservative party. There are also a number of other national confederations that represent the interests of specific segments of business and industry, such as banking, insurance, merchants, and shipowners, as well as an important national organization that is devoted to serving the interests of small firms, the Swedish Organization of Trade and Industry, or *SHIO*.

Another kind of economic interest group that has come to play an important role since the 1930s is the Swedish Union of Farmers, or *RLF*, to which the great majority of farmers belong.[38] This organization was formed in 1929 to defend the interests of farmers. Just as the Agrarian party (now the Center party) was modelled after the Social

Democratic party, so *RLF* was modelled after the successful trade unions of industrial workers. The organization works to present a united front among farmers vis-à-vis the government and other social groups. It is also dedicated to furthering the cooperative movement among farmers, spreading information about agriculture, and encouraging the cultural aspirations of farmers. The organization is also oriented toward including other primary producers, such as those in fishing and forestry, and it has over 2300 local branches that carry on many educational activities. Probably no other major interest group in Sweden has such a vital inner democracy as does *RLF*. While *RLF* is politically neutral, there is much overlapping between its leadership and that of the Center party. While the majority of *RLF* members certainly support the Center party, a minority support the Conservative party and a smaller minority the Liberal party.

Still another kind of economic interest groups that have become well developed in Sweden are the national organizations devoted to the interests of property owners and of renters.[39] The Swedish Association of Property Owners was founded in 1917 to oppose rent regulation, which has remained its primary task to the present. Opposition to rent control has also been an aim of the Conservative party. A number of local renters' associations were formed around 1907 and 1908, but they had little success. A power balance between the property owners and the renters was not possible at this time because of the graded franchise in communal elections, which retained power in the hands of the rich and propertied. During World War I, however, renters' associations were formed in Stockholm and Gothenburg under the auspices of the Social Democrats. They were immediately successful and a number of similar associations were formed in other cities. In 1923 the National Association of Renters was established. The Association was involved in a good deal of strife during the 1930s, and demonstrations and evictions were common. During World War II, however, both the property owners and the renters' associations became represented in the local offices and central organ of The State Rental Council (*Statens hyresråd*). The general importance of these associations is suggested by the observation that more than three-fourths of nonrural Swedish families live in multi-family dwellings and a majority of these families rent.[40]

Cooperatives

There are two fundamental types of cooperative societies, those for consumers and those for producers. In Sweden the two movements are quite distinct and independent from each other. Consumer cooperation developed in the latter part of the nineteenth century, appeals to a broad membership throughout the population, and has had no ambition to become a monopoly, in fact it has vigorously opposed monopolies.[41] Producers' cooperatives, on the other hand, developed mainly among the agricultural population in the 1920s and 1930s as a result of their deteriorating economic situation in what was essentially a class movement.[42] The concern of the producers' cooperatives is with getting the highest prices for their products, and they openly proclaim their desire for monopoly.

Consumer cooperation in Sweden as everywhere else can trace its origins back to the Equitable Pioneers in Rochdale, England, who in the 1840s probably established the first modern consumer cooperative. As in so many other areas, Sweden embarked on consumer cooperation rather late, but has (along with the other Scandinavian countries) gone farther in developing the movement than has anyone else. More than half of all Swedish families belong to consumer cooperative societies. In 1966, 297 of these societies were united in the giant Cooperative Association, or *KF*,[43] which had 3450 shops in 1966 and employed 35,899 persons. Sales were 5.6 billion Swedish *kroner*. Perhaps as high as 15 percent of all retail trade is carried on by cooperatives; for foodstuffs the percentage may now be close to 30 percent.[44] The activities of *KF* enterprises include retail stores, large department stores, insurance, restaurants, travel agencies, and burial societies (which were responsible for 41 percent of all funerals in 1961). *KF* also owns a number of bakeries, meat-processing plants, mills, a light-bulb factory, a soap factory, a publishing house, and a number of other enterprises. The weekly family magazine *Vi*, meaning "We," put out by *KF*, has a circulation of well over a half million.

KF operates according to the principles of the Congress of the International Cooperative Alliance. It has: (1) open membership, (2) democratic management, (3) dividends from surplus in relation to amount of purchase, (4) limited interest on share capital, (5) cash trading, (6) political and religious neutrality, and (7) allocation from surplus for educational work. Granted that the management of the cooperative societies is democratic, it should also be pointed out, however, that in no other major interest organization is such a large proportion of the membership passive. Political neutrality came early to the cooperative movement. The first Swedish cooperatives were imbued with a liberal, self-help ideology.[45] In the 1890s and the early years of this century, there was a strong attempt by the socialists to make the cooperative movement "the third arm" of the labor movement along with the Social Democratic party and the trade-union movement.[46] But KF was one of the first of the great organizations to become unequivocally wedded to a line of political-party neutrality, a position it has consistently held down to the present. The emphasis on educational work in KF is particularly notable. In addition to publishing what is probably the best mass-circulation magazine in Sweden and owning a publishing house, KF has a people's "college," supports adult education, makes educational films, and runs a correspondence school named Brevskolan. KF has taken its seventh principle seriously.

One important economic role that KF has played has been to oppose monopolies and to defend consumer interests in general, vis-à-vis both the government and industry. KF has been responsible for several important laws including one that requires the registration of cartel agreements (passed in 1946) and another that opposes certain kinds of restrictive practices in industry and commerce (passed in 1955). More important than aiding in the passage of these laws, however, have been KF's successes in lowering prices on selected goods by entering into competition with monopoly manufacturers, which has successfully been done in the case of galoshes, light bulbs, and laundry powder.[47]

A very different kind of cooperative is the producers' cooperatives, which are mostly limited to the agricultural sector. A 1962 publication of the Federation of Swedish Farmers' Associations, or SL, claims that not less than 80 percent of agricultural products are handled by organizations within the agricultural cooperative movement.[48] SL further claims that "practically all" farmers producing for the market belong to one or more specialized agricultural cooperatives. All of the cooperatives are national federations of local producers' cooperatives that function in specific natural areas. A list of some of the major agricultural producer cooperatives will give some idea of the extent of specialization:

Swedish Dairies Association (*SMR*)
Meat Marketing Association of Swedish Farmers (*SS*)
Selling and Purchasing Association of Swedish Farmers (*SLR*)
Swedish Egg and Poultry Marketing Association (*SA*)
Association of Swedish Forest Owners (*SSR*)
Association for Swedish Livestock Breeding and Production (*SHS*)
Association of Swedish Producers (*SSF*)
Association of Swedish Distillers (*SBI*)
Association of Swedish Flax and Hemp Growers (*RLH*)
Association of Swedish Oil Seed Growers (*SOC*)
Association of Swedish Fur Breeders (*SPR*).

SL claimed in 1962 that total membership in all of their affiliated organizations totaled over 1,100,000, which works out to around one membership for every man, woman, and child in the agricultural population and to around three to four memberships per farm family.

The Idealistic Organizations

"Idealistic organizations" is the name that the Swedes commonly give to all of the popular movements that do not primarily serve economic ends. Some of the major idealistic organizations in modern Sweden are listed in Table 8.2.

Table 8.2 Membership in Popular Movements and the Free Churches, 1950 and 1967.

	1950	1967
Temperance societies (*Nykterhetssällskap*)	304,666	377,121
Swedish Sports Federations (*Sveriges Riksidrottsförbund*)	735,782	2,241,204
Study Circles	811,132	1,382,393
	(1958–59)	(1966–67)
Free Churches	Ca:394,451*	331,231

* Author's estimate based on incomplete data from *Statistisk Årsbok för Sverige 1961*, p. 283.

SOURCES: *Statistisk Årsbok för Sverige, op. cit.*, for various years.

First are the temperance societies, which have played a surprisingly important role in the development of modern Swedish society. *The Blue Book* (*Blå boken*), a handbook put out by a group of temperance societies, lists twenty-nine national temperance organizations.[49] Some have Christian orientations, others are wholly secular. Some serve only certain categories of the population, such as students, doctors, policemen, or women; others have an open membership. Some are committed to total abstinence; others do not oppose class two beer, which has a low alcoholic content. There are, in addition, two temperance groups in the Riksdag, the Social Democratic Temperance Group and the Riksdag Temperance Group. In 1965 36.8 percent of all members of the Riksdag belonged to these temperance groups.[50]

The temperance movement has placed great emphasis on organizational work and on general popular education in addition to its opposition to alcohol. The high proportion of temperance people in the Riksdag and in much of Swedish organizational life is a result of the organizational training received in the temperance movement. Many Swedish writers and people who are successful in other areas but who came from poor farm and working-class backgrounds have attributed the popular education efforts of the temperance movement as partially responsible for their successes. The very high cost of hard liquor, the campaign against hard liquor and in favor of wine on the part of the state wine and liquor monopoly, and the generally severe liquor laws can be attributed to the disproportionate strength of the well-organized temperance interests. The temperance movement is stronger in the northern Scandinavian countries than in any of the other modern societies.

Related to the temperance movement and an important part of it has been the popular education movement. But popular education is also an important function of the labor movement, the free churches, the Church of Sweden, farmers' groups, civil servants' associations, and other groups. In 1966–1967 almost 1.4 million adults were involved in non-job-related study circles. This figure translates into one student for every four adult Swedes. Exhibit 8.3 lists the subjects studied in all of the registered study circles. More than half were devoted to the study of languages, film, literature, fine arts, and music.

There are also sixty-three people's colleges (sometimes translated "folk high schools") in Sweden, which are supported by all of the various popular movements. The idea of the people's colleges came from Denmark a century ago. They are dedicated to giving a liberal education to young adults who have not had an academic education. The course of study can take from one to three years.

A fast growing movement, though with a rapidly shifting and not

Exhibit 8.3   Member and Subject of Study Circles, 1966-1967.

SUBJECT	Number of study circles
Religion, Philosophy, Psychology	12,089
Languages	26,663
Film, Literature, Fine Arts	21,766
Music	26,389
History, Geography	2,056
Social Science, Law	11,772
Technology, Manufacturing, Communications	10,389
Economics, etc.	15,679
Physical and Medical Science, Sports	7,522
Total Number of Study Circles	134,325
Total Number of Students	1,382,393

SOURCE: *Statistisk årsbok för Sverige 1968, op. cit.*, p. 341.

strongly involved membership, is the sports movement. Membership in 1967 in the Swedish Sports Federations totaled two-sevenths of the entire Swedish population.

Membership in the free churches, as we already noted in our chapter on religion, has been declining for a number of years and is part of the continuing secularization of Swedish society.

The Political Party Organizations

The political parties are quite clearly the most important of "the idealistic organizations." As we have already dealt with the political parties in some detail, we will deal with political parties as voluntary associations here. A political party in Sweden, as in much of Northwestern Europe, is more than only the political apparatus it tends to be in the United States; it also serves as "a civic club, a pressure group, and an organization for the pursuit of leisure time interests." [51] All of the parties with the exception of the Communists have active women's groups, youth groups, and student groups, both in the universities and in the gymnasia. They carry on training programs for party workers, and they offer adult education courses in a broad variety of subjects. The parties also publish a number of political and literary journals, as do the women's organizations and the youth groups. In all of these ways, the Swedish political parties and many of the other interest organizations we have discussed in this chapter serve some of the same functions as churches do in America. In fact, political party identification in Sweden is the closest analogy to religious identity in the

United States. However, Swedes are not as political as their high degree of involvement in political organizations suggests. Table 8.3 shows the percentage of Swedish voters who belonged to political parties in 1964. Membership in political parties was equal to about 30 percent of the total vote. Note that the Social Democrats have the highest percentage, but—as we have already noted in Chapter 2—this high figure is the result of a large proportion of union members being collectively enrolled in branch organizations of the party.

Table 8.3 Number of Members of Political Parties and the Vote for the Parties, 1964.

PARTY	Number of Members	Number of Votes	Members to Voters in Percent
Conservative Party	196,352	582,609	33.7
Center (Agrarian) Party	116,133	569,934	20.4
Liberal Party	89,489	723,988	12.4
Social Democratic Party	867,613	2,006,923	43.2
Communist Party	22,987	221,746	10.4
Other*	—	140,580	—
Total	1,292,574	4,245,780	30.4

* This includes mostly the Christian Democratic Assembly (KDS) with 75,389 votes and the Citizens Coalition (MbS), a combining of the middle-class parties in Malmö with 64,804 votes.

SOURCE: Statistisk årsbok för Sverige 1968 op. cit., pp. 411, 417.

The best theory to explain the much greater membership in political parties in Sweden (and a number of other Western European countries) as compared with America, where it is probably around 5 percent of the adult population,[52] has been suggested by Duverger.[53] He has pointed out that the Socialists, without many material resources, gained power through great emphasis on organization at the local level. The success of the Socialists, in turn, exerted pressure on the bourgeois parties to respond with a greater emphasis on local organization, which appears to be more or less the general pattern in Northwestern Europe. However, this does not appear to be the case in Great Britain, where a high degree of local political organization was developed by the Conservatives even before the formation of the Labour party in 1900.[54] Perhaps the Liberals in Britain can be seen as playing a role analogous to the Socialists elsewhere.

Conclusions

There are a number of summary statements that might be made about Swedish organizations and their role in the greater society. Some of these generalize what we have already said about specific organizations, others make comparative observations.

(1) In none of the modern societies are voluntary organizations as developed as they are in the Scandinavian countries, and the extent of organization is greatest in Sweden, which tends to be the model for Norway and Finland.

(2) The great organizations have close and cooperative relations with the government, yet all are jealous of their independence and sensitive to any kind of legislative regulation. Of particular and unique importance is the extent to which interest organizations of all kinds are brought into the legislative process, both to determine what kind of legislation is needed and later to comment on official reports prior to the enactment of legislation. Lobbying, as we understand it, is not necessary because of the general acceptance of the principle of consulting all groups affected by a given piece of legislation.

(3) Through the years, all of the great organizations, except for *LO*, have come to adopt a policy of strict political-party neutrality. (*LO* continues in its official support of the Social Democrats in spite of much criticism.) This does not mean, however, that organizations do not speak out on issues that concern them or that their lines do not parallel those of one of the political parties.

(4) There is virtually no opposition, one can even say that there is now general acceptance, of the trade-union organization of all groups in the labor force. Trade-union organization begets trade-union organization. For example, it is precisely those countries in which the organization of manual workers is strongest where salaried workers are most prone to organize.[55] Outside of Scandinavia, the country with the strongest blue-collar as well as white-collar organization is Austria. (It is also the Continental country that traditionally has had the strongest Social Democratic movement; the two phenomena correlate rather neatly.) The contrast between Sweden and the United States in this regard is indeed striking: 95 percent of all Swedish manual workers are in trade unions as compared with 50 to 60 percent in the United States; among white-collar workers, the percentage in Sweden is around 60, and in America it is around 11.

(5) The organizations operate in close accordance to their statutes, with practically no internal corruption, even among industrial trade unions. Yet there is sometimes concern with the universal phenomenon of the leadership of the small minority and the passivity of the great majority. Influences between the leadership and the rank and file of organizations move both ways, however, as, for example, a detailed study of the ideological development of Swedish social democracy has shown.[56] The leadership of the political parties, the consumers' cooperatives, the unions, the religious elements, and the temperance groups have continually accommodated themselves to the inclinations of the rank and file. Sweden, significantly, has produced no elite theorist or social scientist in this century with views similar to those of Michels, Mosca, or Pareto—nor even to a James Burnham.

(6) Active participation is least in the cooperative movement in which only a minuscule proportion of the membership is involved in the activities of the local societies. It is probably greatest in the Swedish Union of Farmers, or *RLF*, in which active participation far exceeds the 10 to 15 percent we might take as representing the average degree of active participation in most of the great organizations.[57]

(7) The extraordinary organization of farmers has no counterpart outside of Scandinavia. Many observers, including Karl Marx, who have not known much about Scandinavia have commented on the general inability of farmers to sustain viable political and economic organization.[58] The success of farmer organizations in Sweden in the 1930s insulated them almost completely from any Nazi or undemocratic ideologies.[59]

(8) Equal organizational strength, intelligent legislation, collective agreements, and much experience have laid a basis whereby interest groups fundamentally opposed to each other can compromise their differences as equals. Employees and employers, farmers and consumers, conservatives and socialists, government and private interests have all learned to take half a loaf. There is nothing at all idealistic or even charitable about this capacity to compromise. Its present advanced form has developed since the early 1930s, which was a relatively stormy period. Now, the predominant spirit of negotiation and of compromise is rooted in pragmatic materialism, enlightened self-interest, caution, respect for knowledge, and an awareness that it is preferable to get less than is wished rather than to disrupt the equilibrium of organized interests.

(9) The educational and informational roles of the great organiza-

tions are major ones, the result, perhaps, of the strong socialist and social reform liberalist traditions in Sweden. All the great organizations publish a number of journals and magazines for their membership. They support vast programs of adult education in the form of study circles, special courses, and people's colleges, in addition to well-developed programs of job-related training courses and programs. Of particular note here is the advanced state of popular education in economics resulting from the efforts of the labor-market organizations and other economic interest groups. This is a major force for promoting the spread of information and knowledge, which is a key to Swedish rationality.

(10) In a recent book on German society with no reference to Sweden, Ralf Dahrendorf has spelled out what he regards as the fundamental criteria for the existence of effective liberal democracy, none of which he claims is sufficiently developed in contemporary Germany. No society has ever achieved these to a greater degree than has contemporary Sweden. They are:

(1) *equal citizenship rights have been generalized;*
(2) *conflicts are recognized and regulated rationally in all institutional orders;*
(3) *elites reflect the color and diversity of social interests;*
(4) *public virtues are the predominant value orientation of the people.*[60]

Notes

1. T. L. Johnston, *Collective Bargaining in Sweden* (London: Allen & Unwin, 1962), p. 7.
2. There are two basic works on interest groups in Sweden: Gunnar Heckscher, *Staten och organisationerna*, 2nd ed. (Stockholm: Kooperative Förbundet, 1951), and Nils Elvander, *Intresse organisationerna i dagens Sverige* (Lund: CWK Gleerup, 1968). I have depended greatly on Elvander's up-to-date survey of the role of interest groups in Swedish society. It very much deserves to be translated into English. Some of Heckscher's observations in English on interest groups in Sweden are to be found in his chapter in H. W.

Ehrman (ed.), *Interest Groups on Four Continents* (Pittsburgh: University of Pittsburgh Press, 1960), and in some mimeographed publications of the Swedish Institute in Stockholm: one is entitled "Pluralist Democracy" from the late 1940s, another is entitled "Interest Groups in Sweden: Their Political Role" (1958).

3. Johnston, *op. cit.*, p. 124, uses this phrase in quotation marks. I do not know its source.

4. Some of the observations in this paragraph are from a talk delivered by Alva Myrdal in New Delhi on May 11, 1956: "The Active Participation of Swedish Citizens in Local Affairs" (Stockholm: Ministry for Foreign Affairs, 1956), mimeo.

5. On the origins and development of the party, see Herbert Tingsten, *The Swedish Social Democrats*, Greta Frankel and Richard F. Tomasson (trs.) (forthcoming).

6. On the origins and early development of the trade-union movement, see Tage Lindbom, *Den svenska fackföreningsrörelsens uppkomst* (Stockholm: Tidens förlag, 1938).

7. See the chapter "The Temperance Question" in Tingsten, *op. cit.*

8. The only overview of the modern Swedish feminist movement I have come by is James Rössel, *Kvinnorna och kvinnorörelsen i Sverige, 1850–1950* (Stockholm: YSF förlag, 1950). It contains a bibliography.

9. Fredrika Bremmer, *Hertha*, Mary Howitt (tr.) (London and New York, 1856).

10. The basic work on the early development of *KF* is Olaf Ruin, *Kooperativa förbundet* (Lund, 1960). There is much on *KF* in Elvander, *op. cit.*, passim. See also John Lundberg, *In Our Own Hands* (Stockholm: Ronzo). See latest edition as this is continually revised.

11. Eli F. Heckscher, *An Economic History of Sweden*, Göran Ohlin (tr.) (Cambridge: Harvard University Press, 1954), Chap. 6.

12. Gerard De Gré, "Freedom and Social Structure," *American Sociological Review*, II (October 1946), 529–536.

13. A good and detailed view of the history, structure, and functioning of *LO* is to be found in T. L. Johnston, *op. cit.*, pp. 23–67.

14. Elvander, *op. cit.*, pp. 279–280.

15. Elvander, *op. cit.*, p. 27. The figures given by Johnston, *op. cit.*, are somewhat lower, p. 30.

16. Estimate supplied to me by the labor economist Sanford Cohen.

17. U. S. Department of Labor, *Directory of National and International Labor Unions in the United States 1967* (Washington, D.C.: Bureau of Labor Statistics, 1967), Bulletin No. 1596, p. 65.

18. *Statistisk Årsbok för Sverige 1968* (Stockholm: Statistiska Centralbyrån), p. 241.

19. Johnston, *op. cit.*, p. 15.

20. Johnston, *op. cit.*, pp. 68–91, for a good overview in English of *SAF*.

21. This is a very well known and significant event in modern Swedish history. It is the subject of a 1968 Swedish movie.

22. An English translation of this agreement is available from either *LO* or *SAF*.

23. The Basic Agreement is discussed in detail by Johnston, *op. cit.*, pp. 169–275.

24. It might be noted here that the structure of the other great organizations that do not hold annual congresses is similar to that of *LO*.

25. For a bibliography, see footnotes in Johnston, *op. cit.;* also consult citations in Charles A. Myers, *Industrial Relations in Sweden* (Cambridge: M.I.T. Press, 1951).

26. On the system of labor relations in these two countries, see Walter Galenson's now somewhat outdated studies *Labor in Norway* (Cambridge: Harvard University Press, 1949), and *The Danish System of Labor Relations* (Cambridge: Harvard University Press, 1952); see also his more recent *Trade Union Democracy in Western Europe* (Berkeley and Los Angeles: University of California Press, 1961).

27. Elvander, *op. cit.*, p. 30.

28. Another factor that makes both sides shy away from inflationary wage agreements is that this would drive Swedish goods out of the world market.

29. Elvander, *op. cit.*, p. 30.

30. Again, see the discussion in Johnston, *op. cit.*, pp. 92–112.

31. See Adolf Sturmthal (ed.), *White-collar Trade Unions* (Urbana: University of Illinois Press, 1966).

32. Elvander, *op. cit.*, pp. 48, 50.

33. Estimate cited by Everett M. Kassalow in "White-Collar Unionism in the United States," in Sturmthal, *op. cit.*, p. 11.

34. Johnston, *op. cit.*, pp. 106–109, also has a little to say about *SACO;* see also the informational pamphlet published by *SACO* (Stockholm: *SACO*, 1968).

35. Elvander, *op. cit.*, p. 50.

36. Both of these organizations are also discussed by Elvander, *op. cit.*, passim.

37. Elvander, *op. cit.*, Chap. 1.

38. This organization is also discussed by Elvander, *op. cit.*, passim; see also the English language booklet *SL, Farmers' Cooperation in Sweden* (Stockholm: *SL*, 1962).

39. Also discussed by Elvander, *op. cit.*, passim.

40. See section entitled "Housing," *Statistisk årsbok för Sverige*, *op. cit.*, for any recent year.

41. See Lundberg, *op. cit.*

42. See *Farmers' Cooperation in Sweden, op. cit.*

43. Data from *Statistisk årsbok för Sverige 1968, op. cit.*, p. 143.

44. My estimate based on comments by John Lundberg, *op. cit.*, pp. 6–7.

45. See Tingsten, "Cooperation," in *op. cit.*

46. *Ibid.*

47. See the discussion of the role of the cooperatives in opposing monopolies in Marquis Child's, *Sweden: The Middle Way* (New Haven: Yale University Press, 1961).

48. See *Farmers' Cooperation in Sweden, op. cit.*, p. 5.

49. *Blå Boken* (Stockholm: *Blå Bokens* förlag, annually).

50. *Ibid.*, 1965, pp. 38–41.

51. Dankwart A. Rustow, *The Politics of Compromise* (Princeton: Princeton University Press, 1955), p. 144.

52. Angus Campbell, *et al.*, *The American Voter* (New York: Wiley, 1960),

Chap. 6; see also discussion in Lester W. Milbrath, *Political Participation* (Chicago: Rand McNally, 1965), pp. 16–22.

53. Maurice Duverger, *Political Parties*, Barbara and Robert North (trs.) (London: Methuen University Paperbacks, 1964), passim.

54. See James Cornford, "The Adoption of Mass Organization by the British Conservative Party," in Erik Allardt and Yrjö Littunen (eds.), *Cleavages, Ideologies and Party Systems* (Helsinki: Academic Book Store, 1964), pp. 400–424.

55. See Adolf Sturmthal, "White-Collar Unions—A Comparative Essay," in Sturmthal, *op. cit.*, pp. 365–398.

56. See Tingsten, *op. cit.*

57. Elvander, *op. cit.*, pp. 80–81.

58. See Maurice Duverger, *op. cit.*, pp. 235–237.

59. See discussion of Sten Sparre Nilson, "The Political Parties," in J. A. Lauwerys (ed.), *Scandinavian Democracy* (Copenhagen: Det Danske Selskab, 1958), pp. 112–116.

60. Ralf Dahrendorf, *Society and Democracy in Germany* (Garden City, N.Y.: Doubleday, 1967), p. 31.

IX

Values

"There are, perhaps, two kinds of knowledge—
exact knowledge and the knowledge of values."
—Letter from a Cambridge professor to
ABRAHAM FLEXNER[1]

Values are vague and abstruse and difficult to rigorously pinpoint. But this does not make their study any less meaningful or any less important. Certain values in one society distinguish that society from another, such as the emphases on achievement, egalitarianism, and individual personality, for example, distinguish the American value system from that of most other modern cultures. The function of this chapter is to sum up the distinguishing characteristics—the ethos, if you will—of contemporary Swedish culture. Swedish values will be viewed from the vantage point of other modern cultures, particularly that of the United States.

An intelligent and thoughtful definition of values is given by Florence Kluckhohn, who, along with Robin Williams and others, views values as involving a rank-ordering of possible choices,[2] involving other dimensions, besides being merely an "element of a shared symbolic system." According to Kluckhohn:

Value orientations are complex but definitely patterned (rank-ordered) principles, resulting from the transactional interplay of three analytically distinguishable elements of the evaluative process—the cognitive, the affective, and the directive elements—which give order and direction to the ever-flowing stream of human acts and thoughts as these relate to the solution of common human problems.[3]

There is much that can be said about values. They involve an affective quality. They are generally regarded as fundamental to the well-being of the group. They are not really goals but rather criteria whereby goals are selected. They lie on a continuum of intensity. At one extreme are those that when violated bring forth strong feelings of guilt or shame in the individual; at the other end of the continuum are those values that generally involve little guilt or shame and invoke weak social sanctions. Values differ also in how specific or how general they are.

Our principal concern, as in Robin Williams' well-known discussion of American values, will be with dominant values, those that are pervasive, that are held most intensely, that are persistent, and that take precedence over others. According to Williams, dominant values can be delineated by the following criteria:

1) *Extensiveness of the value in the total activity of the system. What proportion of a population and of its activities manifest the value?*
2) *Duration of the value. Has it been persistently important over a considerable period of time?*
3) *Intensity with which the value is sought or maintained, as shown by effort, crucial choices, verbal affirmation, and by reactions to threats to the value—for example, promptness, certainty, and severity of sanctions.*
4) *Prestige of value carriers—that is, of persons, objects, or organizations considered to be bearers of the value. Culture Heroes, for example, are significant indexes of values of high generality and esteem.*[4]

What follows in this chapter, to a greater extent than in previous chapters, is open to debate and to differences of perspective. This discussion of Swedish value orientations is inevitably shaped by the author's American orientation. A Frenchman or a German would very likely emphasize other considerations. Fundamental value differences, such as those between Western and non-Western cultures and those between modern and developing societies, are ignored. The frame of reference here, as throughout the book, is only with the developed societies. Also, little attempt is made to discuss Swedish values at such an abstract level as universalism-particularism, specificity-diffuseness, performance-quality or other variations of the pattern variables,[5] as such abstractions are so general that they are unwieldy and not very discriminating.

To reiterate Williams, value orientations "do *not operate as single and separate units* but *are in continually shifting and recombining configura-*

tions marked by very complex interpenetration, conflict, and reformulation."[6] Nor are value orientations "disembodied elements which somehow function apart from concrete social relations and personalities." They are high-level conceptions of the desirable abstracted from the complexities of social reality.

Dominant Swedish Values

The order in which certain dominant Swedish values are discussed here is not entirely haphazard. They are presented to some extent in terms of how "distinguishing" they are of Swedish culture as compared with other Western cultures. Values that appear related to each other are discussed sequentially. Those values that are also dominant American values and that also are dealt with by Williams will be discussed in a subsequent section in which the attempt will be made to determine the extent that these American values are also Swedish values. Several of these, such as progress, science and secular rationality, and democracy, are stronger and more pervasive in Swedish culture, several appear to be as characteristic of Swedish as of American culture, and others are less characteristic.

Empiricism. Throughout Swedish culture there is stress on the empirically verifiable. Truth, for the most part, is that which can be measured and counted. In politics there is little ideology; most political debate deals with specific issues. There is a suspiciousness of ideology. Herbert Tingsten has commented that politics has become "a kind of applied statistics. . . . The margin for discussion on principles is exceedingly narrow, and the debates become as dry as wage negotiations."[7] Collective bargaining is shaped by the use of economic data and a pragmatic orientation on the part of both labor and management.[8] Swedish scholarship stays close to the facts and is reluctant to generalize. Social science and sociology place an emphasis on surveys and interviews; history and political science on original historical sources. A. H. Halsey has commented that the research activities of Swedish scientists "express strong preferences for concrete projects with well-defined aims."[9] Even literary criticism is nominalist, shies away from abstract concepts, and tends to use terms with specific and clear referents.[10] There is little interest among Swedish intellectuals in philosophies of history or in abstruse theories. Arnold Toynbee's *Study of History* and Oswald Spengler's *Decline of the West*, for example, have never been translated into Swedish.

A look at government reports and the discussion that ensues from them is another indication of the pervasive Swedish empiricism. The contrast with British government reports is notable. The Swedish reports tend to be factual, filled with statistics, and parsimonious in the use of generalizations and assumptions. A good example is to compare the numerous and analogous education reports of Sweden and Britain.[11] The Swedish reports take little for granted, whereas the British reports are replete with ideological assumptions and general beliefs.

Empiricism is even an important component in interpersonal relations. It is complimentary to refer to a person as *saklig*, which means that one speaks from facts and is objective and has respect for literal truth. Swedes, unlike Americans and English, are reluctant to speak about things in which they do not feel they have competence. There is a fear they may not be thought to be *saklig*.

This pervasive empiricism may be viewed as only one aspect of the intense permeation of Swedish culture by modern values that have replaced the philosophically idealistic and religious values of traditional Swedish culture. Of some significance may be the extraordinarily well-developed statistical heritage of Sweden. Or, perhaps the reason the Swedes have cultivated so much statistical information about themselves is a manifestation of their fundamental empiricism. Probably no other people in the world has a statistical heritage that is comparable to the Swedes. No modern society has or utilizes more knowledge about itself in writing legislation and in running its day-to-day affairs than does Sweden.

Malleability of Institutions. Swedes believe that institutions can and should be restructured to accomplish certain agreed-upon ends. This is true in spite of the fact that the traditional component in many Swedish institutions is great, particularly in the government, the universities, and the legal system. This contrasts with American and English cultures in which many institutions are tinged with the sacred. Contemporary Sweden abounds in examples of change in the most fundamental institutions, which have occurred with little opposition that has its roots in a traditionalism analogous to the conventional American view toward the Constitution or the English view toward the monarchy. The radical restructuring of the school system to make it more egalitarian is an example. The radical revision of the constitution to bring it in accord with contemporary practice is another example; there is no significant opinion urging that practice be brought into accord with principle. Another example is the various radical solutions proposed for changing the relations between the state and the Church. Even sex roles and the relations between the sexes are believed to be amenable to change through changing educational and economic institutions.

Swedish intellectual life in general is like the French in its capacity to be radical, to go to the root of things, and not to accept institutional arrangements as given. Yet, unlike the French, the Swedes have a capacity to effect radical social change through investigation and compromise. The Swedes have little traditionalist orientation toward conventional institutions even though the traditional component is an important aspect in many of them. This in no sense means that most people do not accept conventional institutional arrangements most of the time, an imperative for any stable society, but only that they do have the capacity to rationally contemplate radical change, or they at least have a willingness to follow their leaders on these issues. There is indeed a lack of reverence for traditional institutions. For example, polls asking about the future of the monarchy indicate that one-third of the population wants to see Sweden become a republic with a president after the death of the present king, or they have no opinion on the subject.[12] And, it should be pointed out, Sweden has as regal and egalitarian a monarch as any in the world. And the flag is more decorative than sacred.

It is significant, too, in this regard, that Swedish culture does not tolerate great men as do the Anglo-American cultures. There are no men comparable to our Lincoln, Wilson, or Roosevelt, nor Britain's Disraeli, Lloyd George, or Churchill. When Swedes are asked to name the greatest Swede, most can do no better than to name the present king or some long-dead one, most frequently Gustavus Adolphus.[13] Dag Hammarskjöld, so revered in many Western countries, holds nothing like the honorific place in Swedish opinion that he does here, particularly after the publication of his *Markings* with their peculiar religious revelations.[14] Nor does that very un-Swedish social scientist Gunnar Myrdal or any other intellectual or academic command in Sweden anything like the great respect he holds among American social scientists and intellectuals. What is important in their society are institutions and the use of science and knowledge to change them, not "great men." Perhaps several Swedish writers such as August

Strindberg, Selma Lagerlöf, and Vilhelm Moberg can be regarded as culture heroes, but it would be difficult to maintain that they exemplify any specific values.

Legalism. The Swedes believe in doing things according to rules and regulations. By comparison, American and English societies are casual toward rules and regulations. One of the characteristics of Swedish versus Anglo-American bureaucracy is the literalness with which rules and regulations are followed. Enormous attention is paid to procedure in the whole legal system; much less is left to the discretion of judges than in our legal system.[15] So much of American bureaucracy consists of interpreting rules as guidelines and leaving much room for exceptions. And consider the concept of "humane bureaucracy" which some English writers boast about. In Swedish bureaucracy, however, the emphasis is on doing things according to the rules and not making exceptions. This is certainly one of the great sources (or results) of the universalism of the Swedish value system, a value we might regard as an infravalue.

Some homely examples will illustrate the Swedish emphasis on accepting rules and on orderly behavior. In an apartment house with an elevator in which there is a sign saying that it is limited to three people, one in a party of four will invariably walk, though the elevator could easily accommodate five or six. The orderliness of Swedes in public places and the instinctive queuing up when a number of people are waiting for a bus or are in a store (nearly all of which use a numbering system in order to take people in turn) also suggest general respect for rules, regulations, and orderly procedure. While there are relatively fewer police in Sweden than in America, and consequently less chance of being stopped by one, Swedes—at least Swedish academics—virtually never drive after having a drink or two.

Science and the Usefulness of Knowledge. As mentioned before, there is enormous respect among Swedes for science, technology, and expert opinion. No society in the world utilizes experts and knowledge in the whole process of writing legislation as much as does Sweden. If deference for persons with knowledge and expert opinion is a kind of elitism, then Sweden is an elite society. But, it is important to stress that this is a different form of elitism than the deference to an upper class that characterizes England. There is little anti-intellectualism in Sweden.[16] The belief in the utility of knowledge is another aspect of the penetration of modern values in Sweden. There is a strong belief that expert opinion, knowledge, and science can resolve conflict, or at least that they can narrow the range of conflict. The pervasiveness of this value together with the high degree of organization of basic interest groups with developed traditions of compromise is the key to the extraordinary stability that characterizes Swedish society.

Privacy. Swedes believe that an individual should be left to himself, that one plays many public roles but that these are separate and distinct from one's private roles. There is little publicity given to the private life of politicians or celebrities, with the important exception of the royal family. Whether one gets divorced or commits suicide is considered a private affair and is never mentioned in the newspapers. Nor, in fact, is the cause of death mentioned in obituaries, as this is also in the realm of the "private." If one should be sentenced to a work camp for driving under the influence of alcohol, it will not be in the newspaper even if one is well known; and one has some choice as to when he will serve his time, such as during vacations, so that even his employer need not know. Sexual behavior, too, is very much a private affair, and not, for most Swedes, subject to any special sexual morality. Hardly anyone ever "drops in" on others in Sweden. Business and government provide private offices for almost everyone. And virtually all rooms in university housing are private. There is something very Swedish about Greta Garbo's famous line "I want to be alone."

Proper Performance. Perhaps part of the reason the Swedes value privacy is the result of the great emphasis they put on performing their public roles properly. This is the same "civility" that Johan Goudsblom points out as characteristic of the Dutch "which never indulges in an open display of emotions, but conceals the actor's innermost feelings behind a restrained observance of conventional forms."[17] It also "includes not only good manners and a sense of decorum but also more personal qualities such as self-possession and a sense of duty and responsibility."[18] However, he points out that the Dutch do not "overdo civility: in manners, neither elegance nor modesty is greatly cultivated." From Goudsblom's perspective, one might say that the Swedes "overdo" civility: modesty and elegance are much stressed. Performing well is seen as acting according to correct forms and as sticking close to conventional role definitions and standards. This is manifested in the quiet elegance of their homes, their dress, and the maintenance of a vast amount of ritual in interpersonal relations.

Swedes do not see their roles as having much "play" in them. And here I mean "play" in both meanings, as fun and as tolerance for individual deviations. This is why Swedes are continually described as "formal," "stiff," "reserved," and so forth. It is also the source of some of the jokes that Norwegians and Danes make about them, such as in the joke about the two Norwegians, two Danes, and two Swedes shipwrecked on a desert island: The Danes form a cooperative, the Norwegians begin to fight, while the Swedes just sit around and wait to be introduced. The difficulty the Swedes have in communicating with each other is one of the central themes explored in Ingemar Bergman's films.

Caution. There is a reticence on the part of Swedes to do that which may threaten individual rights or vested interests or that which may have unforeseen or disturbing consequences. We might call this value "caution" or "carefulness," but in any case it can be described as a disdain for passionate behavior, a hesitation to act without weighing all the consequences. Caution, or a slowness to act, is a preëminent feature of Swedish public life. Consider the following example of caution in effecting a desired social change:

the system of entailed estates still exists in Sweden, even though it may well seem one of the most conspicuous remnants of feudalism. In the agricultural provinces of central and southern Sweden, a not insignificant proportion of all the land belongs to a few noble families whose estates were thus kept intact from one generation to another through the rule of primogeniture. Since the 1880's one expert commission after another has attempted to find a formula for the abolition of the system without encroaching upon the rights of those concerned. Finally, in 1963, an Act was passed which provides for the abolition of the special order of succession applicable to these estates.[19]

The failure of the Swedish socialists to carry out any significant nationalization after almost forty years in power, the slow and thorough way in which legislation is drafted, and the striking lack of passion in politics provide ample indicators of this value.

Caution and restraint also characterize interpersonal relations and are related to the emphasis on proper performance that is so characteristic of the Swedes. This is the root of the ubiquitous charge that the Swedes are "dull." Yet it is this cautiousness, this lack of passion, this concern with the consequences of action that is responsible for the extraordinary ability of the Swedes to practice the politics of compromise. It also enhances the conditions for freedom from external pressures for conformity and for rational discourse.

Abhorrence of Violence. There are extremely strong inhibitions on violence and the manifestation of aggression in Swedish culture. While it is now almost commonplace to see nudity and sexual intercourse in Swedish films (though not yet on television), it is not usual to see violence. Most of the violence in the mass media (and much is censored) is in American films and television programs. Herbert Hendin has commented on the strong inhibitions on showing aggression in the suicidal patients that he studied, particularly among the males.[20] Even loud talking or minor altercations in public places will quickly bring the arrival of the police.

Even when Swedes have been drinking heavily at parties, it is rare for any physical aggressiveness to be shown. It may be that the abhorrence of violence is greater in Sweden than in the other Scandinavian countries, though in all of them it is clearly greater than in America. Table 9.1 shows comparative statistics for several Western European countries, which indicate how few willful murders and how few sex offenses are committed in Sweden. Sweden has relatively fewer reported murders and probably the best statistics of any of the countries listed. Only France and Italy have lower rates than Sweden for sexual offenses that are known to the police, and here I would guess that the Italian and French data are grossly incomplete. In any case, if data on willful murder and sex offenses can be used as indicators of how much violence is inhibited in a society, then Sweden is certainly an extreme case. The disdain for violence in Sweden might be likened to the abhorrence of pornography in a puritanical society.

Quality. The quality of things is important to Swedes. First, the Swedes believe that quality is an essential aspect of housing, clothes,

Table 9.1 Willful Murders and Sex Offenses Known to the Police, per 100,000 of the Population, 1962.

	Willful murders	Sex offenses
Sweden	0.7	39.9
Austria	2.00	52.0
Denmark	1.30	80.3
France	5.73	28.14
Germany (FR)	2.1	109.2
Italy	2.64	14.85
Netherlands	2.5	60.7
United Kingdom	0.94	42.01

SOURCE: Reported in *New Society* (London, January 28, 1965), p. 20.

food, and most of the objects of life. Second, they frequently believe
that Swedish products are of particularly high quality. This has long
been a claim of Swedish manufacturers and has been important in the
advertising of Swedish goods, both in the international and in the
domestic markets. The Swedes sell quality steel, quality automobiles,
and quality turbines. In newspaper advertisements the word *qvalitet* is
continually used. An indicator of the belief in the superior quality of
things Swedish is a 1965 survey of automobile owners done by *Dagens
Nyheter* on satisfaction with different make automobiles.[21] Among
the owners of all makes, Swedish and foreign, the rank order of the
quality of cars made in different countries was precisely the same:
Swedish, German, American, English, French, and then Italian. Indeed, while there is doubtless an ethnocentric component to this belief in Swedish quality, it does, probably, have some basis in fact.
First, the quality of housing in the other Scandinavian countries, the
Netherlands, Britain, or America does not generally come up to that
of Swedish standards. The quality of workmanship, construction,
windows, and bathroom fixtures is indeed impressive in Sweden. The
quality of Swedish railroads is probably unsurpassed. The high price
of Volvos and SAABs as compared with automobiles of similar size
manufactured in other countries can be justified only on the basis of
their alleged high quality.

The Aesthetic Component. The Swedes bear a similarity to the Jap-
anese in their sensitivity to the aesthetic component in various aspects
of life. The English writers Kathleen Nott and William Samson have
also made this observation.[22] A concern with the design of household
objects, flower arranging, picture hanging, table setting, and with
beautifying everyday objects with bright colors permeates Swedish
society both in homes and in public places. The art and handicraft
traditions of the rural society still have influence. Such aestheticism is
far less general in the Anglo-American or Continental cultures. The
contrast is most apparent in cross-national comparisons of the lower-
middle and working classes. Perhaps F. S. C. Northrop is right when
he suggests that evangelical Protestantism has lessened the aesthetic
component in Protestant cultures with its de-emphasis of the sensual,[23]
a change of little significance in the Protestant Reformation in Sweden. This well-developed aestheticism is particularly interesting in the
light of the failure of the Swedes to have contributed much to world
painting, architecture, or music.

One of the first observations that Swedes (and other Scandinavians) make of American homes, in general, is the absence of flowers and of paintings on the walls. There is no Swedish counterpart to Richard Hoggart's descriptions of the unalloyed ugliness of English working-class homes.[24] A comparison of catalog furniture in Sweden with Britain or America makes the point. Even the cheapest Swedish furniture is "light" and functional in design with an absence of extraneous decoration. While the aesthetic level of the furniture in the Sears and Montgomery Ward catalogs has improved in recent years, much is still pretty terrible by even modestly sophisticated standards. Barca-loungers and the like would have a small sale in Sweden.

Nature. While the world tends to view the Swedes as a sophisticated and secular people, it is also characteristic of them that they very much value nature and the out-of-doors. Most Swedes give high priority to having access to a place in a deserted area where they can go for part of the summer and perhaps for part of the winter to ski. It is not a quantitative exaggeration to say that most Swedes find this close contact with nature a necessity of life. This value is certainly related to the fact that Sweden is a large country with a relatively small population that has only recently industrialized and modernized. The image of a red farmhouse set among green fir trees has an intense appeal for most Swedes. This need to be in nature, however, may be even stronger among the Norwegians and Finns than the Swedes, though not as much among the Danes in their much smaller and more urbanized country.

To Relate to the World. Swedes tend to regard their country as "a spiritual and physical peninsula on the outskirts of Europe."[25] They have a keen awareness that they live in a "small" country away from the centers of power and influence in the world. They want to know about the world, to relate to the world, and to be heard by the world. They do not want to get lost. This is in contrast to certain other advanced small countries, such as Switzerland and Belgium, which are more provincially oriented. Perhaps no people in the world are so concerned with foreign literature, foreign ideas, and foreign currents of thought as the Swedes. The press devotes an enormous amount of space to foreign books and art, to say nothing of world politics. The plight of the world's unfortunate peoples is given great attention: the discrimination against the blacks in South Africa, the torture of prisoners in Algeria, the starvation of the Biafrans, the slaughter of Brazilian Indians are all front-page news and the frequent subject of editorials and culture page articles. There is much written about, and a number of ad hoc organizations have been formed to oppose, the undemocratic regimes of Greece, Portugal, Spain, and Rhodesia. All of these issues are "causes" for the student political organizations in both the gymnasia and the universities. Sweden is a rich and secure country and, like some rich and secure men, can afford to be concerned with humanitarian and intellectual issues far removed from their immediate world. The continual speaking out of the Swedes on humanitarian issues is both an indicator of their institutionalized humanitarianism and their need to be heard by the world.

Swedish and American Values

None of the dominant Swedish values discussed so far can be regarded as preëminent in American culture as they are in Swedish culture. Yet there is an undeniable similarity in many of the dominant value orientations of these two societies, not excluding some of the values already discussed. After all, these are the two most affluent modern societies in the world and both are liberal democracies in the Protestant, Western tradition. Many Europeans, in fact, look on Sweden as the most "Americanized" country in Europe. It should therefore be revealing to look comparatively at the Swedish value system in terms of the most well known, and I think essentially valid, systematic presentation of American values, that of Robin Williams in *American Society*.[26] He discusses fifteen values to each of which I have posed the question: To what extent is this also a dominant Swedish value? In a few cases, the value is even more dominant in Swedish culture than it is in American, in some cases there seems to be a crude similarity, in several cases the particular value does not apply to the Swedish situation, and in a number of cases the value is less dominant or is not at all a dominant value in Swedish culture. In Table 9.2 the fifteen values are listed together with my estimate of the extent to which each might be considered a dominant Swedish value. Unless otherwise noted, the values are defined as Williams uses them. Again, the concern here is not with similarities in behavior, but with the extent to which there is similarity in the patterned principles of the desirable. Now let us deal with each value in turn.

"*Achievement*" and "*Success.*" Swedish culture does not place the stress on achievement and success that one finds in American culture. They certainly are not important themes in Swedish folklore, novels, plays, or movies.[27] The educational system does not seem to stress

Table 9.2 Williams' "Major Value-Orientations" Compared with Their Role in the Swedish Value System.

AMERICAN VALUE	More Dominant in Swedish Culture	About the Same	Less or Not Dominant in Swedish Culture
"Achievement" and "Success"			+
"Activity" and "Work"		+	
"Moral Orientation"			+
"Humanitarian Mores"			+
Efficiency and Practicality		+	
"Progress"	+		
Material Comfort			+
Equality*		+	
Freedom*			+
External Conformity		+	
Science and Secular Rationality	+		
Nationalism–Patriotism			+
Democracy	+		
Individual Personality*			+
Racism and Related Group-Superiority Themes			+

* These values need to be reinterpreted somewhat when applied to Swedish culture.

SOURCE: Robin M. Williams, Jr., *American Society*, third ed. (New York: Knopf, 1970), pp. 438–504.

competitive success as is done in the United States, and in fact, the emphasis is quite the contrary. At the ideological level there is an attempt to establish the "equality" of theoretical (academic) and practical courses of study. However, it is debatable whether there is really much difference in actual behavior between Sweden and America. Indeed it is suggestive that the Norwegians and the Danes often characterize the Swedes as ambitious. There seems to be about as much mobility in Swedish society as there is in American society, but it is not generally regarded as a source of pride to be a self-made man. This is one of those examples in social life where there does not appear to be much congruence between values, on one hand, and behavior, on the other.

"Activity" and "Work." An emphasis on activity and work seems to be as characteristic of Swedish culture as of American culture. Swedes are doers and joiners as much as are Americans. In fact, insofar as joining unions, political parties, sports clubs, and study circles, they join in far greater numbers than Americans. There is also an emphasis

on being busy and keeping a clean and well-ordered home. These aspects of the Protestant ethic are as descriptive of Swedish as of American culture. Indeed Swedish wives probably work harder at housekeeping than do their American counterparts. There is no role for a gentlemanly upper class such as one finds in England and perhaps in most Continental European countries. One hardly has an identity in Sweden without an occupation.

"*Moral Orientation.*" The difference between Swedish and American cultures in this respect is sharp and unambiguous. There is less of a moral orientation in judging others, in spite of the observation that Swedes are highly critical of each other. Much that is the subject of moral concern in America, such as sexual behavior and personal demeanor, is in the realm of the private in Sweden. In a very basic sense, Sweden is more universalistic than is America, in that "morality" is not a condition of selection or tenure in politics, bureaucracies, and schools. Even the vigorous, but declining, temperance movement is not characterized by much of a moral orientation; it simply sees alcohol as a social problem and emphasizes the incapacity of Swedes to handle alcohol. Sweden's stance in international relations, what has been critically called her "conscience of the world" attitude, may sometimes be an exception to this.

Humanitarian Mores. The "help thy neighbor" attitude so pervasive in American culture, though less apparent in behavior, is little characteristic of Swedish culture. In American culture it is very much a survival from rural life. Helping one's neighbor and welfare in general are, for the most part, seen as the responsibility of duly-constituted governmental agencies. The noblesse-oblige variation of humanitarianism, which is essentially a conservative value, has been more thoroughly discredited in Sweden than in America. Neither voluntary humanitarianism nor "individual responsibility" is an argument against expanding welfare legislation. By contrast with American society, Swedes are very much "unto themselves." The neighborliness ethic, which is now mostly a value rather than reality in American society, is not even a value in urban Sweden.

Efficiency and Practicality. In this area, there does not seem to be substantial difference between American and Swedish culture. Both societies are highly pragmatic and place great value on doing things in the most efficient and practical way. Efficiency and practicality are compelling arguments for choosing how to proceed and as criteria of judgment.

Progress. Swedish culture seems to have a greater commitment to progress than does American culture. A belief in progress may not be regarded as a very sophisticated value in the contemporary world, yet insofar as a belief in progress is limited to the material level of living, optimism about the continued advances of science and technology, and the continued improvement in the benefits and operation of the welfare state, then progress must be reckoned a dominant Swedish value. It is not too much of an exaggeration to say that the conventional view of Swedish history, both popularly and scholarly, is that the past was not good because Swedes were poor and because there was an absence of popular democracy. The present is conventionally viewed as good because of the high standard of living and the great stability of Swedish society, yet the future will be even better in the limited ways previously noted. This generally negative view of their history is interesting considering how tranquil and stable this history has been and in the light of the high degree of freedom that characterized nineteenth-century Sweden. There is nothing like the celebration of their past and its virtues that is so characteristic of American society.

Material Comfort. There does not seem to be as great an emphasis on material comfort among Swedes as there is among Americans. Comfort does not seem to be so prevalent a pitch in advertising; there is a greater stress on quality. The concern with having numerous bathrooms, telephones, television sets, and radios, even among the rich, does not seem as great as with Americans. The capacity of most Swedes to spend substantial periods of time in a primitive summer *stuga* (cabin) without conveniences would indicate a lesser emphasis on material comfort, as does their greater involvement in the out-of-doors, and the greater tendency of middle-aged and older people to walk and hike, swim and bicycle. But, on the other hand, the pervasiveness of this value is probably related to the actual availability of goods, to the material level of living, which is perhaps a half generation behind America.

Equality. This is a most complex value area and one with many ramifications. Yet in the aggregate it is probably as strong and pervasive a Swedish value as it is an American value, although it takes different forms than in American culture. Swedish egalitarianism is shaped by opposition to the traditions of the old hierarchical society, vestiges of which remain in the form of differential terms of address and titles. There is greater respect for authority and for expert opinion and less celebration of the views of "the common man" than one finds in American culture. Yet there is a greater concern in Sweden with economic equality, with the greater privileges of salaried as compared with wage workers, with realizing equality of opportunity in education, as well as with the greater emphasis on sexual equality. Of tangential relevance here is the observation that the range of class differences is narrower in Swedish than in American society. Whether Swedish culture is as egalitarian as American culture, therefore, seems to depend in the last analysis on what is included under the term.

Freedom. In Sweden there is much emphasis on freedom of choice (*valfrihet*), a concept that has become a political slogan for all the political parties. But it is more than that. It is one of the explicit goals of Swedish society to maximize people's choices in education, work, and style of life. Still, however, the concern with freedom as a cultural value does not loom as significantly as it does in American culture. To use Erich Fromm's apt distinction, we might say that in American culture freedom primarily means "freedom *from*," freedom from restraints by institutions and bureaucracies and, above all, the government. An emphasis on this aspect of freedom does not loom large in Sweden; there is a greater stress on "freedom *to*," freedom to have choices in what one wants to do, freedom to realize one's possibilities. On the other hand, the great organizations are very sensitive to any attempts on the part of the government to interfere with their activities. Freedom of religion, of speech, of the press, and even of academic freedom in the American sense are much less salient issues in Sweden; they are just assumed to exist, and, indeed, they do.

External Conformity. One of my favorite questions in Sweden was "What is wrong with Sweden?" One frequent response was that the Swedes are so conformist. This is characteristic of how they play their public roles, in work, at school, in social situations. One of the main criticisms of the Swedes made by Kathleen Nott in her biting attack on Sweden, *A Clean Well-Lighted Place*, was the oppressive conformity of the Swedes as compared with the English.[28] However, in the ideological or intellectual realm this is not the case. External conformity in the intellectual realm, in communal or legal repression of radical and nonconventional ideas, is typically far less in Sweden than in America. Yet in terms of how people play their public roles, the pressures for external conformity seem at least as great as in American society.

Science and Secular Rationality. It is doubtful if any people have such a thoroughgoing commitment to science and secular rationality as have the Swedes. This core modern values is a core Swedish values. Science and reason is the way, the source of truth, the only way for modern men to live. In America, by contrast, the commitment to science and secular rationality is attenuated by much antiscientific and anti-intellectual religious belief and traditionalism.

National-Patriotism. Whereas the people of all societies have some degree of ethnocentrism and pride in their country, the Swedes could hardly be said to have nationalism and patriotism as value orientations. In fact, the Swedes are very much committed to an international point of view, and, in spite of the magnificent success of their social system, they tend to be highly critical of themselves. Conscious nationalism and patriotism are minimal in Sweden. For example, the Swedish school system makes no conscious efforts to inculcate these values. In fact, the situation is quite the opposite. There is an emphasis on the equal value of different peoples and cultures and a strong commitment to internationalism. However, this does not mean that Swedes do not have a frequent unreflective belief that in most respects things are better in Sweden than anywhere else. Yet in some ways this is an assumption that is empirically sound. The general standard of living is as high as in any country outside of the United States without the mass of social problems, and the social system works as well as does any in the world. While children still die in Sweden, relatively fewer do than anywhere else.

Democracy. Democracy is ideologically the most absolute of all modern values in Sweden. It is an ultimate appeal. That is ipso facto good which is democratic. In Sweden, democracy means the right of individuals to choose their leaders in the nation and in organizations, but, at the ideological level, it is frequently confounded with egalitarianism and equality of opportunity. While this is also the case in America, democracy seems to be a more pervasive value in Swedish than American culture. In Sweden it is believed that all organizations should be "democratic," anything that is "not democratic" is liable to suspicion. In recent years there has been much concern with industrial democracy, the bringing of workers into the decision-making process. A common viewpoint is that democracy has been achieved in the political realm, in education, in most of the great organizations, but still not yet in the realm of work. It is clear that there is greater democracy in organizations in Sweden, notably in unions and in political parties, than in America. The students in the universities play a

greater role in the governance of the universities than almost anywhere else. More significant in this context, however, is that there is a
more pervasive *concern* with democracy in organizations than in
America.

Individual Personality. The stress on the rights of the individual
even at the expense of the well-being of the community is certainly
less in Swedish than in American culture. There is more of an organic
conception of the rights of the individual and of the welfare of the
community. The belief in the independence of "the individual" or
"the self" apart from the community is not so great in Sweden. Liberalism and the ideology of individualism have shaped the Swedish value
system much less than the American.

Racism and Related Group-Superiority Themes. There are certainly
fewer group-superiority themes in Swedish culture, but then there is
no more culturally and ethnically homogeneous modern society. If,
however, there should be an influx of Southern Europeans, blacks, or
Asians into Sweden, the reaction might not be much different from
what we have seen in Britain. Yet, the ideological commitment to
antiracism and to equality among diverse peoples is so pervasive in
Sweden that such an influx might be accepted with greater equanimity
in Sweden than in Britain. There is even an antiracist clause in the
program of the Social Democratic party.

It is important to stress that both countries have arrived at their
modern value systems via different routes. Sweden achieved modern
values; America was born to them. Had a De Tocqueville visited
Sweden in the 1830s, or even in the 1890s, we probably would not
find much continuity between his observations of that time and the
description of Swedish values presented here.[29] On the other hand,
one of the striking reactions to reading de Tocqueville on America is
how "contemporary" his description of American values of the 1830s
sounds.[30]

Democracy, egalitarianism, empiricism, malleability of institutions,
and secular rationality, for example, could probably not be regarded
as dominant Swedish values until well into the twentieth century. The
beginnings of the popular acceptance of modern values can be seen
in the leading writers of the 1880s, who, filled with modern ideas
from abroad, found the idealistic, religious, and hierarchical values of
nineteenth century Swedish society "distasteful to the point of
nausea."[31] Liberalism, socialism, the labor movement, and the cooperative and temperance movements all helped spread modern ideas in

the decades around the turn of the century among a literate and homogeneous people living in a tranquil society.

In the second decade of this century the emotive theory of value began to permeate philosophy, law, and social science, and it fundamentally transformed the foundations of Swedish intellectual life. This theory was first put forth by Axel Hägerström in 1911 in what must surely be the most influential essay ever written in Sweden, "On the Validity of Moral Conceptions."[32] This view holds that "moral judgments lack descriptive content, and thus can be neither true nor false but instead have the same status as ordinary emotive expressions, as for example interjection. . . ."[33] This "logical positivism" precedes by a number of years similar ideas put forth by Bertrand Russell, A. J. Ayer, and the "Vienna Circle" of philosophers. The role of this "nihilism of values"—as the Swedes call it—in the final destruction of the intellectual respectability of religious and idealistic values of the Swedish nineteenth century, at least in secular quarters, is difficult to overestimate. A highly self-conscious scientific and empirical orientation toward knowledge and the world became the new foundation of Swedish scholarship and intellectual life and has come to dominate the entire culture. The Hägerström school gave a great boost to rationality in leading to views that were free from the old religious and metaphysical restraints. An example is the rapid popular acceptance in Sweden, which occurred before other countries, of the view that the only grounds for punishing criminals is to prevent the criminal and others from repeating the crime.

Of additional importance in the great transformation of Swedish values in this century has been the rapid industrialization and urbanization of the country. Largely a consequence of this is the coming to dominance of the double radical traditions of social-reformist liberalism and socialism, both of which have been numerically stronger in Sweden than in any other western country. Sweden came late to modern values, but has come to accept them with particular intensity.

Several additional observations might be made about the Swedish value system as compared with the American:

1) The Swedish is a more integrated and harmonious value system that contains fewer internal conflicts and inconsistencies than does the American. There is also a smaller gap between values and the reality they effect. There is not the great emphasis on achievement and success conflicting with pervasive egalitarianism; as Lipset has pointed out, there is a necessary conflict between achievement and egalitarian-

ism.[34] The inherent conflict there, however, seems to be cushioned by the restraint and ritual so pervasive in Swedish society. There is less of a moral orientation toward the world and less everyday idealism than in America, with the consequence that there is less tension and cynicism resulting from the realities of human imperfection in an imperfect world. And, there is not the comparable emphasis on the old liberal value of individual freedom in opposition to bureaucracy and organization, a really dysfunctional value in a modern society where democracy is also a dominant value.

2) In Sweden there is not the gulf between what we might call general values and the values held by intellectuals—a strong theme in American culture. Lars Gustafsson has written about contemporary Swedish authors that "(m)ost . . . exhibit a strong and obvious adjustment to the society they live in. . . ." [35] Such a statement could hardly be made by a contemporary American literary intellectual, certainly not by any German, and probably not by any Continental European.[36] Even New-Left radicals who criticize the "bourgeoisification" of Swedish society and culture are less alienated from the general values of their society than are their American counterparts.[37] The crucial difference is that general values in Sweden have largely permeated down in the society from an essentially sophisticated elite thoroughly embued with modern values. General American values, by contrast, have been shaped by the liberalism of "that 'petit bourgeois' giant . . . the American democrat absorbing both peasantry and proletariat."[38]

3) There is an even greater emphasis on active mastery and control of the world than one finds in American culture, which is an outgrowth of the extraordinarily successful operation of Swedish society.

4) Using William James' distinction, one might classify the Swedish value system in a general way as tough-minded and the American as tender-minded.[39] The tough-minded tends toward empiricism, skepticism, pessimism, nonbelief in the supernatural; the tender-minded toward being less empirical, accepting of the supernatural, idealistic, and dogmatic.

Conclusion: Swedish Values and Modern Values

This chapter and this book will be concluded on a polemical note with a question and an answer. The question is: Which culture, Swedish or American, more manifests modern values? My answer is the Swedish. This may be regarded as comparing the incomparable and as an example of the American tendency to think in terms of rank order. It might also, erroneously I think, be regarded as a meaning-less question because the answer depends on what we subsume under "modern values," a concept about which there is certainly room for some debate and difference of opinion. Yet it is a meaningful question because there is a core of interrelated value orientations that are con-ventionally, even if not always explicitly, regarded as "modern." It is further a question of some importance because it is a common view among both sociologists and laymen that American society embodies modern values to a greater extent than any other society. A gen-eration and more ago this was perhaps unequivocally true. I think it no longer the case.

We might begin with the values of achievement, egalitarianism, universalism, and specificity. These values are derived by Lipset from the pattern variables of Parsons and can be taken as an abstract state-ment of certain modern value orientations.[40] It is true that the value of achievement does not loom so greatly in the Swedish value system as it does in the American. So far as egalitarianism is concerned there does not seem to be much difference in Swedish and American culture, though each emphasizes different aspects of this most abstruse value complex. On the other hand, universalism and specificity seem to be more dominant values in Swedish culture. For example, admission to schools and jobs and conditions of tenure in the civil service in-volve *only* directly relevant criteria; in American society the criteria of personality and character, extraneous characteristics to the Swedes, are commonly considered. The concern with race and ethnic back-ground in government and politics, and more recently in education and industry, are also marked exceptions to universalism and specificity.

An instrumental attitude toward institutions is a core modern value, which is more dominant in Swedish than in American culture; in America elements of the sacred continue to adhere to many insti-tutions, and an anti-institutionalism that is the result of an outworn liberal heritage continues to inhibit planned social change. Belief in science and secular rationality is a core modern value that is mani-fested to a greater extent in Sweden than in America where tradition-alism in a number of areas, most notably in politics, in religion, and in sex roles, plays a greater role. Related to this is the belief in the use of knowledge to shape the environment, which no country manifests more than does Sweden. According to the criteria of Robert E. Lane, Sweden is the most "knowledgeable society" in the world insofar as it consumes knowledge.[41] Another core modern value is democracy, which is a more pervasive value in Sweden, where democracy is of central concern in the church, in education, in industry, and in the great organizations.

We have been discussing values and not social structure. The case for defining Sweden as a more modern society than America is equally great according to structural characteristics. Consider, for example, the ability to affect social change, the national integration of the society, the development of voluntary associations, the advanced level of role segregation and specialization, the extent of economic and social stability, and the other characteristics mentioned at the outset of this book.

While America may be the first new nation, and, indeed, in aggregate and in per capita terms, the most affluent nation in the world, it can no longer be regarded as the foremost embodiment of modern society. However, it would not be unjustified to so regard Sweden. One purpose of this book has been to demonstrate that this is the case.

Notes

1. Abraham Flexner, *Universities: American, English, German* (New York: Oxford University Press), p. 266.
2. See Florence R. Kluckhohn and Fred Strodbeck, *Variations in Value Organizations* (Evanston, Ill.: Row, Peterson, 1961), and Robin M. Williams, Jr., *American Society*, third ed. (New York: Knopf, 1970), pp. 438–504.
3. Kluckhohn and Strodbeck, *op. cit.*, p. 4.
4. Williams, *op. cit.*, p. 448.
5. Lipset has made liberal use of the pattern variables in his comparative discussion of American values; see Seymour M. Lipset, *The First New Nation* (New York: Basic Books, 1963), pp. 248–273.
6. Williams, *op. cit.*, p. 500 (Italics his).
7. Herbert Tingsten, "Stability and Vitality in Swedish Democracy," *Political Quarterly*, XXVI (April–June, 1955), p. 148.

8. T. L. Johnston, *Collective Bargaining in Sweden* (London: Allen & Unwin, 1962), passim.

9. A. H. Halsey, "Science and Government in Sweden," *Minerva*, II (Autumn 1963), p. 60.

10. See Lars Gustafsson, *The Public Dialogue in Sweden: Current Issues of Social, Esthetic and Moral Debate*, Claude Stephenson (tr.) (Stockholm: P. A. Norstedt, 1964), p. 42.

11. See the references to these reports in Chapter 5.

12. *Svenska Institutet för Opinionsundersökningar (SIFO)* (Stockholm: November 28, 1961), mimeo; 65 percent favored continuation of the monarchy, 20 percent favored a president, and 15 percent had no opinion.

13. See polls in Elis Hästad. *"Gallup" och den svenska väljarkåren* (Stockholm: Hugo Gebers, 1950).

14. Dag Hammarskjöld, *Markings*, Leif Sjoberg and W. H. Auden (trs.) (New York: Knopf, 1964).

15. Folke Schmidt and Stig Strömholm, *Legal Values in Modern Sweden* (Totowa, N.J.: Bedminster Press, 1964), pp. 29–30.

16. One young Swedish political scientist, Gustav Lindecrona, went so far as to say to me that there was no anti-intellectualism in Sweden.

17. Johan Goudsblom, *Dutch Society* (New York: Random House, 1967), p. 30.

18. *Ibid.*, p. 126.

19. Schmidt and Strömholm, *op. cit.*, p. 34.

20. Herbert Hendin, *Suicide and Scandinavia* (New York: Grune & Stratton, 1964), p. 72.

21. See, for example, *Dagens Nyheter* (February 14, 1965), p. 11.

22. See Kathleen Nott, *A Clean Well-Lighted Place* (London: Heinemann, 1961), and William Samson, *The Icicle and the Sun* (London: Hogarth, 1958).

23. F. S. C. Northrop, *The Meeting of East and West* (New York: Macmillan, 1946), pp. 169–170.

24. Richard Hoggart, *The Uses of Literacy* (Boston: Beacon Press, 1957), pp. 37–38.

25. L. Gustafsson, *op. cit.*, p. 116.

26. Williams, *op. cit.*, pp. 438–504.

27. An exception to this is the traditional middle-class concern with children taking the *studentexam*.

28. Nott, *op. cit.*

29. A number of observers did visit Sweden in the nineteenth century and wrote books on their travels. These, however, tend to be anecdotal accounts.

30. Alexis de Tocqueville, *Democracy in America* (New York: Vintage, 1955), esp. Vol. II.

31. Alrik Gustafson, *A History of Swedish Literature* (Minneapolis: University of Minnesota Press, 1961), p. 250.

32. See the translation of Axel Hägerström's writings: Karl Olivecrona (ed.), *Inquiries into the Nature of Law and Morals*, C. D. Broad (tr.) (Uppsala: Almqvist & Wiksell, 1953).

33. Quoted from L. Gustafsson, *op. cit.*, p. 26.

34. Lipset, *op. cit.*
35. L. Gustafsson, *op. cit.*, p. 70.
36. According to Edward Shils, such a satisfaction with their society character-
    ized English intellectuals as recently as the middle 1950s; see his essay, "The
    Intellectuals: I. Great Britain," *Encounter*, IV (April 1955), 5–16.
37. See Göran Therborn, *et al.*, *En ny vänster* (Stockholm: Rabén and Sjögren,
    1966), and Richard F. Tomasson and Erik Allardt, "Scandinavian Students
    and the Politics of Organized Radicalism," in Seymour M. Lipset and
    Philip G. Altbach (eds.), *Students in Revolt* (Boston: Houghton Mifflin,
    1969), pp. 96–126.
38. Louis Hartz, *The Liberal Tradition in America* (New York: Harcourt, Brace
    & World, 1955), p. 204.
39. William James, *Pragmatism* (New York: Longmans, Green, 1928), pp. 11–12.
40. Lipset, *op. cit.*, pp. 248–249.
41. Robert E. Lane, "The Decline of Politics and Ideology in a Knowledgeable
    Society," *American Sociological Review*, 31 (October 1966), 649–662.

Name Index

Subject Index